The
Heidelberg Catechism
with
Commentary

400TH ANNIVERSARY EDITION 1563-1963

The Heidelberg Catechism with Commentary

THE PILGRIM PRESS
New York City

Copyright 1962, 1963

UNITED CHURCH PRESS

Fourth printing, 1979

This 400th Anniversary Edition of the Heidelberg Catechism is a translation from original German and Latin texts, by Allen O. Miller and M. Eugene Osterhaven.

The commentary is a translation by Allen O. Miller in collaboration with Mrs. Marie B. Koons from *Le Cathéchisme de Heidelberg* by Andé Péry, published in 1959 by Labor et Fides, Geneva.

The biblical quotations are from the *Revised Standard Version of the Bible* and from *The New English Bible, The New Testament.*

ISBN 0–8298–0062–X
Library of Congress Catalog Card Number 63-10981

The Pilgrim Press
287 Park Avenue South
New York, New York 10010

FOREWORD AND INVITATION

The date January 19, 1963 marks the 400th anniversary of the Heidelberg Catechism. In behalf of the churches belonging to the North American Area of the World Alliance of Reformed and Presbyterian Churches, we are honored to present a new translation of this historic symbol of our catholic Christian faith, "reformed according to the Word of God."

The most ecumenical of the confessions of the Protestant Churches, the Heidelberg Catechism bears the name of the capital city of the German state in which it was written. The Reformation was introduced into the Palatinate in 1546, the year of Luther's death, and soon that region became a veritable battleground for various and contending evangelical views. Looking for advice, Frederick III, the wise prince who became Elector of this important principality in 1559, called upon a native son of the Palatinate, Philip Melanchthon, for assistance. Melanchthon counseled biblical simplicity, moderation, and peace as the gains of reform were being consolidated, and warned against extremes and scholastic subtleties in theological position. After a quarrel between two representatives of the Lutheran and Reformed parties at the altar of the Church of the Holy Spirit in Heidelberg, Frederick ordered a catechism to be written in an attempt to bring the people together.

The men chosen for this important task were Zacharias Ursinus and Caspar Olevianus, then twenty-eight and twenty-six years of age. Ursinus had been trained by Melanchthon and was a professor of theology at Heidelberg. Olevianus was a gifted biblical preacher. In the preparation of this catechism an earlier work of Ursinus, the *Catechesis Minor,* was used. Its threefold division, based on the Letter to the Romans, was taken over and about ninety of its questions were adopted with some modifications. A group of counselors, including the Elector, assisted the principal authors and revised parts of the work.

To Olevianus was given the responsibility for a final revision and translation into German. A man of eloquence, he was one "in whom imagination and pathos combined to clothe the logic of religion with beauty as well as power."

The publication of the Catechism in January, 1563 was a landmark in the German Reformation. According to the provisions of the Peace of Augsburg (1555) the Roman Catholic and Lutheran faiths were recognized, but "Zwinglian" or "Calvinist" views had no legal standing. The gradual reception of the Heidelberg Catechism by emperor, princes, and theologians makes a stirring story. The most significant event was the meeting of the Imperial Diet at Augsburg in the spring of 1566. Here, with the pomp that befitted the occasion, the Emperor read a decree charging the Elector Frederick with having introduced changes in the government and worship of the churches and a catechism dissenting from the Augsburg Confession.

Following a brief recess, the Elector reappeared accompanied by his son, John Casimir, his "spiritual armor-bearer," who carried the Bible and the Augsburg Confession. After a courageous defense reminiscent of Martin Luther's appearance before the Diet at Worms, Frederick, having won the admiration of the majority present, was judged as remaining within the teachings of the Augsburg Confession and to be a prince in good standing in the Empire. Thereafter the Heidelberg Catechism was more widely received and accepted by churches in other states and nations, and the praise accorded it probably exceeds that of any other statement of faith.

The reasons for this praise are to be found in its general characteristics and its theological position. Of its general characteristics the following deserve mention.

1. The Catechism is written in a personal, experiential manner. The mood is existential. Questions are asked in the second person and answered in the first as a confession of faith by the catechumen. Moreover, the approach is dynamic and the progression of thought dramatic. There is no formal beginning with a definition of God or scripture meant to appeal mainly to the intellect, but rather an appeal to the whole person as a religious being with spiritual needs and concerns. The first question and answer, a gem of existential confession, set the tone for the rest.

2. The Catechism is thoroughly biblical in character. Not only

is it fortified throughout with biblical texts which are fundamental and give rise to the separate questions and answers, but, of
equal importance, the entire structure is molded by the biblical
perspective. Its world of thought comes out of the experiences of
profound Christian living when men try to understand God's
Word in his world.

3. The Catechism is a handbook of practical religion. Instead
of raising speculative problems, the Christian faith is presented in
a down-to-earth, utilitarian manner emphasizing its importance
for daily living. In this there is reflected the sharply practical,
ethical side of the Calvinist tradition which has sought to build a
kingdom of God in this world and has been interested in revolution and reform.

4. Unlike other confessional writings, the Heidelberg Catechism is generally irenic in nature. The striking exception to this
mood is the eightieth question, inserted after the first edition as
partial answer to the Roman Catholic Council of Trent which on
September 17, 1562, reaffirmed transubstantiation and the sacrifice of the Mass for the living and the dead, the adoration of the
host, the withdrawal of the cup, and anathematized those who
disagreed.

5. The method is catechetical. Religious and theological truths
are put in the form of questions and answers which are elicited
from the catechumen as thought moves smoothly and logically
from one phase of life in divine-human covenant to another. The
drama of redemption that lies at the heart of scripture is set forth
with beauty and power in dialog which comforts as it informs.

In theological position the Heidelberg Catechism is catholic,
evangelical, and reformed. Thoroughly rooted in the tradition of
the apostles and of the ecumenical councils of the early church, it
has been aptly described as "the flower and fruit of the entire German and French Reformation." Confessional in stance, it never
gets caught in defending speculative notions about either God or
man. It sketches man's sinfulness and the wretched consequences
in bold strokes, and the full effect is to lay greater emphasis on
God's grace. Christocentric throughout, the Catechism strikes the
note of comfort and joy, without seeming to offer cheap grace,
for these fruits of the Spirit accompany the freedom of obedience

7

in the service of the Lord. The divine election and the particularity of salvation are taught but reprobation, found in some Reformed confessions, is not mentioned.

The biblical covenant drama, as the outline for a catechism, was first recognized and taught by Martin Luther in his *Short Exposition* (1520):

"The Decalog teaches a man to know what is wrong with himself . . . to know himself to be a sinful and unrighteous man. Then the Creed shows and teaches him where to find the medicine, that is, divine grace . . . and the Lord's Prayer teaches him to yearn for this grace, to seek it, and take it to heart."

Following this pattern, Luther's own Small Catechism places the Law first, not distinguishing its role as the stern schoolmaster, leading the sinner to Christ, from the positive injunctions to be found in the Ten Commandments for the life of Christian obedience. In the Heidelberg Catechism only the summary of the Law appears in the first section, while its full exposition is placed in Part III, along with the Lord's Prayer, where the Christian life, as an expression of the gratitude we owe to God for our redemption in Jesus Christ, is interpreted.

Thus the Law is seen as serving the gospel both in bringing us to Christ and in our bringing Christ to the world. This emphasis on the continuing significance of the Law in Christian living, which has given Calvinism its disciplined piety and has contributed to its activistic temper, receives a definitive expression in this Cathechism.

In theological position, manner of presentation, and spirit the Heidelberg Catechism retains its eminence as a statement of Christian faith, and its usefulness in Christian nurture and discipline is as great today as when it was written.

We are hopeful that this summary of evangelical teaching may, in our time, become a unitive confession not only for Lutheran and Reformed theologians, as it already was in the sixteenth century, but also for Congregational Christian and Evangelical and Reformed people in the United Church of Christ, for Presbyterian and Reformed Churches within the Alliance, and for an even wider fellowship of churches committed to the twentieth-century venture of reuniting the church, catholic, reformed, and evangelical.

We salute our predecessors, notably Philip Schaff and those who gave us the Tercentenary edition. Along with their very useful printing of the Catechism, with the German, Latin, and English versions in parallel columns, our primary resource has been Wilhelm Niesel's definitive German text, identifying first, second, and third editions, all from 1563, published in 1938. In order to show the biblical and theological precision of the Catechism, we have included in the present translation nearly all the biblical texts cited by the authors, using mainly the *Revised Standard Version* and occasionally *The New English Bible, the New Testament* (N.E.B.). We have received the gracious and invaluable assistance of a score of scholars, both Presbyterian and Reformed, to whom we wish to make this public, though *incognito,* acknowledgment.

It is our conviction that one of the most significant uses of the Heidelberg Catechism, as we enter into the fifth century of its life, may be in adult education. This edition, including a layman's commentary on its questions and answers, is possible because Pastor André Péry of Geneva, Switzerland, has allowed us to present an English translation of his marvelous little book, first published in French in 1959 by Labor et Fides, Geneva, under the title *Le Catéchisme de Heidelberg, un commentaire pour notre temps.*

The chairman wishes to acknowledge the unstinting cooperation of the author and of the original publishers in making this commentary available to the English reader. Pastor Péry has graciously acceded to our request that he elaborate upon his original text at a few key points and has diligently checked our translation for precision and clarity. Special expressions of gratitude are hereby given to Mrs. Marie B. Koons for collaborating with the chairman in producing the first draft from which this English edition of the Commentary has finally emerged; to Allen Hackett, an honored colleague in the ministry of the United Church of Christ, for valued assistance in polishing the English style; to Mrs. Elsie Schult for excellent secretarial services; to my wife, Dorothy E. Miller, for her loving help and boundless encouragement all along the way; and to the Administrative Committee of the North American Area of the World Alliance of Reformed and Presbyterian Churches for their unwavering support of our committee in carrying out the task assigned us.

We invite the reader, both student and teacher, to enter with us as participants in reliving the drama of "man's redemption in Jesus Christ."

ALLEN O. MILLER,
The United Church of Christ, *Chairman*

M. EUGENE OSTERHAVEN,
The Reformed Church in America

ALADAR KOMJATHY,
The Hungarian Reformed Church in America

JAMES I. McCORD,
The World Alliance of Reformed Churches

CONTENTS

PART III

Man's Gratitude and Obedience—
New Life Through the Holy Spirit

INTRODUCTION TO COMMENTARY

The term "catechism" comes from a Greek word which means "to resound, i.e., to sound in one's ears," "to teach by word of mouth."

From the beginning of her life, the church has been obliged to communicate truth which has been revealed, since indeed, and by ·definition, this means "what the heart of man has not conceived" (1 Cor. 2:9). Each generation must therefore be instructed in the knowledge of a truth which does not belong to any of us.

Moreover, it is quite clear that this instruction cannot be acquired once for all and definitively, inasmuch as it is true that we are quickly forgetful of what God has done, and most especially of everything which obliges us to get out of our intellectual and spiritual ruts, to raise the inclination of our response on which we are always inclined to let ourselves slide, in a word, to commit ourselves "to amend our ways and our doings" (Jer. 7:3). This means, therefore, that periodically we should make a thoroughgoing review of our spiritual resources and of our theological confessions. It is the purpose of a catechism to aid us in this enterprise.

At this point, one might pose the question of the place of learning in the church, whether it would not suffice to preach, to pray, to sing the praise of God and to worship him. When Calvin arrived at Geneva and observed the woeful state of the church, he declared: "Nothing has been done in this place but preaching." There is no doubt that preaching is not sufficient. It does not lend itself to the kind of instruction which results from the possibility of a dialogue, an active participation. Preaching is designed to make the Word of God heard so that the Christian community may be helped to live in the world; it provides sustenance for the Christian life. By contrast, the Catechism represents rather the slow and methodical nourishment that one affords a child in order to help him achieve his full stature.

Prayer, adoration, praise are indispensable, but they must be directed toward him who is their object. Therefore, we must *know* him to whom we pray and whom we praise and adore. Everything in the church should begin, therefore, with instruction. All we have to do to believe this is to reread the first chapters of the book of the Acts.

The gospel is never given to the church as a peculiar possession, as a "frozen" asset. This gospel must always be explored and questioned afresh. Let us not hide the fact that it requires work and suffering as well as constant fidelity. But this is what constitutes the *service* which the Christian community owes to God and to humanity.

The basis of this inquiry is the gospel of Jesus Christ as it is witnessed by the holy scripture of the Old and New Testaments. All our interpretative work will consist, therefore, of an explanation of the Scriptures. The exposition of the evangelical doctrine does not depend upon pure speculation; it has to be done in the community of the faithful, in the church, with her, for her (sometimes, against her), and ultimately for the world.

We undertake this study because we are convinced that there exists an urgent and imperious necessity for twentieth-century believers to know what they are believing, and what they are rejecting and why. We cannot live in confusion, and we would risk ceasing to be the church of Jesus Christ—the church which ought to be the salt of the earth and the light of the world—if, for all sorts of reasons, we preferred the vague to the precise.

We have chosen the Heidelberg Catechism because it seemed to us appropriate to resume, along with our fathers in the faith, the attempts at clarification which they undertook in the sixteenth century. We shall reserve for ourselves certain freedom in regard to the book, operating with the very liberty which the Word of God itself gives to us and demands of us.

Let us note once more that the Catechism is not destined for the church alone; it is not a handbook limited to the internal use of the Christian community. This Word is for all men, and it is not for us to decide beforehand which ones will believe or not believe. The good news does not address itself to those worthy or capable of receiving it, but to all men without distinction. It is the Word of God itself which makes the discrimination. Furthermore, when this Word resounds, men are all in the same situation: there are no natural inclinations to be Christian.

The Heidelberg Catechism was produced in 1563 for the Church of the Palatinate, after Frederick the Pious, the Prince of that state, had changed over from Lutheranism to Calvinism. The two theologians who were entrusted with its wording based their work on the Catechism of Zurich and on that of Calvin. It was an outstanding success, and the handbook was soon adopted by one whole part of the Reformed branch of the Protestant movement. It is still used as the official catechism by some of the churches of Switzerland. A contemporary theologian has said of the Heidelberg Catechism that it was "an ingenious presentation of the entire substance of the Reformation."

We hope that our work may be useful to every faithful person who wants to give a more authentic witness to the truth.

ANDRÉ PÉRY

Geneva, June 1959

1 / OUR ONLY COMFORT

❡ QUESTION 1. *What is your only comfort, in life and in death?*

That I belong—body and soul, in life and in death[a]—not to myself[b] but to my faithful Savior, Jesus Christ,[c] who at the cost of his own blood[d] has fully paid for all my sins[e] and has completely freed me from the dominion of the devil;[f] that he protects me so well[g] that without the will of my Father in heaven not a hair can fall from my head;[h] indeed, that everything must fit his purpose for my salvation.[i] Therefore, by his Holy Spirit, he also assures me of eternal life,[j] and makes me wholeheartedly willing and ready from now on to live for him.[k]

a. Rom. 14:8. If we live, we live to the Lord, and if we die, we die to the Lord; so then, whether we live or whether we die, we are the Lord's.

b. 1 Cor. 6:19-20. Do you not know that your body is a temple of the Holy Spirit within you, which you have from God? You are not your own; you were bought with a price.

c. 1 Cor. 3:23. You are Christ's: and Christ is God's.

d. 1 Peter 1:18-19. You know that you were ransomed . . . with the precious blood of Christ, like that of a lamb without blemish or spot.

e. 1 John 1:7; 2:2. If we walk in the light, as [God] is in the light, we have fellowship with one another, and the blood of Jesus his Son cleanses us from all sin. . . . He is the expiation for our sins, and not for ours only but also for the sins of the whole world.

f. 1 John 3:8. He who commits sin is of the devil; for the devil has sinned from the beginning. The reason the Son of God appeared was to destroy the works of the devil.
Cf. Heb. 2:14.

g. John 6:35, 39. Jesus said to them, . . . "This is the will of him who sent me, that I should lose nothing of all that he has given me, but raise it up at the last day."

h. Matt. 10:29-31. "Are not two sparrows sold for a penny? And not one of them will fall to the ground without your Father's will. But even the hairs of your head are all numbered. Fear not, therefore; you are of more value than many sparrows."
Cf. Luke 21:16-18.

i. Rom. 8:28. We know that in everything God works for good with those who love him, who are called according to his purpose.

j. 2 Cor. 1:21-22. It is God who . . . has put his seal upon us and given us his Spirit in our hearts as a guarantee.
Cf. 2 Cor. 5:5; Rom. 8:16; Eph. 1:14.

k. Rom. 8:14, 17. For all who are led by the Spirit of God are sons of God . . . and if children, then heirs . . . with Christ, provided we suffer with him in order that we may also be glorified with him.

The answer to this question sums up in itself the entire content of the Catechism: it forms as it were a majestic portico through which we are invited to enter into the knowledge of our salvation, into the very presence of the grace of God in Jesus Christ.

A preliminary remark is in order here: we are concerned with *comfort*. This refutes at the very outset the argument of those who still think that Christian education, the Catechism, or a theology can be purely abstract, a kind of gratuitous speculation, completely separate from life. The question here, and it will be the theme of the whole Catechism, is focused upon our *comfort,* that is to say, upon our true way of living, our only possibility of living in the world and for him, our happiness here and now and forever. We are men who have been comforted; this is the witness we must make in the world.

This comfort is more a specific succor that God gives in a concrete situation (illness, grief, anxiety, trials of any kind) than a state of well-being in which we might install ourselves in such a way that we should end up forgetting him who is the source of it. We are like a soldier who receives a piece of good news while at the front. It overjoys him, without his being any the less threatened.

What is the basis of this "only comfort"?

1. *It is the assurance that I belong—body and soul, in life and in death—not to myself but to my faithful Savior, Jesus Christ.* The Catechism goes directly to the main point; it does not, for example, begin by demonstrating the possibility or the impossibility of God as a source of true comfort. Rather, it places us in the presence of a staggering and truly existential affirmation, that from now on we know *we belong to Jesus Christ.*

Anyone who wishes to be comforted must begin by acknowledging, that is to say, by admitting through *faith* that he no longer

18

belongs to himself; he has been taken into custody under the protection of the one who will free him from the curse of mortal egoism. We were in the situation of a man in the throes of drowning. The Savior (rescuer) has thrown us a rope to which we have clung. We belong now to this Savior. In this world, we can be only saved men. And this is true, *body and soul.* No part of our being can lay claim to enjoying alone this gracious treatment; it is the whole man who receives the benefit of being saved; body, soul, heart, mind, each belongs to his Savior. Everything in man must then serve the glory of God.

In life and in death we belong to God. That assurance enables us to go right up to the limit that death represents for every man (hero, saint, movie star, and so on). In this dimension of affliction, too, we are comforted.

2. *Who at the cost of his own blood has fully paid for all my sins.* It is an objective act which assures our salvation and our freedom; in Jesus Christ God himself comes to discharge the debt that we have contracted in relation to him through our disobedience. God himself pays for his insolvent debtors. The cross of Jesus Christ is the cross that God makes on the "slate" or "against the score" of our mistakes; therefore, forever after we are free from this burden of debt.

The act of God goes still deeper for it is from the very dominion of the devil that we are set free. Satan is no longer a lord opposed to the true Lord; he is vanquished. He no longer has any resources, no longer any authority. We are no longer in his hands; we are under the *protection* of the true God, and come what may, there is never a sign of God's faltering, or any evidence of his forsaking us. On the contrary, "everything must fit his purpose for my salvation."

All our comfort is bound to the objective work of God in Jesus Christ. If the cross is for us the "greatest crime of history" or a "scandalous error"; if Jesus Christ remains for us an unjustly condemned man, a victim of religious fanaticism, then there is no possible comfort. The cross is our consolation if we lay hold by faith on the fact that God himself comes in Jesus Christ "to pay" for us and to put an end to the old order, or disorder created by the rebellion of man and the power usurped by Satan. Now the **new order begins; the resurrection of Jesus Christ is a positive sign** of the kingdom which has come and which is coming. Such then is our comfort.

3. *Therefore, by his Holy Spirit, he also assures me of eternal life.* The Holy Spirit is God coming to witness in us the work he has accomplished in Jesus Christ for us (Ephesians 1:13-14). The cross is not a work which is purely foreign to us, a historic event from which we might forevermore be separated through the course of the centuries; the Holy Spirit causes the work of God in Jesus Christ to become *my* salvation, *my* assurance, and *my* comfort.

The Holy Spirit is God giving to each man the assurance of his own salvation. This is how Jesus Christ becomes for each man his *only comfort.*

Let us lift up the word "wholeheartedly." It is joyously, with good heart and without constraint that we serve God. We are not heroes nor are we saints; we walk freely on the only road that opens to us, outside of the vicious circle of egoism, pride, and death, in the way of gratitude by the grace of God.

❡ QUESTION 2. *How many things must you know that you may live and die in the blessedness of this comfort?*

Three.[a] First, the greatness of my sin and wretchedness.[b] Second, how I am freed from all my sins and their wretched consequences.[c] Third, what gratitude I owe to God for such redemption.[d]

a. Titus 3:3-8. At one time we ourselves in our folly and obstinacy were all astray. We were slaves to passions and pleasures of every kind. Our days were passed in malice and envy; we were odious ourselves and we hated one another.

But when the kindness and generosity of God our Savior dawned upon the world, then, not for any good deeds of our own, but because he was merciful, he saved us. . . . For he sent down the Spirit upon us plentifully through Jesus Christ our Savior, so that, justified by his grace, we might in hope become heirs to eternal life.

Those who have come to believe in God should see that they engage in honorable occupations, which are not only honorable in themselves, but also useful to their fellow men (N.E.B.) .

b. John 9:41. Jesus said to them, "If you were blind, you would have no guilt; but now that you say, 'We see,' your guilt remains."
  Cf. Rom. 1:18—3:20.

c. John 17:1-3. Jesus . . . lifted up his eyes to heaven and said, "Father, the hour has come; glorify thy Son that the Son may glorify thee, since thou hast given him power over all flesh, to give eternal life to all whom thou hast given him. And this is eternal life, that they know thee the only true God, and Jesus Christ whom thou hast sent."
   Cf. Rom. 3:21—8:39; Phil. 2:5-11; Acts 10:34-43.
d. 1 Peter 2:9-10. You are a chosen race, a royal priesthood, a holy nation, God's own people, that you may declare the wonderful deeds of him who called you out of darkness into his marvelous light. Once you were no people but now you are God's people; once you had not received mercy but now you have received mercy.
   Cf. Rom. 12—14; Eph. 5:8-10.

Let us underscore at once that we are being asked: "How many things must you *know?*" Even before it becomes a question of faith, it is brought to our attention that we must acquire an *understanding* and that we are invited to go to school. The very realities which are going to make faith possible are not to be found in the realm of intuition, of feeling, or of sensibility; they are not possibilities more or less diffuse in man, but a certain number of truths, of objective disclosures which man must receive from without, which he must learn and know well. Calvin said, "Faith does not dwell in ignorance but in knowledge."

The three things that we must know for all our life are: 1. Our *sin and its wretched consequences.* 2. The *deliverance* of which we have been the object. 3. The *gratitude* which we owe to God.

The Christian acknowledgment is summed up in three terms:

wretchedness   *redemption*   *gratitude*

The positive contribution of the Reformation has been precisely to recover the foundation of the gospel, to know that, in the sight of God, the believer can be always only a man who *repents,* who *believes* in his forgiveness and who, therefore, *thanks God.*

PART I

Man's Sin and Guilt—The Law of God

---

2 / OUR HUMAN GUILT

❰ QUESTION 3. *Where do you learn of your sin and its wretched consequences?*

From the Law of God.[a]

a. Rom. 3:20. No human being will be justified in [God's] sight by works of the law since through the law comes knowledge of sin. Cf. Rom. 7:7-25.

❰ QUESTION 4. *What does the Law of God require of us?*

Jesus Christ teaches this in a summary in Matthew 22:37-40:
"YOU SHALL LOVE THE LORD YOUR GOD WITH ALL YOUR HEART, AND WITH ALL YOUR SOUL, AND WITH ALL YOUR MIND.[a] THIS IS THE GREAT AND FIRST COMMANDMENT. AND A SECOND IS LIKE IT, YOU SHALL LOVE YOUR NEIGHBOR AS YOURSELF.[b] ON THESE TWO COMMANDMENTS DEPEND ALL THE LAW AND THE PROPHETS." (Cf. Luke 10:27.)

a. Cf. Deut. 6:5.
b. Cf. Lev. 19:18.

It is the Law, that is to say, the Word of God, which reveals to man his sin and its wretched consequences. It accuses him of having broken the command of God and of having destroyed the relationship God desired of him; in short, of having deprived himself of the *peace* which he is permitted to know on earth as a creature of God.

Man's wretchedness is continually being revealed to him by God. Since, however, none other than God himself reveals it, the situation is not irremediable. At the same time that man becomes aware of his desperate plight, as the condemnation he suffers on account of his disobedience, God announces his *forgiveness*. Thus, the Law is the good news of the God who, in his love, does not abandon man to his illusions or his ignorance. It makes us understand our true position in the eyes of God, that is, that we are and can be only "prone to do evil" and "unable to do good," but it also discloses to us that the grace of God comes to lift us out of this desperate situation.

In summary: By means of the Law, God makes us acknowledge our sin, but since this Law is the Word of the God who is steadfast love, it can do no other than to announce, at the same time, our redemption. The Law is the gospel. It has to do with our only possible chance to live, that is, by the Word of God who, in Jesus Christ, brings us his judgment and his grace.

❰ QUESTION 5. *Can you keep all this perfectly?*

No,[a] for by nature I am prone to hate God and my neighbor.[b]

a. Rom. 3:10, 23. None is righteous, no, not one. . . . All have sinned and fall short of the glory of God.
   1 John 1:8. If we say we have no sin, we deceive ourselves, and the truth is not in us.
b. Rom. 8:7. The mind that is set on the flesh is hostile to God; it does not submit to God's law, indeed it cannot.
   Cf. Eph. 2:1-3; Titus 3:3.

We enter here into the domain of anthropology, that is, into the doctrine of man. It is, however, not going to be a question of man in general, but of man in his relation to God.

Let us begin by taking up the word *perfectly*. Man is bound to do every wish of God.

This impossible demand will make him appreciate the extent of his wretchedness. To the question of the possibility of man's doing the will of God, the Catechism replies with a categorical and absolute "no." If that is so, it is because *by nature I am prone to hate God and my neighbor.*

The impossibility comes then from the nature of man. But what is that nature? Where must one look for it? In primitive man, in an ideal man taken out of the actual human context with the idea that he is going to be studied as a subject in the laboratory?

Such is the illusion with which every optimistic philosophy, most of the reform movements, and very often the philosophies of education rock themselves to sleep. We think that we can learn the nature of man by studying man himself; we claim to improve him merely by modifying the conditions of this "given." Reformed theology reminds us that man can be known only in *the revelation of God.* Man cannot speak authoritatively about man. For him to be able to do that validly, it would be necessary that he should have lived in the primitive state which no longer exists; it would be necessary that the rupture of the fall of man, of his disobedience, sin, and corruption should not have happened at all. The "natural state" of man is no longer an original "state of nature" but that of disobedience. It is precisely this which revelation comes to make known; it lets us see man in the perversion of his nature, in the truth about man today. The essence of man, the nature of man, the truth about man is not in what *we* know and can know but in what *God* knows and gives us to understand in his Word; in knowing precisely that in this nature, we are able only "to hate God and neighbor." As long as we do not understand that, we perpetuate the worst errors. Human affairs will change at the moment when the true nature of man shall be acknowledged and accepted as it is and he shall be established upon truth and no longer on self-deception.

❡ QUESTION 6. *Did God create man evil and perverse like this?*

No.[a] On the contrary, God created man good and in his image,[b] that is, in true righteousness and holiness,[c] so that he might rightly know God his Creator, love him with his whole heart, and live with him in eternal blessedness, praising and glorifying him.[d]

a. Gen. 1:31. God saw everything that he had made, and behold, it was very good.
b. Gen. 1:27. God created man in his own image, in the image of God he created him; male and female he created them.
   Cf. Gen. 2:7.

24

c. Eph. 4:24. Put on the new nature, created after the likeness of God in true righteousness and holiness.
Cf. Col. 3:10.
d. Rev. 21:3. I heard a great voice from the throne saying, "Behold, the dwelling of God is with men. He will dwell with them, and they shall be his people, and God himself will be with them."

This question now arises: *Who is responsible* for this situation? To those who insinuate more or less frankly, more or less rebelliously, that all this is God's fault, that he had the power to prevent the disobedience of man and its troublesome consequences; to all those who indict God and declare him guilty, the Catechism replies once again with a categorical "no." It recalls immediately what God has done for us; God created man *good* and *in his image:* "It is certain that Adam, the father of us all, was created in the image and likeness of God" (Calvin: *Institutes of the Christian Religion,* Book I, Ch. XV. Cf. English translation, John T. McNeill, ed., Vol. 1, p. 186). This last word does not mean merely that Adam "resembles" God, but in truth, that he has been made "to be like" him. In this likeness man possesses *righteousness and holiness.* He comes to participate in all the good qualities of God.

The story of the *creation* reveals to us that man is a good being, essentially bound to God, a creature who exists only in reference to the God of whom he is the image. The biblical revelation does not conceive of man without God. If the situation should occur that the God-man relationship were to come to an end, man would no longer be man. The only place where this relationship ceases is in *hell.*

Whatever may be the evil and affliction which men draw on themselves, they cannot deny their essential belonging to the God who created them, and no one has yet found the way to exist "without God." Practical atheism is an absolute impossibility for man.

The true nature of man is to know God. He can love him or hate him, but he cannot exist without him.

Let us not forget this, however: *even though man cannot destroy* the bonds which unite him with God, *he can pervert them* and it is his fault if now creation bears the mark of corruption.

Man is responsible for the disorder which marks creation today; in no case could this be the Creator himself.

❡ QUESTION 7. *Where, then, does this corruption of human nature come from?*

From the fall and disobedience of our first parents, Adam and Eve, in the Garden of Eden;[a] whereby our human life is so poisoned[b] that we are all conceived and born in the state of sin.[c]

a. Gen. 3:1-6. The serpent was more subtle than any other wild creature that the Lord God had made. He said to the woman, "Did God say, 'You shall not eat of any tree of the garden'?" And the woman said to the serpent, "We may eat of the fruit of the trees of the garden; but God said, 'You shall not eat of the fruit of the tree which is in the midst of the garden, neither shall you touch it, lest you die.' " But the serpent said to the woman, "You will not die. For God knows that when you eat of it your eyes will be opened, and you will be like God, knowing good and evil." So when the woman saw that the tree was good for food, and that it was a delight to the eyes, and that the tree was to be desired to make one wise, she took of its fruit and ate; and she also gave some to her husband, and he ate.

b. Rom. 5:12. As sin came into the world through one man and death through sin, . . . so death spread to all men because all men sinned.

c. Ps. 51:5. Behold, I was brought forth in iniquity, and in sin did my mother conceive me.

Where does the disorder of creation come from and how has our human nature come to be perverted?

The account in Genesis speaks of *temptation* and of *disobedience*. It is the promise of the tempter: "You will be like God" (Gen. 3:5) that lures man to his *downfall*.

The two questions which are being raised here are: (1) Why did God permit man to succumb to temptation? (2) Why did man, who was in such perfect and favorable relationship with God, his Creator, sabotage his Creator's work?

1. God's own essence being freedom, he could not forcibly restrain man without denying himself or without ceasing to be God. God is free and his freedom is that of his love. It is in the very same freedom that he wants to be loved. In order that man may love him with the only love possible, God has had to run a risk: man created *in his image* could not be otherwise than free. It is by this very same freedom that disorder has been introduced

26

into the relationships between God and man. Man has not believed that the freedom which had been given him was for loving God, that is to say, that, really and truly, he should be like God. He thought that the freedom was for loving himself.

2. If man has sabotaged the work of creation, it is because *he has not had confidence in God.* He has not believed God's Word. He has believed that God was holding something back, even though in creating man "in his own image, in true righteousness and holiness," God had already given him everything. *Give me the share of property that falls to me* (Luke 15:12), the prodigal son said to his father, as if in his father's house the son were not already enjoying his whole inheritance.

It is thus that the communication between God and man becomes *poisoned.* From this point onward, the *poison of doubt* runs in man's bloodstream. Like a virus it paralyzes him, handicaps him, and brings about the situation that he can never enjoy to the full his faculties as God's creature. This sickness is *hereditary;* "we are all conceived and born in the state of sin." There is no one who can claim to escape this situation. Henceforth, all the works of man bear the mark of vanity, of pride, of egoism, of anxiety, and of death. The works of man are not meaningless or contemptible but they are *marred, defective.* This is true even of those which seem to us the most accomplished and almost perfect! We cannot know what they would have been had the order of creation not become the disorder we know. It is to Jesus Christ that we must look today to behold genuine perfection, that of God's own image. While appreciating the works of man and rejoicing in them, the believer will always know how to restrain his enthusiasm; he will not shout "a miracle"; he will applaud the works of man with restraint, but he will, in truth, glorify solely God in Jesus Christ.

❰ QUESTION 8. *But are we so perverted that we are altogether unable to do good and prone to do evil?*

Yes,[a] unless we are born again through the Spirit of God.[b]

a. Gen. 6:5. The Lord saw that the wickedness of man was great in the earth, and that every imagination of the thoughts of his heart was only evil continually.

Isa. 53:6. All we like sheep have gone astray; we have turned everyone to his own way.

Job 14:4. Who can bring a clean thing out of an unclean? There is not one.

John 3:6. Jesus answered, . . . "That which is born of the flesh is flesh, and that which is born of the Spirit is spirit."

b. John 3:5. "Truly, truly, I say to you, unless one is born of water and the Spirit, he cannot enter the kingdom of God."

The question that is now being asked concerns the degree of man's perversion. With respect to the issue of knowing whether we are "so perverted that we are altogether unable to do good and prone to do evil," the Heidelberg Catechism replies without hesitation and very categorically: Yes. That man alone who is "born again through the Spirit of God" is capable of doing good.

Man is therefore radically perverted. Such, indeed, is Calvin's view. In the *Institutes of the Christian Religion,* the chapter dealing with "the knowledge of Man," we read: "Man, having been created in the image of God, has been endowed with such favors and distinctions that should enable him to bear witness to the extraordinary liberality of his Creator toward him. Indeed, he was offered an opportunity to share in all these benefits, in the form of eternal life, were he to persevere in the integrity he had received. But he did not remain in that position for long. Because of his ingratitude he suddenly made himself *unworthy of all the benefits which God had given him.* As a result, the heavenly image which he bore was completely obliterated. . . . In place of wisdom, virtue, holiness, truth, and justice, with which adornments he had been clad, there came forth the most filthy plagues, blindness, impotence, impurity, vanity, and injustice; moreover, he has entangled and immersed his offspring in the same miseries" (Book II, Ch. I. Cf. English translation, Vol. 1, pp. 241-246).

In the same chapter, Calvin says later: "We are so vitiated and perverted *in every part of our nature* that by this great corruption we stand justly condemned before God" (*Ibid.,* p. 251). And furthermore, "whatever is in man, from the understanding to the will, from the soul even to the flesh, has been defiled and crammed with this concupiscence. Or, to put it more briefly, *the whole man is of himself nothing but concupiscence*" (*Ibid.*, p. 252; italics by Péry).

It is clear that for Calvin, as for the Heidelberg Catechism and for the reformers in general, man is *totally and radically perverted*.

This position has the advantage of not laying itself open to misunderstanding: man being completely fallen can be saved solely by an act of God's pure grace. God's work is all the more striking because man's effort has resulted in such a pitiful failure.

Even so, the dogma of radical or total perversion, upon reflection, presents a number of difficulties: if man is completely fallen, he is no longer a man, and consequently the incarnation becomes unthinkable. If man is merely nothing, how will God be able to assume human form? If Jesus Christ is "*true* God and *true* man," according to the definition of the Chalcedonian Council and the Heidelberg Catechism (Question 15), it is necessary to make some reservations with respect to the dogma of total perversion as it has been defined by the theology of the sixteenth century. We declared in the introduction to this study that we would not feel ourselves bound by the Catechism itself. We are not here to confirm the established truths of an infallible system, but to consider the meaning of our faith together with the men of the sixteenth century, with our contemporaries, and with some other fathers and brothers in the faith as well. Our guide is the biblical revelation and not this or that human system. What we are looking for is a better understanding of this revelation itself. As useful as a guide may be, still it will never take the place of direct knowledge of the goal to which it wishes to lead us.

It is to Jesus Christ himself that one must go in order to understand man. Because he is *true man*, Jesus Christ belongs to the order of creation in its fallen condition, perverted by human sin. If this nature no longer exists, Christ cannot assume it, even to save it.

In order to avoid any confusion, let us state carefully the following two points:

1. It is not man (that is to say we) who has soft-pedaled the perversion, as if we all at once were to say: "After all, things are

not as serious as we have been led to believe up to now: therefore let us put our minds at ease; we are not so bad, and everything will be fixed up between God and men!" The cross of Jesus Christ will always keep us from reasoning thus. Rather, God in the revelation of himself in Jesus Christ, the "true God and true man," obliges us not to take sin more seriously than the Lord himself does, as if any sin of man could possibly have ruined the work of the Creator of heaven and earth.

2. If man is fallen to the point of being annihilated, it is God who is made to suffer and is deprived of the one who represents and epitomizes all creation.

In short we can say: "Man has kept most of the admirable qualities with which God has endowed him. *But he no longer knows how to use them,* neither for the glory of God nor for his own well-being. *It is the use* of these faculties that is found to be perverted radically, but not the powers themselves although they too have suffered from the results of the fall" (Jacques de Senarclens: *Bulletin du Centre protestant d'études,* September 1957, p. 10).

Let us reaffirm that this criticism of the dogma of radical perversion by contemporary theology cannot be interpreted as pure speculation, a venture of the mind, or a theologians' quarrel. We are dealing, Karl Barth reminds us, with God's own truth. The purpose of all this thoughtful reflection based upon revelation is "the better to know who *God* is by recognizing who he is in *Jesus Christ*" (Karl Barth: *The Humanity of God,* p. 47).

Barth says again in the same work: "It is when we look at Jesus Christ that we know decisively that God's deity does not exclude, but includes his *humanity.* . . . In his deity there is enough room for communion with man. . . . How could we see and say it otherwise when we look at Jesus Christ in whom we find man taken up into communion with God? No, God requires no exclusion of humanity, no nonhumanity, not to speak of inhumanity, in order to be truly God. On the contrary, not merely does his deity not exclude humanity, it actually *encloses humanity in itself.* . . . All false deities are by Jesus Christ once for all made a laughingstock. In him the fact is once for all established that God does not exist without man" *(Ibid.,* pp. 47, 49-50; the italics are Dr. Barth's).

Thus we come to the end of these four questions dealing with the doctrine of man. It is most interesting to note the fact that we have finally been brought back to God himself. *Man does not exist without God:* this must be our most significant discovery.

Summary

1. It is in God himself, in his revelation that one must seek man and not elsewhere, in what could only be mere abstractions about man, be they optimistic or pessimistic.

2. Since Jesus Christ is both "true God and true man," it is to him that one must go in order to know both God and man.

3. The truth about God is that of a God who puts on humanity while agreeing to be borne by it.

4. The truth about man is that he is still able to put on God, therefore once again: "true man," "image of God."

5. Satan has sown the seeds of disorder in the relation between man and God by making man doubt the very reality of the love of God.

6. The perversion of man does not make him lose his manlike qualities, it debases them; it corrupts the use of them. Man wishes to use his freedom against God when in the order of creation everything was to be for God, and consequently, for man.

❡ QUESTION 9. *Is not God unjust in requiring of man in his Law what he cannot do?*

No, for God so created man that he could do it.[a] But man, upon the instigation of the devil,[b] by deliberate disobedience, has cheated himself and all his descendants out of these gifts.[c]

a. Gen. 1:31. God saw everything that he had made, and behold, it was very good.

b. John 8:44. Jesus said to them, "You are of your father the devil, and your will is to do your father's desires. He was a murderer from the beginning, and has nothing to do with the truth, because there is no truth in him. When he lies, he speaks according to his own nature, for he is a liar and the father of lies."

c. Rom. 5:12, 18-19. As sin came into the world through one man and death through sin, . . . so death spread to all men because all men sinned. . . . One man's trespass led to condemnation for all men. . . . By one man's disobedience many were made sinners. Cf. Gen. 3.

The question of responsibility bounces back again: things being what they are, man being unable to do what God demands of him, is not God at fault with respect to man? Is it not ultimately he who wrongs man, so that he is himself responsible for the situation? Man can then accuse him as Adam did, saying to God: "The woman whom *thou gavest* to be with me, she gave me fruit of the tree" (Gen. 3:12).

The Catechism recalls again that since God created man good, the latter is capable of fulfilling the Law. This is the fundamental gift which frees God from any responsibility. God does not change, he is *faithful* (Isaiah 49:7); it is not he who tempts man (James 1:13-15) but the *devil*.

Devil is the translation of the Hebrew word "Satan," the adversary, the accuser; "Satan" comes from a root that means to separate, to divide, to disunite. Satan destroys the unity of God's work; he rises up against God. He exhibits before man what he intends to propose to him: he uses his freedom for his own profit and introduces division thereby in the world God has created. He is, therefore, "the tempter" (Matt. 4:3; 1 Thess. 3:5), "a liar" and "the father of lies" (John 8:44) or the "evil one" or the "malevolent one" (2 Thess. 3:3; Matt. 6:13; 1 John 2:13).

However that may be, Satan remains subject to God *in spite of his disgrace* (Job 1:6); "he presents himself before God"; he must ask his permission before doing anything.

Satan tries to drag man into the way that he himself followed and he has permission to do it, but even in doing so he has not the power to jeopardize the lordship of God. The death and resurrection of Jesus Christ are the assurance given to men of Satan's defeat.

On the other side of the coin, however, let us not forget that God can toy with Satan by playing the trick of turning even evil to his glory. Calvin has pointed out that "the evil deeds of men are the righteous works of God."

We have to watch out when we speak of Satan and his power that we do not fall into the heresy of *Manicheanism* or *dualism*, which posits two gods of equal power, squaring off against each other. The biblical revelation knows only one God and it is precisely so that men may confess him as the living and victorious God who reveals himself to them.

Satan therefore is responsible for the disorder of the creation, for the sinfulness of man and for our sin. It is on his account henceforth that man is *evil* (Ephesians 2:3; Romans 3:10-23).

Let us remember that it is the very same Law of God, the one that man cannot fulfill, which reveals his true situation to him. It could not be his conscience or the state of the world around him or this or that philosophy which informs him. Only God himself through his Word, God in Jesus Christ, can do so. It is this name, when all is said and done, which frees us from all fear, however compromised our situation is, as men tempted by Satan.

Knowing what God wants of us and not being able to do it, our situation would be desperate had not God himself come to put an end to this condition through Jesus Christ. In him God makes known his *judgment* and his *grace*.

3 / THE JUDGMENT AND THE GRACE OF GOD

❡ QUESTION 10. *Will God let man get by with such disobedience and defection?*

Certainly not, for the wrath of God is revealed from heaven, both against our inborn sinfulness and our actual sins,[a] and he will punish them according to his righteous judgment in time and in eternity, as he has declared: "Cursed be everyone who does not abide by all things written in the book of the Law, and do them."[b]

a. Rom. 1:18. The wrath of God is revealed from heaven against all ungodliness and wickedness of men.
b. Gal. 3:10. All who rely on works of the law are under a curse; for it is written, "Cursed be every one who does not abide by all things written in the book of the law, and do them."
Cf. Deut. 27:26; 28:15.

Even though Satan is the one responsible, man is nonetheless *guilty* of having acceded to his seductions, of having yielded to the entreaties, the lure, and the enticement of evil. "Each person is tempted when he is lured and enticed by his own desire" (James 1:14). Man is therefore subject to the *righteous judgment* of God: he is punished by the very righteousness he has himself offended. The *righteousness of God* is the order of creation in which man had the *right* to live with God, sharing in the very life of his Creator. Since, however, man has willed to arrogate to himself another right, righteousness must be reestablished, for there could be only one righteousness, that of the living God. Man is therefore punished by the good and merciful God who *must* restore order. In letting his judgment act, God not only restores his own righteousness, but that of man as well.

The wrath of God means *the salvation of man;* it announces the end of disorder: the living God cannot tolerate that man live without him.

We are always in danger when we treat the wrath of God as an old and worn-out notion, in the framework of the evolutionist treatment of "religion." If Christianity represents a superior state of spiritual evolution, the wrath of God can only belong to the past; it can only be an attribute of the one called the "God of the Old Testament" (as if there could be two different "gods," according to whether one opens the Old or the New Testament).

If we read the scripture without prejudices, freeing ourselves from the pagan idea which insists that human affairs should always move from smaller to greater, from the inferior to the superior, from a primitive stage to a more developed stage; if, indeed, we come to the point of disregarding some of the humanistic prejudices that speculative philosophy has imposed upon us, we will see that there is only one God who reveals himself throughout the entire Bible as the righteous God who loves man. It is because *God loves man* that he does not let sin go unpunished. Those who reproach him for the expressions of his anger, simply show that they have not understood the meaning of God's love, which alone can be true love.

The wrath of God is nothing other than a demonstration of his *grace;* the righteousness of God is the gospel. If God were the "good God" that men thoughtlessly wish for, if he did nothing but pardon without punishing, he would be guilty in the same way that man is; he would be responsible for the human situation himself and would be powerless to save us from despair.

Question 10 adds that when man is subject to God's wrath, he is "cursed." "According to the Bible, the one who is cursed is no longer inside, but outside" (Barth: *The Heidelberg Catechism for Today*, Questions 10, 11). The man who brings down the wrath of God upon himself is in truth rejected. He can no longer avail himself of the privileges of his election. He no longer participates in the life which God has given him. He returns to chaos, to an existence "without ground or meaning." He passes into the camp of the enemy, into the domain of darkness and enmity toward God. Such is the downright misery of man cursed by God.

⟨ QUESTION 11. *But is not God also merciful?*

God is indeed merciful[a] and gracious, but he is also righteous.[b] It is his righteousness which requires that sin committed against the supreme majesty of God be punished with extreme, that is, with eternal punishment of body and soul.[c]

a. Exod. 34:6-7. The Lord passed before [Moses], and proclaimed, "The Lord, the Lord, a God merciful and gracious, slow to anger, and abounding in steadfast love and faithfulness, keeping steadfast love for thousands, forgiving iniquity and transgression and sin."

b. Exod. 20:5. "I the Lord your God am a jealous God, visiting the iniquity of the fathers upon the children to the third and fourth generation of those who hate me."
   Ps. 5:4-6. Thou art not a God who delights in wickedness; evil may not sojourn with thee. The boastful may not stand before thy eyes; thou hatest all evildoers. Thou destroyest those who speak lies; the Lord abhors bloodthirsty and deceitful men.

c. Matt. 25:45-46. Then [the King] will answer them, "Truly, I say to you, as you did it not to one of the least of these, you did it not to me." And they will go away into eternal punishment, but the righteous into eternal life.

Even when the Catechism speaks of God's mercy and grace, it does not cease to speak of his righteousness. The two motifs ought to go hand in hand and it is on purpose that Question 11 picks up again the theme of righteousness. It would have been very dangerous to speak no longer of anything but the mercy of God, since we tend so naturally to forget what establishes it and makes it possible.

In other respects, too, the question that we take up now does not repeat what has already been said about punishment. It directs our faith toward the One who has been "punished with extreme, that is, with eternal punishment of body and soul." Jesus Christ was man in his deepest anguish, utterly and absolutely forsaken. He alone has borne all the weight of the curse; he alone has known hell and that on our account (Isaiah 53). He suffered the "eternal punishment" of being separated from God. Jesus Christ recapitulates all mankind.

The suffering which the sin of man imposed upon him is *eternal* (Colossians 1:12-20). Nevertheless, the punishment declared against man on that Good Friday was not God's last word. The last word is that of grace, mercy, and forgiveness. After having said no to man and Satan, God now says yes by means of the resurrection of Jesus Christ who "bore our sins in his body on the tree" (1 Peter 2:24).

The guilt has been blotted out; disorder has been changed into order. God has restored his right. In this event and in this event alone, man too has been reestablished in his own right through Jesus Christ and in him. Righteousness reigns again on earth and in heaven; relationships between God and man have become normal; today they are so for every man who believes that Jesus Christ is himself the righteousness *and* the steadfast love of God.

"One could speak endlessly about the wretchedness of man, but thanks to God this situation is not endless" *(Ibid.,* Question 10, 11).

It was necessary for us to plunge to the very depth of despair in order that every illusion regarding our own capabilities might be destroyed. Only the Word of God, only Jesus Christ, could give us this awareness. God, however, is not like the philosophers who excel in destroying man's illusions, but have nothing to put in their place. They are in a sense half-prophets. God himself never speaks merely to judge man and condemn him. He comes to save him: "I have set you this day . . . to destroy and to overthrow, to build and to plant," God says to Jeremiah (1:10).

PART II

Man's Redemption and Freedom— The Grace of God in Jesus Christ

It is worthwhile to point out the proportion of questions devoted to each of the three parts of the Catechism: nine dealing with *Man's Sin and Guilt,* seventy-four with his *Redemption,* and forty-four with the *Gratitude* he owes to God.

For the authors of the Catechism what matters most is the fact that man has been freed. This is what constitutes the gospel, the new life, the opportunity man has been offered. It is clear that if the church's preaching is to be evangelical, that is to say, faithful to the scriptural revelation, it must speak more (eight times more!) of the redemption of man than of his guilt and condemnation, of the grace of God than of the sin of man. The knowledge of man's anguish could never be regarded as an end in itself; its only significance is to make the grace of God toward us better understood.

Questions 12-18 form a whole which is logically linked together. The words "since . . . therefore . . . because . . . so that" convey the rigor of the argument up to the moment when it culminates in the very basis of our comfort, for today and for the future—*"our Lord Jesus Christ,* who is freely given to us for complete redemption and righteousness" (Question 18).

The entire Bible makes clear to us that Jesus has suffered and died in our place, in order to satisfy the righteousness of God against which we have offended, to establish God and man again in their respective rights and that *he alone has been able to do it.* The event constituted by the birth, death, and resurrection of Jesus Christ is not a happenstance; it is not an accident (not even a "happy accident") but something which has a meaning, a necessity, a logic (in Greek *logos* means "word," the Word of God, Jesus Christ, the revelation that God gives of himself).

God's decision not to let sin go unpunished could, by itself, only enslave us to despair. We would be caught in the very necessity that God had to lay down by virtue of his holiness, if he had not come himself to shatter this inexorable logic. The name of Jesus Christ means that God has decided to put an end to the tragic situation of sinful man; it is thus that, at the end of this terse and painful reasoning, Question 18 can declare triumphantly that our Lord Jesus Christ "is freely given to us *for our complete redemption and righteousness.*"

4 / JUSTIFICATION BY GRACE

❡ QUESTION 12. *Since, then, by the righteous judgment of God we have deserved temporal and eternal punishment, how may we escape this punishment, come again to grace, and be reconciled to God?*

God wills that his righteousness be satisfied;[a] therefore, payment in full must be made to his righteousness, either by ourselves or by another.[b]

a. Exod. 23:7. God said: "I will not acquit the wicked."
   Cf. Exod. 20:5; 34:7; Deut. 7:9-11.
b. Rom. 8:3-4. Sending his own Son in the likeness of sinful flesh and for sin, [God] condemned sin in the flesh, in order that the just requirement of the law might be fulfilled.

God wills that his righteousness be fulfilled, that the pattern of his normal relationship with man be restored. He decided, therefore, to punish man, to make him acknowledge his Law, the full demand of his holiness. Accordingly, if man wants to "come again to grace," to live in the presence of God, it will be necessary for him to pay; if he is insolvent, it will be necessary that someone else pay for him. The debt cannot remain unpaid. The relationship of man with God must be opened for renewal on an absolutely new, that is, a perfectly "sound" basis, or else be poisoned forever. God would not know how to settle for a "certificate of bankruptcy." Man's situation is so desperate that one cannot wait for him to work out the reparation for himself. We have our backs to the wall: we must pay it ourselves (but we cannot) or else find someone who, knowing full well our position, will *agree to pay in our place.*

In one way or another, the debt *must* be paid without any unnecessary delay. The revelation of God in Jesus Christ has created for man a situation of urgency. As long as he did not know the exact amount of his debt, as long as he had not met his creditor, he could live in relative unconcern and tell himself that his situation was not so catastrophic, that, in some way, things would come out all right without having to face a reckoning. Now, because Jesus Christ has come, because the kingdom is at the gate (Mark 1:15, "the kingdom of God *is at hand")*, and the time of squaring accounts has arrived, man's situation is positively critical; there is no time to lose, no more illusions to be held—we have to work fast.

This note of urgency resounds throughout the Gospels. Thus, in the parable of the unfaithful steward, "there was a rich man who had a steward, and charges were brought to him that this man was wasting his goods. And he called him and said to him: 'What is this that I hear about you? *Turn in the account of your stewardship.'* The steward said to one of his master's debtors: 'Take your bill, sit down *quickly'* " (Luke 16:1-2, 6). Having been backed into acknowledging his infidelity, man absolutely has to find a solution.

℅ QUESTION 13. *Can we make this payment ourselves?*

By no means. On the contrary, we increase our debt each day.[a]

a. Job. 9:3. If one wished to contend with [God], one could not answer him once in a thousand times.
   Rom. 2:4-5. Do you not know that God's kindness is meant to lead you to repentance? But by your hard and impenitent heart you are storing up wrath for yourself on the day of wrath when God's righteous judgment will be revealed.
   Matt. 6:12. "Forgive us our debts, as we also have forgiven our debtors."

Man's first idea is to turn to himself in order to take stock of his resources; even in the face of a tremendous over-draft, he maintains the illusion that he will be able to meet it.

Such is the origin of the idea of *atonement:* man wants to do something for God; he wants to pay his debt. Such is the illusion that the "religions" keep alive in the heart of man. All, in one way or another, pretend to furnish man with the means of paying off his debt toward God. *Evangelical Christianity is not a religion,* it is not a human system of atonement. That is what Paul learned in the bosom of the Jewish religion and Luther in the bosom of the Roman Catholic system. When the apostle Paul says that the gospel "is the power of God for salvation to every one who has faith," and that "he who *through faith* is righteous shall live" (Rom. 1:16, 17); when Luther writes that "the glory of God appears in all its splendor when sinners are *received in grace,* for it is the glory of God to *heap blessings* upon us"; when Calvin states positively that "faith accepts the righteousness *offered* in the gospel"—the apostles and reformers agree, in fidelity to the gospel of Jesus Christ, that man cannot satisfy the righteousness of God, that he cannot pay off his debt and that help must come to him from outside of himself. A bankrupt man cannot pay his creditors by himself; a drowning man cannot save himself by pulling himself up by the hair.

"Good" deeds are quite useless; they cannot compensate for the bad ones; they cannot restore the balance. Our acts are all tainted by the curse; we cannot produce a single pure deed, that is to say, a completely unselfish act motivated by love alone. Everything that we do bears the mark of our own deep-seated egoism and pride. Such is our tragic situation, that even in wanting to do what is right and especially when we want to do it in order to save ourselves, we can only increase our debt. Therefore Jesus came not "to call the righteous, but sinners" (Matt. 9:13). This means those men and women who have given up trying to extricate themselves through their own efforts and are relying upon no other than the grace of God. As long as we do not accept this gift, *we increase our debt each day.*

It is important to understand clearly that our good deeds and our good will are only relatively good. Since God wants perfection (Matthew 5:48), our acts can in no way be used to satisfy God, that is, they cannot help bring him to declare himself fully repaid.

There is no place in the gospel which says that God will take into consideration our good will, our good works, our good intentions. "It is the road to hell that is paved with good intentions, not the road to heaven" (Jean de Saussure: *Cours supérieur d'Instruction religieuse basé sur le Catéchisme de Heidelberg,* p. 10).

The only thing God considers in man is his *repentance,* that is, the acknowledgment of his own guilt and his personal incompetence. Our good works are simply what we *owe* God; they cannot be anything more.

❡ QUESTION 14. *Can any mere creature make the payment for us?*

No one. First of all, God does not want to punish any other creature for man's debt.[a] Moreover, no mere creature can bear the burden of God's eternal wrath against sin and redeem others from it.[b]

a. Ezek. 18:20. The soul that sins shall die.
    Heb. 2:14-15. Since therefore the children share in flesh and blood, [Jesus] himself likewise partook of the same nature, that through death he might destroy him who has the power of death, that is, the devil, and deliver all those who through fear of death were subject to lifelong bondage.
b. Ps. 130:3. If thou, O Lord, shouldst mark iniquities, Lord, who could stand?
    Ps. 49:7. Truly no man can ransom himself, or give to God the price of his life.

Man himself cannot make the payment. Then could perhaps another man, another creature pay for him?

In paganism and Judaism a sacrificial animal pays and atones for man. In Roman Catholicism it is the saints. Certain creatures "merit" by their good works and their virtue a portion of grace over and above that which they owe for their salvation. This excess comes to supply "the treasury of compensation" with merits. God has always at his disposal a bit of credit which he can use for the benefit of his creatures whose liabilities are too heavy. Such is the Catholic doctrine of the transfer of merits.

"The church's treasury of graces *(thesaurus ecclesiae)* is formed of the superabundant atoning works of Christ and of the saints. These works do not lose their value, even when they are of no use to their author but, by virtue of a practice instituted by the head of the church, they drop into the treasury of the church and can thus be a benefit to the communion of saints, as a power of indulgence" (Bernhard Bartmann: *Précis de théologie dogmatique,* Tome II, p. 452. Original German title: *Lehrbuch der Dogmatik,* 2 Band).

At the heart of this doctrine, which could be called a stupendous illusion, we find the fact that man is considered capable of paying the contracted debt to God. If this is not true of all men, certain ones at least succeed in it and others are the beneficiaries of their surplus.

Protestantism is not safe from this error. To the same extent that the members of the Reformed churches cease believing in salvation by grace, they reintroduce the notion of merit into their belief. These Protestant works, although not being obligatory, are nonetheless real. How many times do we not find men and women, who, in one way or another, think they ought still to satisfy God? But when God reveals himself as he really is in Jesus Christ, when he ceases to be a creation of the human imagination, it becomes clear immediately that he could not allow anyone to *bargain* with him over his grace.

In Jesus Christ, the living God acquaints us with the nature of his holiness; he reveals to us that before his own face there is *no one* who can lay claim to the title of saint. The greatest "saints" and the most venerated remain and will remain debtors to the holy God. Not only can they provide nothing for the others, but not being themselves able to pay their own debt, they need someone to pay for them.

Therefore, the veneration of the saints and of the Virgin can be only a trap. It serves no purpose to beg from those who are as poor as we and who can in no way pull us out (Psalm 49:7; Matthew 25:8-9). No, it is the author of the offense who is responsible; it is he who is being examined and accused; it is he who must stand up and answer for his default.

If he cannot do so, there is no use for him to turn to another man, since all are in the same situation. It is, therefore, very clear that we cannot extricate ourselves from it without aid coming from the outside. *Jesus Christ is the one who comes to make us understand this, at the same time that he brings us succor.*

¶ QUESTION 15. *Then, what kind of mediator and redeemer must we seek?*

One who is a true[a] and righteous man[b] and yet more powerful than all creatures, that is, one who is at the same time true God.[c]

a. 1 Cor. 15:21. As by a man came death, by a man has come also the resurrection of the dead.
b. Isa. 53:9. They made his grave with the wicked and with a rich man in his death, although he had done no violence, and there was no deceit in his mouth.
Heb. 7:26. It was fitting that we should have such a high priest, holy, blameless, unstained, separated from sinners, exalted above the heavens.
2 Cor. 5:21. For our sake [God] made him to be sin who knew no sin, so that in him we might become the righteousness of God.
c. Isa. 9:6. To us a child is born, to us a son is given; and the government will be upon his shoulder, and his name will be called "Wonderful Counselor, Mighty God, Everlasting Father, Prince of Peace."
Cf. Jer. 23:5-6.

¶ QUESTION 16. *Why must he be a true and righteous man?*

Because God's righteousness requires[a] that man who has sinned should make reparation for sin, but the man who is himself a sinner cannot pay for others.[b]

a. Rom. 5:12, 15. Sin came into the world through one man and death through sin . . . but the free gift is not like the trespass. For if many died through one man's trespass, much more have the grace of God and the free gift in the grace of that one man Jesus Christ abounded for many.
b. 1 Peter 3:18. Christ also died for sins once for all, the righteous for the unrighteous, that he might bring us to God, being put to death in the flesh but made alive in the Spirit.
Cf. Isa. 53:3-5, 10-11.

¶ QUESTION 17. *Why must he at the same time be true God?*

So that by the power of his divinity he might bear as a man the burden of God's wrath,[a] and recover for us[b] and restore to us righteousness and life.[c]

43

a. Isa. 53:8. By oppression and judgment [the Lord's Servant] was taken away; and as for his generation, who considered that he was cut off out of the land of the living, stricken for the transgression of my people?

b. Acts 2:23-24. "This Jesus . . . you crucified and killed by the hands of lawless men. But God raised him up, having loosed the pangs of death, because it was not possible for him to be held by it."
John 1:4. In him was life, and the life was the light of men.

c. John 3:16. God so loved the world that he gave his only Son, that whoever believes in him should not perish but have eternal life.
2 Cor. 5:21. For our sake [God] made him to be sin who knew no sin, so that in him we might become the righteousness of God.

❡ QUESTION 18. *Who is this mediator who is at the same time true God and a true and perfectly righteous man?*

Our Lord Jesus Christ,[a] who is freely given to us for complete redemption and righteousness.[b]

a. Matt. 1:23. "Behold, a virgin shall conceive and bear a son, and his name shall be called Emmanuel" (which means, God with us).
Luke 2:11. "To you is born this day in the city of David a Savior, who is Christ the Lord."
Cf. 1 Tim. 3:16.

b. 1 Cor. 1:30. You are in Christ Jesus by God's act, for God has made him our wisdom; he is our righteousness; in him we are consecrated and set free (N.E.B.).

Since God is righteousness himself, he is the only one able to restore it. If a child sets fire to a house, it is not the child who can rebuild it. The proof of our inability being shown, we are obliged to call upon God to pull us out of our untenable situation. Such is the basis of the Reformed doctrine of *salvation by faith alone.* Faith is the act by which man acknowledges his own inability and the ability of God, and henceforth expects nothing except from him.

In Jesus Christ, God himself comes to the rescue of men; he runs to meet them (Luke 15:20). In order to be able to pay for human guilt, God becomes man. He enters into our condition; he takes our debt to his account because he is the only one who can do so.

Jesus is *true man.* It is important to understand this very clearly and never, in any way, to water down his humanity if we would accept him and acknowledge him as the one who saves man.

As early as the second century a heresy had come to light which cast doubt upon the humanity of Jesus Christ; this was *Docetism* (from the Greek verb that means "to seem, to appear to be"). According to this view, Christ would not really have known the weaknesses, the suffering, and tragic distress of men; he would merely have "seemed" to suffer and even "appeared" to die. God, in some way, would have "disguised" himself as a man in order to come to observe the human situation; he really would not have taken human status; he would only have pretended to do so. God would then be comparable to a king who puts on the outfit of a miner, goes down into the mine, smudges his face, and climbs up again to pose for the photographer. The gospel writings would be documents telling of this memorable event of God playing man. If this is all that has happened, we are not saved, God has not taken upon himself once for all and forever the burden of our eternal punishment; he has scarcely been smirched by contact with human realities, when, this unhappy moment being over, he returns to his royal prerogatives.

The opposite heresy is that of *Arianism* (from a fourth century theologian named Arius). According to this view, Jesus Christ was not *really God,* but simply a creature, the chief one to be sure, but nonetheless a creature. Once again, Jesus could not save us, if he is only a man who was mistaken for God. Faith in Jesus is, therefore, a human illusion, the first and fertile source of many others.

Let us recall the words of the Nicene Creed produced in the fourth century under the influence of Athanasius precisely in order to fight against the Arian heresy. Here are the interpretations added to the second article of the Apostles' Creed:

"And in one Lord Jesus Christ, the only begotten Son of God, begotten of the Father before all worlds, very God of very God, light of light, begotten not made, being of one essence with the Father by whom all things were made."

We note that these careful theological definitions which may appear useless to the faith of a simple heart are made necessary by heresy, that is, by sin. It is not that the theologian is enamored of subtleties as such; his precise task is one that sin makes obligatory.

These heresies are hardy and perennial; under one form or another, with some variations, they constantly recur in the course of history. Today they are represented by spiritualistic philosophers on the one hand, and by liberal theologians on the other. It is necessary, therefore, always to be precise in putting forward the right definition of Jesus Christ as "true God and true man," and our only Savior.

As far as the *humanity* of Jesus is concerned, it already appears in those outward marks of his life which attest to his true sharing in human existence: Jesus knows hunger (Matthew 4:2), thirst (John 19:28), sleep (Mark 4:38), joy (Luke 10:21), sorrow (Luke 19:41). Jesus asks to be *baptized* (Matthew 3:13-17) in order to stress that he is entering fully into our human situation. "Let it be so now," he says to John the Baptist, "for thus it is fitting for us to fulfill *all righteousness*" (Matt. 3:15). At the moment of baptism Jesus knows that he is being asked to fulfill the righteousness of God, to reestablish God and man in their respective rights; baptism is already a preview of the *cross*.

Jesus is fully man, truly one of us, completely involved in our humanity and our anguish. In him is neither shame nor deceit. God becomes man in Jesus Christ in order to bear the burden of man's guilt.

As to the *divinity* of Jesus, it appears constantly in the gospel records. The New Testament in its entirety bears witness to this fact that, in Jesus of Nazareth, in this man born in wretched surroundings at Bethlehem, God himself is present. When a disciple looked at Jesus, he could not doubt his being human, but when he heard him speak or saw him work, he could not doubt that this man was indeed the Son of God, the one who according to the testimony of the Old Testament signified the coming of God among men. Indeed, Jesus can assert positively: "I and the father are one" (John 10:30), he can announce himself (John 10:9-11), he can forgive sins (Matthew 9:2-3), he can require his followers to leave everything behind (Matthew 10:37-39).

The New Testament has no other goal than to attest to the word which Jesus spoke about himself and in which he presented himself as very God. We cannot cast doubt on this word or on the acts which give it authenticity. Either we believe what Jesus said about himself, or else like the Jews we make of him an imposter.

Either we believe that he is true God and true man, or else we are willing to be completely wrong on this matter.

Let us sum up the possibilities regarding the humanity of Jesus Christ. There are only three of them.

1. *Jesus is only a man.* What he has done, however, proves that he was a great man, the ideal which ought to draw mankind to him, the great example recommended but impossible to achieve. In this regard, Jesus is not superior to Muhammad or Buddha; Christianity is only one religion among others and perhaps not the best. Indeed, "if Jesus is only a man, he is not even an honest man" (Gaston Frommel). He has perpetrated the greatest hoax in history. He wanted to pass himself off for God even though he was not God.

2. *Jesus is an imposter,* a blasphemer, and the leaders of the Jews are right in condemning him as such (Mark 14:61-65). Indeed, what must one make of the scripture? Can one suppose that all this had been faked, having been arranged and harmonized in order to defend the thesis of the divinity and the messiahship of Christ Jesus? Further, how are we to explain the authority of Jesus in his words and acts (Mark 1:27; Luke 4:32)? When Jesus cured the sick and raised the dead, it was not only for the purpose of acquainting men with God's love, and making them well; it was also meant to offer them a demonstration of his divinity (John 3:2). We can only embrace the third solution, unless we are, in the most literal sense of these words, "men of bad faith," refusing to believe God even when he comes himself, to tell us who he is.

3. *Jesus Christ is God-in-man.* As such, he is the mediator between God and men, the only one who can save us, the only one capable of bearing the weight of the divine wrath, the only one who is absolutely righteous (1 Peter 3:18; Matthew 3:17).

Therefore, God in Jesus Christ, true God and true man, offers himself as the perfect satisfaction of the righteousness he demands of man. It is only in this way that we can be totally freed, without God's righteousness being impaired (which would be the case if he were only indulgent, or if he had not become truly a man).

In Jesus Christ God comes to restore the fullness of his claim upon man, and thereby he reestablishes man's right. "All goes back into order." It is, of course, only in this setting that such an expression can ever be used.

Jesus Christ is, therefore, our *only comfort.*

Through faith, we receive right now the fullness of what we are in the eyes of God (1 John 3:1-3).

Such is the ambiguity, however, of the Christian life: we have received everything in Jesus Christ, but we still are sinful men (Mark 9:24); we believe in our deliverance and in our new righteousness, we have really come again to grace in the presence of God, we are reconciled to him and no longer have to fear him as a judge; we know peace and joy, but we are not for that reason exempt from the struggles and pain of our life. Our faith is not a haven or refuge against the sufferings of life, but a witness that we make in the midst of these very sufferings, a proof of our liberation by Jesus Christ. Thus we arrive at the logical conclusion, based upon the Scriptures, that it is the *judgment of God* which gives us the assurance of our salvation.

SUMMARY

1. Our sin has offended the righteousness of God; it has perverted the order that God himself has established in the creation.

2. It is necessary that this order be reestablished, that the righteousness of God be fulfilled, that is, that our relations with God become normal again.

3. God, therefore, decided to punish sin by having man make a "complete payment" of what he owes him, that is, of the righteousness that he has flouted.

4. Man himself cannot pay; in wishing to do so, he accumulates new debts to God.

5. No creature can pay for the man who is responsible for his own sin. Moreover, no one can give back to God the righteousness that is due him.

6. Therefore, God himself comes in Jesus Christ to set man free. Because he is a real man, he bears the burden of the punish-

ment deserved by man; because he is truly God, he is perfectly righteous and can discharge the debt of righteousness that man has contracted toward God.

In Jesus as the Christ, God reveals his righteous and gracious love toward us. Moreover, in him *God gives his love to us.*

We cannot fail to acknowledge Jesus Christ as true God and genuine man, as attested by the Scriptures, without losing all the benefits of our redemption.

5 / THE HOLY TRINITY

❡ QUESTION 19. *Whence do you know this?*

From the holy gospel, which God himself revealed in the beginning in the Garden of Eden,[a] afterward proclaimed through the holy patriarchs[b] and prophets[c] and foreshadowed through the sacrifices and other rites of the Old Covenant,[d] and finally fulfilled through his own well-beloved Son.[e]

a. Gen. 3:14-15. The Lord God said to the serpent: "I will put enmity between you and the woman, and between your seed and her seed; he shall bruise your head, and you shall bruise his heel."

b. Gen. 22:18. "By your descendants shall all the nations of the earth bless themselves, because you have obeyed my voice."
Gen. 49:10. "The sceptre shall not depart from Judah, nor the ruler's staff from between his feet, until he comes to whom it belongs; and to him shall be the obedience of the peoples."

c. Heb. 1:1-2. In many and various ways God spoke of old to our fathers by the prophets; but in these last days he has spoken to us by a Son, whom he appointed the heir of all things, through whom also he created the world.
Acts 10:43. "To [Jesus of Nazareth] all the prophets bear witness that everyone who believes in him receives forgiveness of sins through his name."
Cf. Rom. 1:1-6; Acts 3:22-26.

d. Heb. 9:13-15. If the sprinkling of defiled persons with the blood of goats and bulls and with the ashes of a heifer sanctifies for the purification of the flesh, how much more shall the blood of Christ, who through the eternal Spirit offered himself without blemish to God, purify your conscience from dead works to serve the living

God. Therefore he is the mediator of a new covenant.
Cf. Heb. 9:1—10:10.
e. Gal. 4:4-5. When the time had fully come, God sent forth his Son, born of woman, born under the law, to redeem those who were under the law, so that we might receive adoption as sons.
Cf. Rom. 10:4.

The reply to this question is fundamental, for it discloses to us the basis of our assurance. What has been stated up to this point concerning our freedom through Jesus Christ, our redemption from sin and death, is not a speculative theory or a spiritual vision. Our assurance rests upon a certain number of revelatory historical events of which mankind has been *witness*. Jesus Christ, our Redeemer, did not come into the world as a meteor fallen from the sky (one would then be able to ask all sorts of questions of him, and the revelation that it would claim to bring would be conjectural). No, the coming of Jesus as the Christ has been planned from the beginning of the covenant relationship between God and man; the whole Bible bears witness to it.

The entire scripture therefore can qualify here as the "holy gospel": it bears witness to this fact that from the moment when he bound himself to man in creating him, God has disclosed himself as man's Savior. Our assurance does not rest upon a single fact, one that could be discussed by itself, but on a series of events in human history, recorded and reduced to writing for the purpose of strengthening our faith.

The revelation of God regarding the Savior already appears in the promise made to the woman that her posterity "will bruise the head" of the serpent (Gen. 3:15). This promise becomes more explicit and positive for the patriarchs of whom Abraham is the model: "By your descendants shall all the nations of the earth bless themselves, because you have obeyed my voice" (Gen. 22:18). As for the prophets, they openly announced the coming of a Savior in the person of the servant of the Lord (Isaiah 53), of a branch of David (Jeremiah 23:5-6), of the one who will rule in the name of God (Micah 5:1-4), of the king of Israel (Zachariah 9:9). Psalm 22, from which Jesus will quote on the cross, is a prophetic announcement of the messianic Savior. Again, one must mention here the text of John 8:58: "Before Abraham was born, I *am*."

As to the sacrifices and ceremonies of the Old Testament, they announce and prefigure the act of him who would come as the "high priest of good things to come" (Heb. 9:11, KJV).

"God testified concerning his Son, whenever in past times he held out to the ancient people hope of salvation" (Calvin: *Commentary on the Gospel according to John;* 5:37, p. 216). Jesus Christ has accomplished in his person the whole ministry of the Old Testament. He is king, priest, and prophet. Those who did not see him knew *by faith* that he would come (Hebrews 11:39-40). The acts of God manifested in the history of Israel engendered the faith of the "cloud of witnesses" (Heb. 12:1), just as today their witness nourishes our faith.

God's decision, to redeem mankind in Jesus Christ and by him, has not been a hypothetical one; it has been disclosed among men who could bear witness to it. The Bible, from Genesis to the book of Revelation, constitutes the foundation of our faith: it is the gospel, the good news of our salvation that all men can recognize today.

❰ QUESTION 20. *Will all men, then, be saved through Christ as they became lost through Adam?*

No. Only those who, by true faith, are incorporated into him and accept all his benefits.[a]

a. John 1:11-13. He came to his own home, and his own people received him not. But to all who received him, who believed in his name, he gave power to become children of God; who were born, not of blood nor of the will of the flesh nor of the will of man, but of God.

Rom. 11:17-20. If some of the branches were broken off, and you, a wild olive shoot, were grafted in their place to share the richness of the olive tree, do not boast over the branches. If you do boast, remember it is not you that support the root, but the root that supports you. You will say, "Branches were broken off so that I might be grafted in." That is true. They were broken off because of their unbelief, but you stand fast only through faith. So do not become proud, but stand in awe.

Heb. 4:2; 10:39. Good news came to us just as to them; but the message which they heard did not benefit them, because it did not meet with faith in the hearers. . . . But we are not of those

who shrink back and are destroyed, but of those who have faith and keep their souls.
Cf. Isa. 53:11; Heb. 11.

God comes to make himself known and the acts of the divine initiative are clearly attested. "When we hear a summons as simple as that, our first inclination is to think that everybody is going to accept such a godsend" (de Saussure: *Op. cit.,* p. 14). In fact, this is not so! The great majority pass up this privilege. Why?

It is not because of ignorance, for these events, at least in the main, are well known. For some people, it is because "their deeds [are] evil" (John 3:19) and they do not want to be obligated to God for anything; for others, it is because they are "too busy" and they do not lack excuses for postponing until later their giving attention to God (Luke 14:18-20). Above all, it is because the *decision of faith* is God's work through the Holy Spirit (Matthew 16:17; Acts 16:14). When God reveals himself, he does not automatically drop into the hands of men in such a way that they could manipulate him as they wish. No, God always keeps the initiative, and although he reveals himself, he *chooses* those whom he *summons* to the decision of faith. God in Jesus Christ comes among men, but it is God the Holy Spirit who enables men to recognize him (1 Corinthians 12:3).

By the preaching of the gospel, a new people grafted into the trunk of Israel appears in the world (Romans 11:17-19); these men are "incorporated" into Jesus Christ, forming his body on earth (1 Corinthians 12:27) and as such are closely linked to his ministry among men. They extend and renew the sovereign act of God, our Creator and Savior, from generation to generation. They keep alive the knowledge of the living God for the people of their own times. They are called together not for themselves, for their own satisfaction, but for the glory of God. They are "the light of the world" (Matt. 5:14). This is the counterpart of election; the church exists to glorify God in the world.

℘ QUESTION 21. *What is true faith?*

It is not only a certain knowledge by which I accept as true all that God has revealed to us in his Word,[a] but also a wholehearted trust which the Holy Spirit creates in me[b] through the gospel,[c]

52

that, not only to others, but to me also God has given the forgiveness of sins, everlasting righteousness and salvation, out of sheer grace solely for the sake of Christ's saving work.[d]

a. John 17:3. "This is eternal life, that they know thee the only true God, and Jesus Christ whom thou hast sent."
Cf. James 1:18.

b. Rom. 4:13, 16. The promise to Abraham and his descendants, that they should inherit the world, did not come through the law but through the righteousness of faith. . . . That is why it depends on faith, in order that the promise may rest on grace.
Matt. 16:15-17. Jesus said to them, "But who do you say that I am?" Simon Peter replied, "You are the Christ, the Son of the living God." And Jesus answered him, "Blessed are you, Simon Bar-Jona! For flesh and blood has not revealed this to you, but my Father who is in heaven."
2 Cor. 1:21-22. It is God who . . . has put his seal upon us and given us his Spirit in our hearts as a guarantee.

c. Rom. 1:16. I am not ashamed of the gospel: it is the power of God for salvation to everyone who has faith, to the Jew first and also to the Greek.
Rom. 10:17. Faith comes from what is heard, and what is heard comes by the preaching of Christ.

d. Rom. 3:21-26. Now the righteousness of God has been manifested apart from law, although the law and the prophets bear witness to it, the righteousness of God through faith in Jesus Christ for all who believe. For there is no distinction; since all have sinned and fall short of the glory of God, they are justified by his grace as a gift, through the redemption which is in Christ Jesus, whom God put forward as an expiation by his blood, to be received by faith. This was to show God's righteousness, because in his divine forbearance he had passed over former sins; it was to prove at the present time that he himself is righteous and that he justifies him who has faith in Jesus.
Cf. Eph. 2:4-9; Gal. 2:15-16.

The reply to this question insists rightly upon the fact that true faith is a *knowledge* (recognition) and a *trust* (confidence). Theology, since the Reformation, has not always given faith an exact definition. Sometimes the accent is put upon knowledge, at other times upon trust. In the first case it has ended in intellectualism or dogmatism, that is to say, in a doctrinaire orthodoxy, utterly cold and dead, without any relevance to life. This explains the prejudices of certain individuals against all elaboration of a Christian doctrine which they fear will always become pure speculation, only a word game, and no longer be a confession of the faith commonly held among us. In other times and precisely in reaction to these intellectualistic tendencies, there were those who did not want to speak of faith as knowledge at all, in order to guard faith as trust. When, however, trust was no longer tied to anything, they wound up with the vaguest kind of sentimentalism, a mystical subjective Christianity, an individualistic piety, which in the end had no more relevance for the world than the intellectualism they had wished to avoid.

The reformers were very precise about the relationship that should exist, in the matter of faith, between knowing and trusting. Calvin said: "Faith is a firm and certain knowledge of God's benevolence toward us, founded upon the truth of the freely given promise in Christ, *both revealed to our minds and sealed upon our hearts through the Holy Spirit*" (*Institutes,* Book III, Ch. II. Cf. English translation, Vol. 1, p. 551).

The response that man makes to God's election demands his entire being: spirit, soul, mind, will. All his faculties come into play in order that he may avail himself of God's gift of freedom.

Faith in the gospel is not just any faith, its character is determined by revelation. Man called to faith through the preaching of the gospel (Romans 10:17) must consult the evidence of the scripture if he wants to know what he should believe regarding the God who comes to him. He can have no "true faith" without study, without seeking to meet the God who manifests himself in person. Study of the scriptural evidence must always be the answer of the man called to faith. We can know God only on this one condition.

Indeed, in order that this knowledge may claim man completely and that he be encouraged to pursue his quest to know all its implications and all its applications, the Holy Spirit must give him the assurance that God's work concerns him personally. The Holy Spirit tells me that my salvation, my forgiveness, my reconciliation with God, my redemption are all involved here. Then, faith becomes a wholehearted trust which carries me through all the circumstances of life.

Let us add that this personal recognition of God's work in Jesus Christ does not isolate man. It does not separate him, nor does it shut him up in the selfish enjoyment of his privilege. On the contrary, it opens up at the same time the recognition that there exist around him men and women to whom the same revelation has been given. Where true faith is confessed, that is, where the work of God in Jesus Christ is acknowledged and confidence is bestowed by the Holy Spirit, there the church is truly gathered together. Of small import is the number of those who belong, their culture, their intellectual level, their social status. Only one thing counts from now on: that their faith be addressed to the God who has made himself known in the gospel.

This community of believers becomes therefore "the light of the world." The church can be many things; but if it is not first of all the place where, through his Word and his Spirit, Jesus Christ rules unchallenged, all our witness becomes sterile and men continue, because of the church's failure, in their hunger for the knowledge of God's righteousness.

€ QUESTION 22. *What, then, must a Christian believe?*

All that is promised us in the gospel,[a] a summary of which is taught us in the articles of the Apostles' Creed, our universally acknowledged confession of faith.

a. John 20:31. These are written that you may believe that Jesus is the Christ, the Son of God, and that believing you may have life in his name.
Cf. Matt. 28:18-20; Acts 10:34-43.

What is the *content of the faith,* the object of the believer's knowledge? It is what is "promised us in the gospel," what the church has clearly expressed in its confessions of faith and particularly in the Apostles' Creed.

We cannot just believe any way or any thing. The church's confession of faith, at the same time that it defines exactly what the church ought to believe in loyalty to the gospel, tells her what she cannot believe without ceasing at that point to be the church of Jesus Christ.

We believe only what God tells us of himself. "Free from the limitations of reason, faith is strictly bound to the framework of revelation" (de Saussure: *Op. cit.,* p. 16). A true confession of faith does not imprison God. On the contrary, it gives him his full freedom. God the Holy Spirit is never bound, but we are bound to the testimony of his revelation.

The Apostles' Creed *(Symbolum Apostolicum)* is a document whose formulation can be placed between the third and fourth centuries. It was not written by the apostles themselves but by the church faithful to their teaching. The Latin word *symbolum* originally meant "sign," "banner," "standard." Every Roman legion had its own standard. When a soldier became lost in the midst of battle, he knew where to find his unit again and thus he did not run the risk of joining the camp of the enemy by mistake.

Still today the Apostles' Creed rises above the changing opinions of men and their intellectual moods and theological fashions. It constantly reminds the church what she must preach, what she must believe. The Creed is the rallying "standard" for all believers. Certain ones are pretty far away from their unit of combat; they are struggling and working hard to rejoin it. The important thing is that this banner permits them to know their direction so that they may not waste their energy in futile efforts that lead them nowhere.

The confession of faith recalls for all Christians, generation after generation, the mandate that God hands to the people whom he calls to be his witness on earth. It becomes, so to speak, the life-sustaining food of believers, the "iron ration" of the church.

We must add that the confession of faith also constitutes the *answer* which the church gives to the God who examines her in the gospel.

The Apostles' Creed was the baptismal formula for the first centuries of Christianity. It was explained to the catechumen, who was required to recite it before entering the membership of the church. This confession of faith links us to the Christians of all ages. It reminds us that we have fathers and brothers in the faith. We cannot pass lightly over the fact that men and women have believed this way before us. We are to a large extent bound by their testimony.

¶ QUESTION 23. *What are these articles?*

I BELIEVE IN GOD THE FATHER ALMIGHTY, MAKER OF HEAVEN AND
EARTH;

AND IN JESUS CHRIST, HIS ONLY-BEGOTTEN SON, OUR LORD: WHO WAS
CONCEIVED BY THE HOLY SPIRIT, BORN OF THE VIRGIN MARY; SUF-
FERED UNDER PONTIUS PILATE, WAS CRUCIFIED, DEAD, AND BURIED;
HE DESCENDED INTO HELL, THE THIRD DAY HE ROSE AGAIN FROM THE
DEAD; HE ASCENDED INTO HEAVEN AND SITS AT THE RIGHT HAND OF
GOD THE FATHER ALMIGHTY; FROM THENCE HE SHALL COME TO JUDGE
THE LIVING AND THE DEAD.

I BELIEVE IN THE HOLY SPIRIT; THE HOLY CATHOLIC CHURCH; THE
COMMUNION OF SAINTS; THE FORGIVENESS OF SINS; THE RESURRECTION
OF THE BODY; AND THE LIFE EVERLASTING.

¶ QUESTION 24. *How are these articles divided?*

Into three parts: The first concerns God *the Father* and our
creation; the second, God *the Son* and our *redemption;* and the
third, God *the Holy Spirit* and our *sanctification.*

¶ QUESTION 25. *Since there is only one Divine Being,*[a] *why do*
you speak of three, Father, Son, and Holy
Spirit?

Because God has thus revealed himself in his Word, that these
three distinct Persons are the one, true, eternal God.[b]

a. Deut. 6:4. "Hear, O Israel: The Lord our God is one Lord."
b. Matt. 3:16-17. When Jesus was baptized, he went up immediately
   from the water, and behold, the heavens were opened and he saw
   the Spirit of God descending like a dove, and alighting on him; and
   lo, a voice from heaven, saying, "This is my beloved Son, with whom
   I am well pleased."
   Cf. Matt. 28:19; 2 Cor. 13:14.

The Apostles' Creed, the church's confession of faith, the articles of "our universally acknowledged confession of faith" constitute an "epitome," a summary of "all that is promised us in

57

the gospel" (Question 22). The articles of the Creed are true to the revelation that God gives of himself and it is on this ground that they can be believed. The articles of faith are also an *explanation of the meaning* of the gospel, a development of what it contains as a seed. The Creed is not a graft, but the normal growth of the same plant.

Thus, God is revealed in the gospel, in his Word, as Father, Son, and Holy Spirit; that is, as the Lord who *creates* men, who *frees* them and finally *redeems* them. Such is the *doctrine of the Trinity* which the Catechism sets forth.

This doctrine is not the invention of the church, a "find" by theologians, or a human theory to explain God. It would then deserve the reproach which people made against it during the centuries following the Reformation: that it was obscure, and that it was itself responsible for the divisions of the church. No, the doctrine of the Trinity is deeply rooted in revelation; it is biblical and we cannot produce an evangelical theology without speaking of God in the very manner in which the Bible speaks of God. We have to get out of our minds the prejudices against the Trinity which the centuries of liberal theology, rationalism, and humanism have left upon them.

The intransigence of Calvin in the Servetus affair, for example, is not to be laid to an authoritarian character nor to an irritable temperament! To think so is to oversimplify the matter. Calvin did not set out to achieve a personal-opinion triumph, no more than he wished to wreak vengeance against any opponent. He was convinced, however, that to deny the Trinity would inevitably lead to denying the gospel itself. It is true that where God is not believed and received as the Father, Son, and Holy Spirit, Christianity no longer exists. The severity of the condemnation pronounced upon Servetus attested the seriousness of the heresy which he taught.

Let us notice, however, that several of the difficulties raised by the doctrine of the Trinity have come about because theology itself has, again and again, wandered down the road of speculative philosophy. In the past century, there was proposed a higher, eternal and all-powerful, God-Spirit which some theologians wished to demonstrate was identical with the God of revelation. Since it became an impossibility to prove that this God conceived by human reason could be a one-in-three, they were led to eliminate the doctrine of the Trinity as incompatible with reason. It is clear that if God is the eternal mind (pure reason) and the guarantor of the moral order (practical reason), neither the Son nor the Holy Spirit have any longer a role to play. The Son cannot be of the "same essence" with the Father. For a rationalistic theology and for a moralistic theology, Jesus is only a man. As for the Holy Spirit—and this is worth noting—either he is ignored or he is identified with the universal spirit among men, which they corporately experience within themselves.

Another difficulty has arisen from a faulty use of terms: the reformers have spoken, and the Heidelberg Catechism does it too, of the three persons of the Trinity, at the risk of setting forth in God an irreconcilable distinction so that one has, in fact, three Gods (Calvin said three "marmousets") even though one takes the trouble to state exactly *one God in three persons.*

Contemporary theology has given back to the doctrine of the Trinity its true worth: it is the very expression of the God who reveals himself in his acts, of which the scripture bears witness. The God who creates, who frees man, and who makes his salvation known to him, is God the Father, Son, and Holy Spirit, the Lord, the only God of whom Christian theology could speak.

Again, it has been proposed that we no longer speak of the three "persons" of the Trinity, but of the three "modes" of God's being. God exists, is revealed and manifested in three distinct modes, but it is always the same God with whom we are dealing. In Jesus Christ God reveals himself as the Father and this revelation becomes effective for man through the Holy Spirit.

All the knowledge that man can have of God comes from Jesus Christ. In order that the doctrine of the Trinity can be received as the revelation of the "one, true, eternal God," man must first of all be freed by Jesus Christ.

Once *freed by Jesus Christ* man knows through the *Holy Spirit* that he is already a member of the kingdom of which *God* is the Lord. He is introduced into the covenant of grace by the God who, in Christ, reveals himself to him as his Father. God's work as Creator and Savior is witnessed to him by the Holy Spirit as being God's work for him.

The triune God is *precisely* as he reveals himself. It is literally impossible to describe God in any other way. Through these three ways of being corresponding to the three fundamental acts of God the Creator, the Reconciler, and the Redeemer, God gives us the only human possibility of speaking of him.

Moreover, the triune God is *completely* as he reveals himself. There is nothing of what he allows men to know which is hidden. He answers our questions about God's being in a fully satisfying way. He is the Father of Jesus Christ and our Father; the Holy Spirit is his Spirit and the Spirit of Jesus Christ. We can say nothing else and nothing more about God.

Finally, the triune God is *definitively* what he reveals himself to be. We no longer have to look for other revelations that might be more complete, more accessible, more amenable to human understanding. What God has done in Jesus Christ he need not do again, and the Holy Spirit who makes this deed known speaks no differently today than formerly.

Let us note further:

1. The Heidelberg Catechism speaks of God the Father as being the *Creator,* of God the Son as being the *Redeemer,* and of God the Holy Spirit as being the *Sanctifier.*

For Karl Barth and a great number of today's theologians, he is God the *Creator,* God the *Reconciler,* and God the *Redeemer.* Thus, it is to the Holy Spirit that contemporary theology attributes the work of redemption which traditional theology entrusted to Jesus Christ. In this way a faulty independence of the Holy Spirit is prevented. It has happened and it will happen again that he may be considered as a kind of "outsider," that he may be represented, one could say, as "a solitary knight," so that the work of sanctification attributed to him is in no way linked to anything else. Such is the tendency with pentecostal movements; they put an almost unique emphasis upon the Holy Spirit and end by making him an autonomous power working directly and immediately upon man. The "baptism of the Holy Spirit," of which certain Christians avail themselves, is dissociated from true baptism, which is a death and a resurrection *with Christ* (Romans 6); it is thus no more than a kind of enthronement in glory, making useless the cross of Jesus Christ. Indeed, since man is left in his actual wretchedness, the gifts that the Holy Spirit bestows upon man always run the risk of being poisoned by his perverted nature.

In attributing the role of redemption to the Holy Spirit, contemporary theology underscores the fact that his work is not different from that of Jesus Christ; the Holy Spirit actualizes the work of Jesus Christ for the man who thereby becomes the beneficiary of it, and is thus truly redeemed.

2. Notice that the question of the procession of the Holy Spirit was one of the causes of eleventh-century schism between the Eastern Church and that of the West. In the beginning, they agreed that the Holy Spirit proceeded "from the Father and the Son" (*Filioque*). By the sixth century, however, it became necessary, in the face of the heresy of Arius who contested the divinity of Christ, to define the doctrine more explicitly. Later still, when Charlemagne showed more and more clearly his intention to break off with the Eastern empire which was in competition with him, the question of Filioque became an instrument of imperial policy. Despite the pleas of Pope Leo III who did not wish to see any change in the text of the ancient Nicene Creed, the practice developed of reciting the Creed with the Filioque added. By the eleventh century, when the schism occurred, the practice was established. If the Filioque was not the issue which provoked the break, it certainly contributed the last straw. Confronted with the heresy confessed by the Western See, Byzantium erased the name of the pope from the list of liturgical prayers (marking the break). What the East blamed above all was less the doctrinal deviation than the schismatic and divisive act of modifying the sacred text (despite the formal defense given it by the councils) without consulting the Eastern family of the *Una Sancta*. (Paul Evdokimov: *L'Orthodoxie*, p. 138.)

3. Let us recall finally the deviations that are produced in theology whenever one pretends to put aside one of the three modes of God's being: those who neglect God the Father, God the Creator, fall into *pantheism* for which God is everywhere diffuse in the creation. Those who disregard the Son fall into *deism:* God abandons the world he has created to its own devices (such was the point of view of Voltaire in making God a great clockmaker who no longer busied himself with keeping his "clock" in work-

ing order). Those who overlook the Holy Spirit end by embracing a *purely philosophical faith* or by falling into *metaphysics,* God and his work being no more than an object of human speculation instead of being man's salvation.

Let us remember from this that the doctrine of the Trinity is the only way to give a true account of God, as he is, as he is revealed, and as man must believe in him in order to be *saved.*

6 / GOD THE FATHER

❡ QUESTION 26.   *What do you believe when you say: "I believe in God the Father Almighty, Maker of heaven and earth"?*

That the eternal Father of our Lord Jesus Christ, who out of nothing created heaven and earth with all that is in them,[a] who also upholds and governs them by his eternal counsel and providence,[b] is for the sake of Christ his Son my God and my Father.[c] I trust in him so completely that I have no doubt that he will provide me with all things necessary for body and soul.[d] Moreover, whatever evil he sends upon me in this troubled life he will turn to my good,[e] for he is able to do it, being almighty God, and is determined to do it, being a faithful Father.[f]

a. Ps. 90:1-2. Lord, thou hast been our dwelling place in all generations. Before the mountains were brought forth, or ever thou hadst formed the earth and the world, from everlasting to everlasting thou art God.

Isa. 44:24. Thus says the Lord, your Redeemer, who formed you from the womb: "I am the Lord, who made all things, who stretched out the heavens alone, who spread out the earth by myself."

Cf. Gen. 1; John 1:1-5; Ps. 33:6.

b. Matt. 10:29. Are not two sparrows sold for a penny? And not one of them will fall to the ground without your Father's will.

Cf. Ps. 104; Heb. 1:1-3.

c. Rom. 8:15-16. You have received the spirit of sonship. When we cry, "Abba! Father!" it is the Spirit himself bearing witness with our spirit that we are children of God.

Cf. John 1:12-13; Gal. 4:4-7.

d. Luke 12:22. [Jesus] said to his disciples, "Therefore I tell you,

do not be anxious about your life, what you shall eat, nor about your body, what you shall put on."
Cf. Matt. 6:25-44.

e. Rom. 8:28. We know that in everything God works for good with those who love him, who are called according to his purpose.

f. Matt. 7:9-11. "What man of you, if his son asks him for a loaf, will give him a stone? Or if he asks for a fish, will give him a serpent? If you then, who are evil, know how to give good gifts to your children, how much more will your Father who is in heaven give good things to those who ask him?"

We deal here with the first Article of the Apostles' Creed devoted to *God the Father.*

The knowledge of God the Creator comes from revelation. By ourselves, we cannot know anything for certain about the origin of the world. Science studies the world as it now is, but can only form hypotheses with respect to its origin.

What permits the Catechism to declare that "out of nothing" God "created heaven and earth with all that is in them," is that God is also "the eternal Father of our Lord Jesus Christ."

Moreover, what God has done for us in Jesus Christ, known to us through the *re-creation* of which we have been the object, bears witness to what God has done for the world as its creator, what he is doing today in his providence (Question 27) for this world, and finally what he will do again for it in the final consummation of his steadfast love. God is revealed in Jesus Christ as the true creator God and merciful Father.

Not only is God the Creator, but he "upholds and governs" his creation "by his eternal counsel and providence." Our world is not abandoned to itself; God is not disinterested in the work which he has created. On the contrary, he is concerned with it to the point of providing his creatures "with all things necessary for body and soul." God continues to act in this world. Jesus Christ, the living Lord to whom the living church bears witness, is the pledge of this activity (John 5:17; read also verse 18). The entire world is sustained and borne by the will of God; if his will ceased to function, the creation would return to nothingness Psalm 104:25-30. "It is so utterly impossible for the world to exist without God that, if God should forget it, the world would immediately perish" (Sören Kierkegaard: *The Journals*).

Accordingly, we can never think of ourselves in this world in any other way than as creatures of God. Man cannot claim autonomy. If God were to grant him that complete independence for which he constantly clamors, he would return to the nothingness from which his creator has brought him forth.

Even though we have our existence only in total and unconditional dependence upon God *almighty,* we are not thereby under the thumb of a tyrant. God is a "faithful Father" and what he does for us, he does for the love of his Son Jesus Christ. We need nòt fear anything or anyone in this world. Nothing in it appears to us as essentially dark and obscure.

The world is not an enigma against which we happen to be pitted; my life is not surrounded by mysteries which exhaust my vitality and destroy my courage. Jesus Christ has come to give meaning to this world (John 1:3); he gives us an explanation of its source and an understanding of what is happening to us.

That is what we proclaim when we confess "God the Father Almighty, Maker of heaven and earth," and it is through Jesus Christ that we can call him "our Father" (Question 120).

❡ QUESTION 27. *What do you understand by the providence of God?*

The almighty and ever-present power of God[a] whereby he still upholds, as it were by his own hand, heaven and earth together with all creatures,[b] and rules in such a way that leaves and grass, rain and drought, fruitful and unfruitful years, food and drink,[c] health and sickness,[d] riches and poverty,[e] and everything else, come to us not by chance but by his fatherly hand.[f]

a. Acts 17:24-25. The God who made the world and everything in it, being Lord of heaven and earth, does not live in shrines made by man, nor is he served by human hands, as though he needed anything, since he himself gives to all men life and breath and everything.
Cf. Acts 17:26-28.
b. Heb. 1:3. He reflects the glory of God and bears the very stamp of his nature, upholding the universe by his word of power. When he had made purification for sins, he sat down at the right hand of the Majesty on high.

c. Acts 14:15-17. "You should turn from these vain things to a living God who made the heaven and the earth and the sea and all that is in them. In past generations he allowed all the nations to walk in their own ways; yet he did not leave himself without witness, for he did good and gave you from heaven rains and fruitful seasons, satisfying your hearts with good and gladness."
Cf. Jer. 5:24.
d. John 9:3. Jesus answered, "It was not that this man sinned, or his parents, but that the works of God might be made manifest in him."
e. Prov. 22:2. The rich and the poor meet together; the Lord is the maker of them all.
Cf. Matt. 10:29-31.
f. Eph. 1:11. In Christ indeed we have been given our share in the heritage, as was decreed in his design whose purpose is everywhere at work (N.E.B.).

The revelation of the fatherhood of God is what theology calls his *providence*. This idea has been so debased, however, that, for many men and women today, speaking of providence is equivalent to speaking of chance, of luck, at best of good luck. Taken in this sense, the expression: "It is providence!" is not far from meaning: "It is the work of fate!"

If we confess that God is the Father Almighty, we cannot admit another power besides him; that would become "fatal." This is the basic claim of the Christian faith, that always we be brought back to the confession of the absolute sovereignty of God over his creation. There is no other alternative: either God is Lord or someone else is—Satan, man himself, Evil, Fate. To believe in God the Father Almighty comes to be choosing one's true master.

The providence of God is the "almighty and ever-present power" by which he provides all that is necessary for his creation. As contradictory as the matter may appear to our human reason, God in his providence is concerned with even the smallest detail of our life (Matthew 6:24-34). The very fact that that appears to us contradictory, or putting the matter in its best light, as an ideal not consistent with reality, reveals to us our lack of faith. We do not "seek first the kingdom of God," we do not have faith enough to dare to put God to the test (Malachi 3:10-12). Too often we behave like overcautious bookkeepers, although God expects from us the trust of a little child.

In reality, we are very much in the hand of God, in his right hand, in the hand that saves, protects, and guides. Everything in this world is ordered according to the design of God himself, the Creator and the Savior. Creation is the scene of his activity, and his work among men demonstrates to them that the kingdom is already present.

"In all trials and afflictions," Luther said, "man should first of all *run* to God; he should realize and accept the fact that everything is sent by God, whether it comes from the devil or from man" *(The Seven Penitential Psalms,* 1517, Ps. 6: Weimar I, p. 159; *Luther's Works,* edited by Jaroslav Pelikan, Vol. 14, p. 140).

Faith in the providence of God is not fatalism, but an active assent to his will.

❡ QUESTION 28. *What advantage comes from acknowledging God's creation and providence?*

We learn that we are to be patient in adversity,[a] grateful in the midst of blessing,[b] and to trust our faithful God and Father for the future, assured that no creature shall separate us from his love,[c] since all creatures are so completely in his hand that without his will they cannot even move.[d]

a. Rom. 5:3-4. We rejoice in our sufferings, knowing that suffering produces endurance, and endurance produces character, and character produces hope.
   Cf. James 1:3; Job 1:21.
b. Deut. 8:10. "You shall eat and be full, and you shall bless the Lord your God for the good land he has given you."
c. Rom. 8:38-39. I am sure that neither death, nor life, nor angels, nor principalities, nor things present, nor things to come, nor powers, nor height, nor depth, nor anything else in all creation, will be able to separate us from the love of God in Christ Jesus our Lord.
d. Acts 17:28. "In him we live and move and have our being."
   Cf. Acts 17:25; Job 1:12; Prov. 21:1.

The doctrine of providence gives to the believer patience, gratitude, and trust.

Patience "in adversity" is not the resignation of the Stoic, which is actually a living death, a petrification of man. "Resignation is always the disconsolate consolation of unbelief" (Barth: *Church Dogmatics,* Vol. II, I, p. 510).

No, the patience of a believer is a dynamic and living operation, an act of faith which permits him to count upon the freely given grace of God as it has been manifested in Jesus Christ. The believer is not dimmed in spirit by adversity; he keeps his gaze upon him who is the pledge of his victory (Romans 5:1-5).

The patience of faith is not to be mistaken for detachment from earthly realities or the mere contemplation of "the higher realties." Those who have understood it in this manner have deserved the just reproach of making Christianity into a narcotic. The doctrine of the providence of God reminds us that God is not disinterested in the material realities of our life. The patience of the believer allows him to expect with confidence nothing less than the actual demonstration of this providence.

With respect to *gratitude,* it is the very life of the believer in his obedience. He rejoices not only in his new freedom in Jesus Christ, but in his whole existence in this world where blessings, like adversities, are the signs of God's work today and of the kingdom which is coming.

Finally, *trust* comes to the believer from the assurance that he has of being in God's own hand. His life henceforth has meaning. He knows through Jesus Christ the love and faithfulness of the one who never abandons his own.

Summing up: faith in the providence of God Almighty gives us assurance that the work of God in Jesus Christ is manifested in this world in spite of all appearances. The works of providence are signs of the kingdom that is coming, a "demonstration" made for faith of "things not seen" (Heb. 11:1).

7 / GOD THE SON

⊂ QUESTION 29. *Why is the Son of God called* JESUS, *which means* SAVIOR?

Because he saves us from our sins,[a] and because salvation is to be sought or found in no other.[b]

a. Matt. 1:21. "She will bear a son, and you shall call his name Jesus, for he will save his people from their sins."
Cf. Heb. 7:25.
b. Acts 4:12. "There is salvation in no one else, for there is no other name under heaven given among men by which we must be saved."

The name *Jesus* comes from two Hebrew roots meaning "Jahweh saves." We find it in the Old Testament either in the form of "Jehoshua" or "Joshua." This name was given to Jesus by Joseph, but at the command of an angel. On the one hand, Jesus of Nazareth is a Jewish child bearing a name identifying his civil status; on the other hand, this name defines the divine mission which will be entrusted to him among men: "He will save his people from their sins" (Matt. 1:21).

Thus Jesus bears a name which others have borne in the tradition of the people of Israel and that fact reassures us of his historicity. He is not a figment of the imagination, an ideal figure. He did exist, his name was registered like that of other Jewish children. However, Jesus is not only recorded in our history, he takes it on himself.

By a decision of divine mercy, this Jesus is the Savior (Luke 2:11; John 4:42; Acts 5:31; Philippians 3:20).

It was so important to state this exactly in the context of the apostolic preaching. Indeed, for the pagan world, there used to exist numerous hero-gods, that is, saviors upon whom men counted for their deliverance from all kinds of perils, particularly from war. It often happened that a victorious military leader qualified as "savior." Jesus, however, is presented as the one and only Savior whom God sends to men. He comes to save all men (1 Timothy 2:3; 4:10). The salvation he brings is cosmic in dimension, the *whole* creation will participate in it (Philippians 3:20; Colossians 1:12-20).

If such is the meaning of the name *Jesus,* salvation is truly "to be sought or found in no other."

❡ QUESTION 30. *Do those who seek their salvation and well-being from saints, by their own efforts, or by other means really believe in the only Savior Jesus?*

68

No. Rather, by such actions they deny Jesus, the only Savior and Redeemer, even though they boast of belonging to him.[a] It therefore follows that either Jesus is not a perfect Savior, or those who receive this Savior with true faith must possess in him all that is necessary for their salvation.[b]

a. 1 Cor. 1:12-13. Each one of you says, "I belong to Paul," or "I belong to Apollos," or "I belong to Cephas," or "I belong to Christ." Is Christ divided? Was Paul crucified for you? Or were you baptized in the name of Paul?
Cf. Gal. 5:4.
b. Col. 1:19-20. In him all the fullness of God was pleased to dwell, and through him to reconcile to himself all things, whether on earth or in heaven, making peace by the blood of his cross.
Cf. Isa. 9:6-7; John 1:16.

If Jesus is the "only Savior," it is either he or nothing! Either we put all our trust in him or else, by the very fact that we require him to share the role with others, we clearly and simply deny him even though we "boast of belonging to him."

Thus the claims of Roman Catholicism and of Protestant humanism, in particular, are to be refuted once more. No salvation is possible save in Jesus Christ and through him. And it is the unique task of evangelical theology always to bring us back to the only name that saves. In the final analysis, all that we teach has only one purpose, namely, to understand that we vow to Jesus Christ a love and trust that tolerates no division of loyalty. Indeed, if Jesus Christ is the Savior, the one who redeems us from the curse of the law, the one who pays in our behalf the debt of righteousness that we have contracted toward God, he can be none other than the only Savior. Therefore, our prime concern is that we receive him with "a true faith," that is, that we accept the decision of God the Lord who wishes to save us himself through Jesus Christ as Savior.

◖ QUESTION 31. *Why is he called* CHRIST, *that is, the* ANOINTED ONE?

Because he is ordained by God the Father and anointed with the Holy Spirit[a] to be *our chief Prophet* and *Teacher*,[b] fully revealing to us the secret purpose and will of God concerning our redemption;[e] to be *our only High Priest*,[d] having redeemed us by the one sacrifice of his body and ever interceding for us with the Father;[e] and to be *our eternal King*, governing us by his Word and Spirit, and defending and sustaining us in the redemption he has won for us.[f]

a. Luke 3:21-22. When all the people were baptized, and when Jesus also had been baptized and was praying, the heaven was opened, and the Holy Spirit descended upon him in bodily form, as a dove, and a voice came from heaven, "Thou art my beloved Son; with thee I am well pleased."

Cf. Luke 4:14-19 (Isa. 61:1-2) ; Heb. 1:9.

b. Acts 3:22. "Moses said, 'The Lord God will raise up for you a prophet from your brethren as he raised me up. You shall listen to him in whatever he tells you.' "

Cf. Deut. 18:15, 18.

c. John 1:18. No one has ever seen God; the only Son, who is in the bosom of the Father, he has made him known.

Cf. John 15:15.

d. Heb. 7:17. It is witnessed of him, "Thou art a priest forever, after the order of Melchizedek."

e. Heb. 9:12, 28. He entered once for all into the Holy Place, taking not the blood of goats and calves but his own blood, thus securing an eternal redemption. . . . Christ, having been offered once to bear the sins of many, will appear a second time, not to deal with sin but to have those who are eagerly waiting for him.

Rom. 8:34. Is it Christ Jesus, who died, yes, who was raised from the dead, who is at the right hand of God, who indeed intercedes for us?

f. Luke 1:32-33. He will be great, and will be called the Son of the Most High; and the Lord God will give to him the throne of his father David, and he will reign over the house of Jacob forever; and of his kingdom there will be no end.

Zech. 9:9. Rejoice greatly, O daughter of Zion! Shout aloud, O daughter of Jerusalem! Lo, your king comes to you; triumphant and victorious is he, humble and riding on an ass, on a colt the foal of an ass.

Cf. Mark 11:1-10; Matt. 21:1-11.

Matt. 28:18. Jesus came and said to them, "All authority in heaven and on earth has been given to me."

The word *Christ* translates the Hebrew "Messiah," meaning

"the Anointed." Anointing with oil is the sign of divine election. The one who receives it enters into God's plan for the salvation of men; he becomes the agent God uses to accomplish his purpose on earth. Jesus is preeminently the Anointed One, he is *the* Christ, he is "the power and the wisdom of God" (1 Cor. 1:24). It is in him that the whole promise of the Old Testament is accomplished; it is through him, definitively and completely, that God saves his people. The title of Christ explains how Jesus is the Savior; he has been *ordained by God the Father and anointed with the Holy Spirit.* Thus, Christ is not a kindly individual thrown up on the bosom of history to save mankind; he is the very fulfillment of God's plan of salvation. The title of Christ is to reassure us fully of Jesus' ability to be the Savior.

Jesus Christ fulfilled the promise of salvation announced in the Old Testament, in three ways:

1. He is "our chief Prophet and Teacher." Jesus speaks of God with full authority (Mark 1:21-22); furthermore, it is God who speaks in him and through him (John 1:18). All that God means to men and wants them to know about him is said through Jesus; Jesus is the Word of God (John 1:1-3, 14). Whereas God expressed himself *through* the mouth of prophets (Isaiah 6:5-7; Jeremiah 1:7-9), he now speaks *directly* through Jesus Christ. Jesus Christ is the prophet par excellence.

2. Jesus is still "our only High Priest," that is, the one and only *priest.* In the Old Testament the high priest was charged with making atonement for the sins of the people by sacrificing an animal (Leviticus 16). Jesus Christ offers himself in sacrifice in order to reconcile men with God and he is the only one able to do it (Hebrews 7:26-27). His sacrifice is unique and the act is final (Hebrews 10:1-3, 11-14). Jesus Christ is the priest who intercedes for all men in the presence of God (Hebrews 7:25). Not only does he fulfill the priesthood of the Old Testament so that he becomes *the* priest, but henceforth he makes every other priesthood useless: his sacrifice being perfect, men do not need any longer to offer anything to God for their salvation. The sacrifice of ourselves can only stand as an act of gratitude to God for the salvation given in Jesus Christ.

3. Finally, Jesus is "our eternal King." Because he acquired us by his sacrifice, we belong to him; he rules over us and is our

only Lord. We no longer belong to ourselves; no longer have we the possibility of deciding by ourselves the use of our lives. Moreover, we no longer belong to human masters, since Christ himself has laid claim to us. The believer respects the governing authority God has established over us (Romans 13), but in no way would he be able to belong to this authority. Christians cannot "serve two masters" (Matt. 6:24). This is an absolute impossibility, since Jesus Christ alone is God and the only Lord of men.

In these three ways, as prophet, as priest, and as king, Jesus Christ is our Savior.

¶ QUESTION 32. *But why are you called a Christian?*

Because through faith I share in Christ[a] and thus in his anointing,[b] so that I may confess his name,[c] offer myself a living sacrifice of gratitude to him,[d] and fight against sin and the devil with a free and good conscience throughout this life[e] and hereafter rule with him in eternity over all creatures.[f]

a. Acts 11:26. In Antioch the disciples were for the first time called Christians.
   1 Cor. 12:27. You are the body of Christ and individually members of it.
b. Acts 2:17. "And in the last days it shall be, God declares, that I will pour out my Spirit upon all flesh, and your sons and your daughters shall prophesy, and your young men shall see visions, and your old men shall dream dreams."
   Cf. Joel 2:28; 1 John 2:27.
c. Matt. 10:5, 32. These twelve Jesus sent out, charging them, . . . "Everyone who acknowledges me before men, I also will acknowledge before my Father who is in heaven."
d. Rom. 12:1. I appeal to you therefore, brethren, by the mercies of God, to present your bodies as a living sacrifice, holy and acceptable to God, which is your spiritual worship.
   1 Peter 2:5, 9. Like living stones be yourselves built into a spiritual house, to be a holy priesthood, to offer spiritual sacrifices acceptable to God through Jesus Christ. . . . You are a chosen race, a royal priesthood, a holy nation, God's own people, that you may declare the wonderful deeds of him who called you out of darkness into his marvelous light.

e. 1 Tim. 1:18-19. Inspired by [prophetic utterances] you may wage the good warfare, holding faith and a good conscience.

f. 2 Tim. 2:11-13. The saying is sure: If we have died with him, we shall also live with him; if we endure, we shall also reign with him; if we deny him, he also will deny us; if we are faithless, he remains faithful—for he cannot deny himself.

This has been said to be "one of the most interesting questions of the Catechism." Here we learn what *a Christian* is!

He is first of all a man who bears the name of his Lord. What was a nickname in the beginning has become a veritable "birth certificate." Still it is necessary for the merchandise to correspond to the label! What in reality is a Christian?

1. He is a man who is *a member of Christ* by faith: he literally belongs to the one who raised him from the dead. It is not a question of mystical union, but one of confident gratitude, because the death and resurrection of Christ mean our dying and rising with him. Indeed, it is due to this decisive act of God's judgment and mercy that, from now on, we are members of Christ (1 Corinthians 12:27).

2. By virtue of this name we *share in his anointing:* we receive the same grace that Jesus Christ received, God's own Holy Spirit. As Christians we share in the benefits of Christ. We live in the forgiveness God manifests in Christ Jesus and through him.

3. We are able therefore *to confess his name:* The Christian cannot be merely a tax collector. It is not his profession which makes him a Christian but his confession of faith, that is to say, his words, his actions, his entire behavior are such that no one can doubt that this man truly belongs to Jesus Christ. That a man's entire life may be a testimony to Jesus Christ and to him alone, does not depend upon a human decision, even though this is indispensable, but upon the grace of God.

4. The Christian life is therefore *a living sacrifice of gratitude.* The Christian, owing everything to his Savior, can no longer keep back anything for his own use and his personal glory. He shares everything as a sign of his gratitude, he needs no longer to ask what he ought to do with his life, he knows to whom he owes it.

5. The Christian life is *a battle:* not merely our personal struggle against temptations and doubts, but sharing in Christ's great battle on earth. Because the Christian lives in the confidence

of God's faithfulness, he is already victorious in the victory which God has won over the devil and of which the resurrection of Jesus Christ is his pledge. The words "with a free and good conscience" signify that the Christian lives, acts, and fights as a man who has been freed by Christ; he never seeks his own advantage; he never "makes" his salvation; he has no fear regarding the outcome of the battle. Liberated by Jesus Christ he already possesses everything in him and through him.

6. Therefore, the Christian is assured of *ruling eternally* with Christ over all creatures. His life today as a member of Christ is for him the pledge that he shall live with Christ in the kingdom of heaven. The Christian does not await the kingdom as a hypothetical possibility; by his faith, he already lives in the kingdom and he knows, because of Christ, that this life will have no end.

⁋ QUESTION 33. *Why is he called* GOD'S ONLY-BEGOTTEN SON, *since we also are God's children?*

Because Christ alone is God's own eternal Son,[a] whereas we are accepted for his sake as children of God by grace.[b]

a. John 1:1-3, 14, 18. In the beginning was the Word, and the Word was with God, and the Word was God. He was in the beginning with God; all things were made through him, and without him was not anything made that was made. . . . The Word became flesh and dwelt among us, full of grace and truth; we have beheld his glory, glory as of the only Son from the Father. . . . No one has ever seen God; the only Son, who is in the bosom of the Father, he has made him known.
   Cf. Heb. 1:2.
b. Eph. 1:5-6. He destined us in love to be his sons through Jesus Christ, according to the purpose of his will, to the praise of his glorious grace which he freely bestowed on us in the Beloved.
   Cf. John 1:12; Rom. 8:15-17.

The reply to this question shows how Jesus Christ can be the Savior: he is "God's only-begotten Son"; he is "God's own eternal Son." Question 35 will say that he is "true and eternal God." Let us be quite clear that if Jesus Christ is God's own eternal Son (the German reads *"natürliche Sohn Gottes"*), the essential nature and activity of God is the point at issue.

If Jesus Christ saves us, it is because God himself saves us through him. The whole possibility of redemption rests upon this reality of the divine nature of Jesus Christ. It is by virtue of this very presence of God that the name of Jesus has its worth and meaning.

With regard to the Christian, he is a child of grace and not of God's own nature. The difference between Jesus and us is one not of degree but of nature. He alone is the Son. As for us, we are only adopted children.

Whatever may be the reality of our participation in the grace of Jesus Christ, let us never forget the essential difference between him and us. A too great familiarity with Jesus Christ, an uncontrolled "fraternization" on the part of the Christian is never a good omen; it generally signifies that this "big brother," this "friend" is no longer the *God* who saves.

The apostles never call Jesus anything other than "Master" and "Lord."

¶ QUESTION 34. *Why do you call him* OUR LORD?

Because, not with gold or silver but at the cost of his blood,[a] he has redeemed us body and soul from sin and all the dominion of the devil, and has bought us for his very own.[b]

a. 1 Peter 1:18-19. You know that you were ransomed from the futile ways inherited from your fathers, not with perishable things such as silver or gold, but with the precious blood of Christ, like that of a lamb without blemish or spot.
   Cf. 1 Peter 2:9-10.
b. 1 Cor. 7:23. You were bought with a price; do not become slaves of men.
   Cf. 1 Cor. 6:20.

Jesus Christ is truly "our Lord." We are literally his property by virtue of the act by which he bought us back. This is the import of a true recognition of the meaning of the name of Jesus Christ.

This is our assurance for today, our comfort and our joy: we are not abandoned, we are not handed over to all possible tyrannies, for we belong to Jesus Christ. He is our Lord, he has taken charge of us and makes us participants in his victory and in his eternal rule.

The name of Jesus Christ is truly the only "name given among men by which we must be saved" (Acts 4:12).

❡ QUESTION 35. *What is the meaning of: "Conceived by the Holy Spirit, born of the Virgin Mary"?*

That the eternal Son of God, who is and remains true and eternal God,[a] took upon himself our true manhood from the flesh and blood of the Virgin Mary[b] through the action of the Holy Spirit,[c] so that he might also be the true seed of David,[d] like his fellow men in all things,[e] except for sin.[f]

a. John 1:1. In the beginning was the Word, and the Word was with God, and the Word was God.
b. John 1:14. The Word became flesh and dwelt among us, full of grace and truth; we have beheld his glory, glory as of the only Son from the Father.
   Cf. Gal. 4:4.
c. Luke 1:35. The angel said to her, "The Holy Spirit will come upon you, and the power of the Most High will overshadow you; therefore the child to be born will be called holy, the Son of God."
   Cf. Matt. 1:18, 20.
d. Rom. 1:1-3. The gospel of God [is] . . . the gospel concerning his Son, who was descended from David according to the flesh.
   Cf. Ps. 132:11; 2 Sam. 7:12-17.
e. Phil. 2:5-7. Christ Jesus . . . emptied himself, taking the form of a servant, being born in the likeness of men.
f. Heb. 4:15. We have not a high priest who is unable to sympathize with our weaknesses, but one who in every respect has been tempted as we are, yet without sinning.

❡ QUESTION 36. *What benefit do you receive from the holy conception and birth of Christ?*

That he is our Mediator,[a] and that, in God's sight, he covers over with his innocence and perfect holiness the sinfulness in which I have been conceived.[b]

a. 1 Tim. 2:5-6. There is one God, and there is one mediator be-

76

tween God and men, the man Christ Jesus, who gave himself as a ransom for all.

b. Rom. 4:7. Blessed are those whose iniquities are forgiven and whose sins are covered.

Cf. Ps. 32:1; 1 Cor. 1:30.

These two questions reckon with the fact that Jesus Christ is *true God* and *true man*.

According to the witness of the scripture and that of the ancient church, Jesus is *God:* it is God himself who manifests his being in Jesus Christ. Jesus has no human father; he is a unique act of creation by almighty God. Human action has been excluded from the conception of Jesus Christ; on account of man's fall and disobedience, he was unfit to become the author of the new creation; God alone could beget the second Adam (Romans 5:12, 18-19; 1 Corinthians 15:45). Such is the meaning of the words "conceived by the Holy Spirit."

However, Jesus *is born of the Virgin Mary* and thereby God became true man, "because it was necessary that the disobedience committed by man against God should be redressed in human nature" (Calvin: *Geneva Catechism,* 1541, No. 51). God is no longer removed from us; he does not reveal to us our forgiveness from his glorious heaven above; he is with us, in our nature, nearer to us than anyone else will ever be able to be. Thus it is that "the mercy of God has reached *us* in Jesus Christ; God's redemption has been accomplished in our person" (Barth: *The Faith of the Church,* p. 82). In Jesus Christ, the man of Nazareth, God himself manifests himself fully and definitively as God the Savior. We no longer have to seek God, God himself has sought and found us.

This is what the event called Jesus Christ means. It is through him alone that we can attain the assurance of our salvation: Jesus is beyond any possible doubt true God and true man. We are saved because God has actually taken our human nature.

It is necessary here to consider the miracle of the Virgin's conception. Now and then it has been believed, and some still believe, that it is possible to dispense with this sign (as with that of the empty tomb), while keeping the reality of the thing signified. One ought not to labor under any delusions on this subject. Theological experience shows that those who, for one reason or another, wanted to dispense with the sign have ended by losing the reality as well. This sign is there for the purpose of reminding us that *faith* is indispensable to the understanding of the mystery of the incarnation, that is, of God's being made man. The fact that one claims to get along without the sign makes us see, more or less quickly, that one has thereby come to make faith itself useless; the mystery as a result is no longer meaningful. One falls into rational explanations. The question of the birth of Jesus is reduced to this: either it is a spontaneous generation or his father is actually Joseph. For this kind of reasoning, Jesus is no longer God and redemption through him becomes unthinkable. There is a necessary relationship between the sign, the actual event of the Virgin's conception, and our salvation accomplished by God in human form. Theological reasoning and the event of which the scripture bears witness join and clarify each other. Our faith must grasp the event of Jesus Christ in its total meaning.

Jesus is true God, therefore, because he has been "conceived by the Holy Spirit," and on this account alone he is *our Mediator* (Question 36). It is no one else than God himself who comes to fulfill his righteousness; there is no third person between God and man, but God who joins himself to man and unites man to him in Jesus Christ, so that, "in God's sight, he covers over with his innocence and perfect holiness the sinfulness in which I have been conceived."

Let us note again that the words "the sinfulness in which I have been conceived," like those of Calvin's confession of sin, "born in corruption," do not imply a negative judgment on sexual relationships. It is not necessary to believe that Jesus was "conceived by the Holy Spirit" because sex would in itself have brought the taint of a specific sin upon him. As Karl Barth has said, "sexual asceticism is a pagan notion and not a biblical one." It is very regrettable that the Christian church, in the Middle Ages in particular, believed that it ought to profess, in regard to this area of life, a distrust of which one finds no trace in the scripture. If we want to be able to say something to the men and women of our time concerning this question, first we must be freed from the prejudice that wants these sexual relationships to constitute in themselves a sin. It is the whole man who is the sinner. Actually, the mind or human reasoning, as well as sexuality, can become the occasion of sin.

When the Catechism speaks of the "sinfulness in which I have been conceived," it means that we were born carriers of the hereditary sinfulness that men transmit to their descendants, in the same way as we pass on the color of our eyes or any such trait, whether it be flattering or calamitous for their character.

It is this kind of sin that in God's sight Jesus Christ "covers over." Because of the sacrifice of the cross, God determined not to see the sin which is still in us (Psalm 85:3); we are really covered. To be sure, we will not treat our sin lightly, for we know that "God is not mocked" (Gal. 6:7), but at least we will no longer be overwhelmed; our sin will no longer prevent us from believing in the mercy of God. We realize from now on that God is no longer dealing with us as we are in ourselves but as we are in Jesus Christ.

❰ QUESTION 37. *What do you understand by the word "suffered"?*

That throughout his life on earth, but especially at the end of it, he bore in body and soul the wrath of God against the sin of the whole human race,[a] so that by his suffering, as the only expiatory sacrifice, he might redeem our body and soul from everlasting damnation, and might obtain for us God's grace, righteousness, and eternal life.[b]

a. Isa. 53:12. He poured out his soul to death, and was numbered with the transgressors; yet he bore the sin of many, and made intercession for the transgressors.

1 Peter 2:24. He himself bore our sins in his body on the tree, that we might die to sin and live to righteousness. By his wounds you have been healed.

b. Rom. 3:24-25. They are justified by his grace as a gift, through the redemption which is in Christ Jesus, whom God put forward as an expiation by his blood, to be received by faith. This was to show God's righteousness, because in his divine forbearance he had passed over former sins.

Cf. 1 John 2:2.

❰ QUESTION 38. *Why did he suffer "under Pontius Pilate" as his judge?*

That he, being innocent, might be condemned by an earthly judge,[a] and thereby set us free from the judgment of God which, in all its severity, ought to fall upon us.[b]

a. John 19:13-16. Pilate . . . brought Jesus out and sat down on the judgment seat at a place called The Pavement, and in Hebrew, Gabbatha. Now it was the day of Preparation for the Passover; it was about the sixth hour. He said to the Jews, "Here is your King!" They cried out, "Away with him, away with him, crucify him!" Pilate said to them, "Shall I crucify your King?" The chief priests answered, "We have no king but Caesar." Then he handed him over to them to be crucified.
Cf. Luke 23:13-24; Acts 4:27-28.

b. Isa. 53:4-5. Surely he has borne our griefs and carried our sorrows; yet we esteemed him stricken, smitten by God, and afflicted. But he was wounded for our transgressions, he was bruised for our iniquities; upon him was the chastisement that made us whole, and with his stripes we are healed.
Rom. 5:6. While we were yet helpless, at the right time Christ died for the ungodly.
Cf. 2 Cor. 5:21; Gal. 3:13.

❡ QUESTION 39. *Is there something more in his having been crucified than if he had died some other death?*

Yes, for by this I am assured that he took upon himself the curse which lay upon me, because the death of the cross was cursed by God.[a]

a. Gal. 3:13. Christ redeemed us from the curse of the law, having become a curse for us—for it is written, "Cursed be everyone who hangs on a tree."
Cf. Deut. 21:23.

❡ QUESTION 40. *Why did Christ have to suffer "death"?*

Because the righteousness and truth of God are such that nothing else could make reparation for our sins except the death of the Son of God.[a]

a. Heb. 2:9. We see Jesus, who for a little while was made lower than the angels, crowned with glory and honor because of the suffering of death, so that by the grace of God he might taste death for everyone.

Cf. Rom. 8:3-4.

❡ QUESTION 41. *Why was he "buried"?*

To confirm the fact that he was really dead.[a]

a. Acts 13:29. When they had fulfilled all that was written of him, they took him down from the tree, and laid him in a tomb.
Cf. Matt. 27:59-60; Luke 23:50-55; John 19:38-42.

❡ QUESTION 44. *Why is there added: "He descended into hell"?*

That in my severest tribulations I may be assured that Christ my Lord has redeemed me from hellish anxieties and torment by the unspeakable anguish, pains, and terrors which he suffered in his soul both on the cross and before.[a]

a. Isa. 53:5. He was wounded for our transgressions, he was bruised for our iniquities; upon him was the chastisement that made us whole, and with his stripes we are healed.
Matt. 27:46. About the ninth hour Jesus cried with a loud voice, "Eli, Eli, lama sabach-thani?" that is, "My God, my God, why hast thou forsaken me?"

The suffering of Jesus Christ is a sign of his being a true human being. In Jesus Christ, however, it is God himself who suffers in his encounter with man, and from this encounter. Inasmuch as we are God's enemies, in that we are by nature "prone to hate God" (Question 5), we can only show him our hostility at the precise moment in which he presents himself to us. Jesus took to himself all the hatred of men against God, and in this sense he has suffered.

His entire life from the beginning (the account of the nativity attests to it) was a Passion. Furthermore, Jesus suffers not only in behalf of man but in behalf of God whose wrath he bears. The origin of this suffering is sin, and that suffering is absolute, complete; no man will be able to suffer as Jesus did, either as God or as man. The incarnation truly signifies the suffering of God by man and of man by God in Jesus Christ. It was necessary that

Christ should suffer in order that reconciliation might be effected (Matthew 16:21; Luke 24:26).

The cross is the decisive sign of redemptive suffering. To be precise, there is no other. Our own sufferings do not save us; they make us share in the suffering that, because of man's hostility toward God, Christ endures until his return.

The words "under Pontius Pilate" signify in part that this suffering was historical and that Jesus actually appeared before a human tribunal (Calvin). The passion of Christ was neither theoretical nor entirely internal (for example, the pain of the defeat that he suffered); it was real suffering, physical, moral, and spiritual; it was inflicted upon him by men at a definite time in our history. At the moment when Jesus appears before Pilate, he is presented as the culprit, the one to be judged, the condemned one. The court of Pilate represents the court of God where Jesus appears in our place as the accused par excellence. Pilate, however, declared Jesus innocent and it is prophetic that he testifies that Jesus is without sin; it is prophetic also that "he washes his hands"; he is not competent in this affair. God alone can condemn Christ to take our place. He alone can effect this double substitution of ourselves in Christ and of him in his Son in order that it may be God who pays in our place, since only he is capable of doing so. Thus our condemnation is eliminated and this is what Pontius Pilate announces in declaring Jesus innocent.

One is surprised that the Christ should die on the *cross* and that he was not stoned to death, since that was the means of capital punishment practiced among the Jews (Acts 7:59). The cross in Israel was the sign of a *curse* (Deuteronomy 21:23; Galatians 3:13). On the cross Jesus appeared as cursed by God. He becomes what we are: men whom God curses because of our enmity toward him. But in Jesus Christ the accursed one is God himself who accepts being so for the sake of his righteousness, because of his mercy. Thus the curse could be removed and completely abolished. Because Jesus died on the cross, we are no longer cursed and no one can ever be so again in this world.

The Creed is precise in affirming that Christ *died* and that he *was buried*. It was necessary not only that the Christ suffer but also that he die. Having agreed to submit to the curse of sin, he had to suffer the final consequence of this curse. The death of Christ is the final completion of his humanity; at the moment when his loved ones take him down from the cross they no longer doubt that he is true man, truly standing in our place. Without any reserve, he became the man that we are, the man driven to this terrifying end that is death.

Christ bears the brunt of this curse to the last extreme, since he is left alone in the solitude of the tomb: "Man is not entirely dead until he is alone in his tomb after other men have gone away" (Barth: *The Heidelberg Catechism for Today,* Questions 35—44).

But because it is God himself, in Jesus Christ, who underwent it, this stage is not the last, the absolute and ultimate end, total solitude. No, in Jesus Christ, God himself conquers death; so for us, too, who are in covenant with Jesus Christ, death will mean nothing more than a transition.

The *descent into hell* is the crowning blow of the punishment that Jesus Christ has endured and, because he has known it himself, no one of us will be allowed to know it in this degree, either now or hereafter. In hell Christ undergoes the utmost of inner torments: he is abandoned by God and handed over to total despair; such is the extreme of punishment which results from our enmity toward God. Inasmuch as we declare ourselves his enemies, God abandons us and it is hell, the place and time in which man is no longer sustained by God, when he ceases to be a creature of the Father, a being who shares in the blessing of God, becoming no more than nothing, nothing in the strictest sense that can be given to this term. That is what Christ has learned for us by descending into hell in our place. The curse, at this juncture, has borne all its fruit; man in Jesus Christ has been finally annihilated and can no longer put forth any claim. All that might happen to him hereafter and what the resurrection of Jesus Christ guarantees him can only be the result of an act of pure grace done by the God who is "righteous and merciful."

This is the starting point of evangelical theology.

❡ QUESTION 42. *Since, then, Christ died for us, why must we also die?*

Our death is not a reparation for our sins,[a] but only a dying to sin and an entering into eternal life.[b]

83

a. Rom. 7:24. Wretched man that I am! Who will deliver me from this body of death?

Ps. 49:7. Truly no man can ransom himself, or give to God the price of his life.

b. 1 Thess. 5:9-10. Our Lord Jesus Christ . . . died for us so that whether we wake or sleep we might live with him.

Cf. John 5:24.

❆ QUESTION 43. *What further benefit do we receive from the sacrifice and death of Christ on the cross?*

That by his power our old self is crucified, put to death, and buried with him,[a] so that the evil passions of our mortal bodies may reign in us no more,[b] but that we may offer ourselves to him as a sacrifice of thanksgiving.[c]

a. Rom. 6:6. We know that our old self was crucified with him so that the sinful body might be destroyed, and we might no longer be enslaved to sin.

Cf. Col 2:12.

b. Rom. 6:12. Let not sin therefore reign in your mortal bodies, to make you obey their passions.

c. Rom. 12:1. I appeal to you therefore, brethren, by the mercies of God, to present your bodies as a living sacrifice, holy and acceptable to God, which is your spiritual worship.

These two questions are going to help us state precisely in what sense the work of Jesus Christ has been accomplished in our behalf as an efficacious demonstration of the faithfulness of God, so that we may truly and actually be *freed* from the weight of the curse of sin and death.

Our own death will no longer appear as an inevitable punishment, the failure of our life, a terrifying end that we try to treat more or less casually, while wishing to forget it as often as possible. No, the death toward which we are going means the death of our old humanity already promised at our baptism (Romans 6:3-4). This moment will mark our ultimate freedom from the sin which still holds us and our entrance into a state where, depending in no sense upon ourselves, we will depend this time entirely upon the grace of God. When Paul said that death was for him a "gain" (Phil. 1:21), he did not mean that in itself death appeared to him as preferable to life, but that, through the work of Jesus Christ, death signifies, to the believer, the admission into a new life for which he has paid the "earnest money" (Ephesians 1:14).

Such are the fruits of the sacrifice of Jesus Christ for us. By virtue of God's mercy, life is for us *a possibility* today. The Christian can be the new man who proclaims in this world "the new heaven and the new earth," according to the promise of the scripture: *The kingdom of God is upon you* (Mark 1:15, N.E.B.).

◖ QUESTION 45. *What benefit do we receive from "the resurrection" of Christ?*

First, by his resurrection he has overcome death that he might make us share in the righteousness which he has obtained for us through his death.[a] Second, we too are now raised by his power to a new life.[b] Third, the resurrection of Christ is a sure pledge to us of our blessed resurrection.[c]

a. Rom. 4:24-25. It will be reckoned [as righteousness] to us who believe in him that raised from the dead Jesus our Lord, who was put to death for our trespasses and raised for our justification.
Cf. Heb. 2:14-15; 1 Peter 1:3, 21.

b. Rom. 6:3-4. Do you not know that all of us who have been baptized into Christ Jesus were baptized into his death? We were buried therefore with him by baptism into death, so that as Christ was raised from the dead by the glory of the Father, we too might walk in newness of life.
Cf. Col. 3:1-5; Eph. 2:4-6.

c. Rom. 8:11. If the Spirit of him who raised Jesus from the dead dwells in you, he who raised Christ Jesus from the dead will give life to your mortal bodies also through his Spirit which dwells in you.
Cf. 1 Cor. 15.

It probably appears surprising that the Catechism devotes only one question to the resurrection and eight to the death of Christ and that it speaks of the benefit of the resurrection of Christ for us without taking the trouble to establish the event.

It was important to give in detail the circumstances of the death of Jesus in order that we might understand he "was really dead" (Question 41) *for us.* As for the resurrection, it has already been affirmed in all the questions that tell us of Christ, "God's only-begotten Son," "our Lord," "conceived by the Holy Spirit" (Questions 31, 33, 34, 35). Because he was a real man, it was necessary that Jesus die in our place, but because he is true God, he could not remain a prisoner of death. The resurrection is the confirmation of the divinity of Christ: he is really God, who becoming man in the form of Jesus died in our place; it is he who appears on Easter morning as the all-powerful and forgiving Lord.

This work of God is for mankind—for us. The authors of the Catechism were right in showing us especially in what way the resurrection of Jesus Christ serves us.

Something completely new begins to happen through the resurrection of Jesus Christ: sin, the curse, suffering, death, hell have been annihilated, overthrown, and rendered inoperative by the victory of God. What happened there has been compared with a game of chess: the game still continues for a while but the men are so arranged on the chessboard that victory in fact is already won; the result of the game can be in no doubt for the believer who sees in Jesus Christ the victor, the conquering hero, the one who causes the game of life to enter its final phase.

The resurrection of Jesus Christ benefits us in three ways:

1. It makes us *share in the righteousness which he has obtained for us through his death.* We have already seen that we cannot achieve righteousness ourselves, we cannot do what is pleasing to God. Through our own efforts we can only sink a little deeper into evil and unrighteousness. Only one can carry out the will of God perfectly; from his baptism to his death Jesus has actually fulfilled all righteousness (Matthew 3:15). The resurrection means that God accepts this righteousness; that the obedience which Jesus put into practice was identical with that which the righteous God demands. Moreover, in the same way that the death of Jesus Christ was *for us,* his resurrection signifies our sharing in the benefits of his obedience (Romans 5:1-11). Such is the newness of Easter: God loves us, God forgives us, and God receives us as his children *because of the obedience* of Jesus Christ.

2. We too *are now raised by his power to a new life.* The resurrection of Jesus Christ is for us the revelation of what his death

has done for us (Question 43). From now on we know our old humanity has been put to death and buried with him (Romans 6:3-4). Now, therefore, we can live the new life that Christ has acquired for us, actually knowing peace, forgiveness, joy; we can do the will of God, no longer as an irksome duty and in the fear of not doing enough or of doing it too badly to deserve his forgiveness. We are no longer stopped by this kind of scrupulousness; we act in joy and gratitude. Having been raised with Christ (Romans 6:5-7), we are freed from preoccupation with our own salvation. Now we can serve God joyously, freely, and heartily.

3. We receive through his victory *a sure pledge of our blessed resurrection.* We cannot reach any certainty of immortality beyond the demonstration which the resurrection of Christ affords us. It is an act of re-creation by the God who is at once all-powerful and merciful. When Jesus Christ appears alive to his disciples, he shows to his church what she can and must believe concerning immortality; the whole man is to live in a new body. The risen Jesus Christ is the promise of a "new heaven and a new earth" (Rev. 21:1).

Because of the resurrection of Jesus Christ, the believer cannot help but believe in the resurrection of the body. "If we do not admit it," says a contemporary theologian, "at least let us acknowledge that it is the fault of our eyes which do not see, of our ears which do not hear well, and of our imagination which replaces God's reality with sad illusions." Besides: "If we should find it difficult to believe, rather than modify the message, let us pray God that he give us faith through his Holy Spirit." Finally, this last quotation, reminding us that the church is founded upon the witness of the resurrection: "Fortunately, God has never ceased to work in men's hearts and send the faith needed to see those things" (Barth: *The Faith of the Church,* pp. 105, 107-108).

❡ QUESTION 46. *How do you understand the words: "He ascended into heaven"?*

That Christ was taken up from the earth into heaven before the eyes of his disciples[a] and remains there on our behalf[b] until he comes again to judge the living and the dead.[c]

a. Luke 24:50-51. [Jesus] led them out as far as Bethany, and lifting up his hands he blessed them. While he blessed them, he parted from them.
Cf. Acts 1:9.

b. Heb. 9:24. Christ has entered, not into a sanctuary made with hands, a copy of the true one, but into heaven itself, now to appear in the presence of God on our behalf.
Cf. Rom. 8:34; Eph. 4:8.

c. Acts 1:11. "Men of Galilee, why do you stand looking into heaven? This Jesus, who was taken up from you into heaven, will come in the same way as you saw him go into heaven."
Acts 10:42. He commanded us to preach to the people, and to testify that he is the one ordained by God to be judge of the living and the dead.
Cf. Matt. 25:31-46.

❡ QUESTION 49. *What benefit do we receive from Christ's ascension into heaven?*

First, that he is our Advocate in the presence of his Father in heaven.[a] Second, that we have our flesh in heaven as a sure pledge that he, as the Head, will also take us, his members, up to himself.[b] Third, that he sends us his Spirit as a counterpledge[c] by whose power we seek what is above, where Christ is, sitting at the right hand of God, and not things that are on earth.[d]

a. Rom. 8:34. Is it Christ Jesus, who died, yes, who was raised from the dead, who is at the right hand of God, who indeed intercedes for us?
Cf. 1 John 2:1.

b. John 14:2. "In my Father's house are many rooms; if it were not so, would I have told you that I go to prepare a place for you?"
Cf. John 17:24; 20:17.

c. John 14:16-17. "I will pray the Father, and he will give you another Counselor, to be with you forever, even the Spirit of truth."
Cf. Acts 2; 2 Cor. 1:22; 5:5.

d. Col. 3:1. You have been raised with Christ, seek the things that are above, where Christ is, seated at the right hand of God.
Cf. Phil. 3:20.

❡ QUESTION 50. *Why is there added: "And sits at the right hand of God"?*

Because Christ ascended into heaven so that he might manifest himself there as the Head of his Church,[a] through whom the Father governs all things.[b]

a. Eph. 1:20-23. [God] raised [Christ] from the dead and made him sit at his right hand in the heavenly places, far above all rule and authority and power and dominion, and above every name that is named, not only in this age but also in that which is to come; and he has put all things under his feet and has made him the head over all things for the church, which is his body, the fullness of him who fills all in all.
Cf. Col. 1:18.

b. Matt. 28:18. Jesus came and said to them, "All authority in heaven and on earth has been given to me."
Cf. John 5:22.

❡ QUESTION 51. *What benefit do we receive from this glory of Christ, our Head?*

First, that through his Holy Spirit he pours out heavenly gifts upon us, his members.[a] Second, that by his power he defends and supports us against all our enemies.[b]

a. Acts 2:33. Being therefore exalted at the right hand of God, and having received from the Father the promise of the Holy Spirit, he has poured out this which you see and hear.
Eph. 4:8. "When he ascended on high he led a host of captives, and he gave gifts to men."

b. John 10:28. "I give them eternal life, and they shall never perish, and no one shall snatch them out of my hand."

The words *he ascended into heaven* have sometimes been understood in a purely spiritual sense. It is necessary to take notice that the real issue here is a change of place; Jesus left the scene of our human struggle for domination in order to go back to the indisputable dominion of almighty God. The ascension confirms the divinity of Christ. It does not constitute it, however, for Jesus is not a man raised by God to the rank of the gods, but the one who being God must manifest himself as such.

He is "our Advocate in the presence of his Father" (Question 49). He does not do it, however, merely by speaking for us; he takes us with him, where God is: "we have our flesh in heaven as a sure pledge that he, as the Head, will also take us, his members, up to himself." In the incarnation, Jesus lowers himself to us and assumes the form of sinful humanity. His ascension signifies that from now on he does not abandon this flesh, this human reality, like an unwanted garment; he has taken it there with him, in the presence of God. Such is the final phase of the solidarity which binds Jesus, true God and true man, to the sinful form of man that we are. Freed by him, we share with him in his glorification. The Holy Spirit is the pledge of this participation.

The words *sits at the right hand of God* signify, according to the expression of Calvin, that Jesus is from now on "God's lieutenant." It is to him that all of God's power has been entrusted. This recognition of the lordship of Jesus as the Christ spells the end of all dictatorships. No human power will ever be able to compete with or threaten the fullness of power given to Christ by God, actually and effectually executed through his Word and the power of the Holy Spirit.

Let us note again these words: *the Head of his Church, through whom the Father governs all things* (Question 50).

The church recognizes in him who is "seated at the right hand of God" her own Head, and she reminds the world that he is its Lord also. The command to teach and baptize "all nations" (Matt. 28:19) shows us that the revelation, God's mighty deed in Jesus Christ, really concerns the whole world; the world's destiny is being fulfilled in Jesus Christ. Every now and then we are tempted to think that history is determined by economic phenomena to such a degree, for example, that a new distribution of wealth could mean an ultimate improvement. The revelation, this historic phenomenon par excellence, shows us where the true reality of history is to be found: in Jesus Christ, in whom God has brought to pass the decisive event for our world. The death, the resurrection, and the ascension of Jesus Christ make clear to us what God wills and does for this world. In him and through him, we know where we come from and where we are going. The events of history, those which have occurred and those which will still occur between the ascension of Christ and his return, are of only relative value and significance. They are epiphenomenal, events which arise along side of and because of the decisive event. They are unable to modify the result in any way. Jesus Christ sums up all things (Ephesians 1:10 says literally "recapitulates" not "unites" as in the Revised Standard Version).

Today more and more this must be the justification for the church's *evangelism* and *missionary work:* the Christ must be presented to men of all conditions, all political affiliations, all tongues, all colors, as the one who perfects and fulfills the universal history of mankind and not merely as a Savior of individuals. Jesus Christ is Savior because he is Lord.

Such is the meaning of the message of *the ascension.*

❡ QUESTION 47. *Then, is not Christ with us unto the end of the world, as he has promised us?*[a]

Christ is true man and true God. As a man he is no longer on earth,[b] but in his divinity, majesty, grace, and Spirit, he is never absent from us.[c]

a. Matt. 28:20. "Lo, I am with you always, to the close of the age."
b. John 17:11. "Now I am no more in the world, but they are in the world, and I am coming to thee. Holy Father, keep them in thy name which thou hast given me, that they may be one, even as we are one."
   Cf. John 16:28.
c. John 14:18-19. "I will not leave you desolate; I will come to you. Yet a little while, and the world will see me no more, but you will see me; because I live, you will live also."

❡ QUESTION 48. *But are not the two natures in Christ separated from each other in this way, if the humanity is not wherever the divinity is?*

Not at all; for since divinity is incomprehensible and everywhere present,[a] it must follow that the divinity is indeed beyond the bounds of the humanity which it has assumed, and is nonetheless ever in that humanity as well, and remains personally united to it.[b]

a. Jer. 23:23-24. "Am I a God at hand, says the Lord, and not a God afar off? Can a man hide himself in secret places so that I cannot see him? says the Lord. Do I not fill heaven and earth? says the Lord."

Cf. Ps. 139:7-10.

b. John 3:13. No one has ascended into heaven but he who descended from heaven, the Son of man.

Col. 2:9. In [Christ] the whole fullness of deity dwells bodily.

These two questions are intended to sharpen the mode of Christ's presence after the ascension.

Everyone knows that opposition was very lively in the sixteenth century between the Lutherans and the members of the Reformed Church, particularly on the subject of the holy Communion. The Lutherans have always affirmed a real presence of Christ in the elements. Luther at the Marburg Colloquy held his finger obstinately poised over the "is" of the inscription "this *is* my body" that he himself had traced on the table.

The members of the Reformed Church, by opposition to this localization which seemed too materialistic to them, reached the point of considering it no more than a completely spiritual presence of Christ, "in his grace and Spirit." They postulated, at the same time, an opposition just as irreducible between the human nature and the divine nature of Christ.

Karl Barth, at the end of the exposition he devotes to the problem of "The Unity and Omnipresence of God" (*Church Dogmatics,* Vol. II, I, pp. 440-490) proposes to the Reformed and to the Lutherans that on other grounds they should resume the discussion that has remained ever since at a standstill. If Jesus Christ is the only Mediator between God and man, he is present in his entirety where his Spirit and grace are found. Thus, Barth says: "The whole Jesus Christ is there at the right of God in one way, and the same Jesus Christ is here in Israel and the church, but also in the entire world, in another way" (p. 490).

Thus it will no longer be a question of minimizing one of the forms of this presence in favor of the other. Christ sits at the right hand of God; he is the Lord in the presence of his Father, but at the same time he is also completely present on earth through his Word and in the sacraments that confirm it. The Spirit then, is no longer a different reality from Jesus Christ, but his Spirit and the Spirit of God coming to bring to life his very presence on earth.

¶ QUESTION 52. *What comfort does the return of Christ "to judge the living and the dead" give you?*

That in all affliction and persecution I may await with head held high the very Judge from heaven who has already submitted himself to the judgment of God for me and has removed all the curse from me;[a] that he will cast his enemies and mine into everlasting condemnation,[b] but he shall take me, together with all his elect, to himself into heavenly joy and glory.[c]

a. Luke 21:28. "When these things begin to take place, look up and raise your heads, because your redemption is drawing near."
   Phil. 3:20. Our commonwealth is in heaven, and from it we await a Savior, the Lord Jesus Christ.
b. Matt. 25:41-43. "He will say to those at his left hand, 'Depart from me, you cursed, into the eternal fire prepared for the devil and his angels; for I was hungry and you gave me no food, I was thirsty and you gave me no drink, I was a stranger and you did not welcome me, naked and you did not clothe me, sick and in prison and you did not visit me.' "
c. Matt. 25:34. "The King will say to those at his right hand, 'Come, O blessed of my Father, inherit the kingdom prepared for you from the foundation of the world.' "

The words of the Creed, "from thence he shall come," are a comfort to us because we are here being told that our time is not ultimate. We are not condemned to live forever in an empty eternity: he who is the glorious Christ, he who is Lord, will *come to judge the living and the dead*. Our comfort does not rest upon the vague idea of an abstract eternity but on Christ's promise to return as King of his kingdom. The Christian does not believe in "the beyond" but in the one who has fulfilled everything and who will return to make it known to the whole creation in a definitive convincing manner.

Every now and then the doctrine of the return of Jesus Christ has been interpreted in a way that does not correspond to the reality of the judgment made by the Lord himself. Christ has been seen to return brandishing the thunder of his wrath, chastising some and blessing others. Certain biblical texts seem to authorize this interpretation (Matthew 25:34, 46). A more accurate understanding of the person and the work of Christ would have allowed us, we believe, to avoid making a too narrow schematization with respect to these very texts.

Question 52 asks us: "What comfort does the return of Christ to judge the living and the dead give you?" The first part of the answer is wholly satisfying: "I may await with head held high the very Judge from heaven who has already submitted himself to the judgment of God for me and has removed all the curse from me."

We have seen that in Jesus Christ God has taken upon himself the burden of the judgment, the punishment, and the curse which ought to fall upon men. If Jesus Christ is God coming to fulfill the requirements of his righteousness because he alone can do it, the work which he accomplished for us is perfect. We are truly *freed* by the sacrifice of the one who has been true God and true man for us (Question 38).

The judgment accompanying the return of Christ can no longer be a pure and simple condemnation, but a definitive and compelling demonstration to all men of his lordship, a final revelation of his divinity.

In the Scriptures the verb "to judge" has not only the restricted sense of "rendering justice" that we give it today; this verb means "to rule," "to govern," "to guide" (Judges 3:10; 4:4; 15:20; Psalms 9:7-8; 82:8; 1 Corinthians 6:2).

Thus on his return Jesus Christ will be revealed as he is both to *the living and the dead;* he will appear as Lord of his creation, as the King of his kingdom.

In short, the return of Jesus Christ, the Judge, signifies at once his ultimate and final manifestation as Lord of heaven and earth.

Moreover, let us be moderate in our descriptions and avoid setting ourselves up as judges. God alone is Judge; God alone is Lord. That is what the promise of his return teaches us.

8 / GOD THE HOLY SPIRIT

Questions 53-58 define the reality of the Holy Spirit and describe his work in and for man.

⊂ QUESTION 53. *What do you believe concerning "the Holy Spirit"?*

First, that, with the Father and the Son, he is equally eternal God;[a] second, that God's Spirit is also given to me,[b] preparing me through a true faith to share in Christ and all his benefits,[c] that he comforts me[d] and will abide with me forever.[e]

a. Gen. 1:1-2. When God began to create the heavens and the earth, the earth was without form and void, and darkness was upon the face of the deep; and the Spirit of God was moving over the face of the waters.
   John 4:24. God is Spirit, and those who worship him must worship in spirit and truth.
   Cf. John 14:7-17; Acts 5:3-4.
b. Matt. 28:19. "Go therefore and make disciples of all nations, baptizing them in the name of the Father and of the Son and of the Holy Spirit."
   1 Cor. 3:16. Do you not know that you are God's temple and that God's Spirit dwells in you?
   Cf. 2 Cor. 1:22.
c. 1 Cor. 6:17, 19. He who is united to the Lord becomes one spirit with him. . . . Do you not know that your body is a temple of the Holy Spirit within you, which you have from God? You are not your own.
   Cf. Gal. 4:6-7.
d. Acts 9:31. The church throughout all Judea and Galilee and Samaria had peace and was built up; and walking in the fear of the Lord and in the comfort of the Holy Spirit it was multiplied.
e. John 14:16. "I will pray the Father, and he will give you another Counselor, to be with you forever."

Let us note immediately that the Creed says: "I believe in the Holy Spirit" just as it said "I believe in God. . . . I believe in Jesus Christ." The one who confesses the Christian faith believes in the Holy Spirit in no different way than in God and Christ. "I believe in the Holy Spirit" means: "I believe in God the Holy Spirit; I believe that God himself by the Holy Spirit, reveals to me the work which he has fulfilled for me in Jesus Christ."

God the Holy Spirit makes us aware of:

1. **Salvation in Jesus Christ** (Question 53).

95

2. The church as a community of fathers and brothers in the faith (Question 54).

3. Freedom through the forgiveness of sins (Question 56).

4. Life, now and forever, through the resurrection of Jesus Christ (Questions 57 and 58).

Thus, the Holy Spirit renders the work of God in Jesus Christ actual and effectual for us. "To have the Holy Spirit is not to have more than Jesus Christ; it is really to have Jesus Christ" (Roland de Pury: *Je suis le Seigneur ton Dieu,* p. 49).

We will never separate this third mode of God's being from the other two. The Holy Spirit does not bring anything new. He does not complete the revelation. He makes the revelation accessible. However, the Holy Spirit does not establish a direct, private relationship between God and man or between man and God as the mystics and spiritualists understand it. Man can never be directly connected with God. One must always ask for a connection through "Central"—that is to say, through Jesus Christ and his Word.

The word "spirit" (Greek, *pneuma*) means "wind," "breath." When it signifies the Spirit of God, it betokens a movement of God toward man. The Holy Spirit is God coming into man.

The Holy Spirit must not be confused with the spirit of man. It cannot be identified with some sort of exaltation of the human spirit, with enthusiasm or inspiration. This kind of confusion is impossible since the Holy Spirit *is* God (John 4:24).

Let us repeat that, if the Holy Spirit means that God gives himself to man and that he enters into man, he could never become man's property. The word *pneuma* (wind, breath) indicates a movement: the Holy Spirit is continuously given to man, daily reminding him of God's righteousness and mercy toward him. Faith is the constantly renewed gift of God. One cannot "lose faith" as one loses his purse. Those who think so have really lost nothing but an entirely human acquisition. God himself can help destroy this false faith in order to give us back the true one, that is to say, a daily renewal of confidence in the reality of his work for us, a true "comfort" in all the circumstances of life. This can be so precisely because it is the fruit of the Holy Spirit, the gift of himself which God makes to us.

The Holy Spirit not only promises us the presence of God, *he is this very presence.*

⟪ QUESTION 54. *What do you believe concerning "the Holy Catholic Church"?*

I believe that, from the beginning to the end of the world, and from among the whole human race,[a] the Son of God,[b] by his Spirit and his Word,[c] gathers, protects, and preserves for himself, in the unity of the true faith,[d] a congregation chosen for eternal life. Moreover, I believe that I am and forever will remain a living member of it.[e]

a. Gen. 26:3b-4. "I will fulfill the oath which I swore to Abraham your father. I will multiply your descendants as the stars of heaven, and will give to your descendants all these lands; and by your descendants all the nations of the earth shall bless themselves."

   Rev. 5:9. They sang a new song, saying, "Worthy art thou to take the scroll and to open its seals, for thou wast slain and by thy blood didst ransom men for God from every tribe and tongue and people and nation."

b. Col. 1:18. [Christ] is the head of the body, the church; he is the beginning, the first-born from the dead, that in everything he might be preeminent.

c. Isa. 59:21. "This is my covenant with them, says the Lord: my spirit which is upon you, and my words which I have put in your mouth, shall not depart out of your mouth, or out of the mouth of your children, or out of the mouth of your children's children, says the Lord, from this time forth and forevermore."

   Cf. Rom. 1:16-18; 10:14-17.

d. Acts 13:47-48. The Lord has commanded us, saying, "I have set you to be a light for the Gentiles, that you may bring salvation to the uttermost parts of the earth." And when the Gentiles heard this, they were glad and glorified the word of God; and as many as were ordained to eternal life believed.

   Cf. Isa. 49:6.

   Eph. 4:3-6. [Be] eager to maintain the unity of the Spirit in the bond of peace. There is one body and one Spirit, just as you were called to the one hope that belongs to your call, one Lord, one faith, one baptism, one God and Father of us all, who is above all and through all and in all.

   Eph. 5:25-27. Christ loved the church and gave himself up for her, that he might sanctify her, having cleansed her by the washing of water with the word, that the church might be presented before him in splendor, without spot or wrinkle or any such thing, that she might be holy and without blemish.

e. John 10:28. "I give them eternal life, and they shall never perish, and no one shall snatch them out of my hand."
Cf. Rom. 8:29-39.

◖ QUESTION 55. *What do you understand by "the communion of saints"?*

First, that believers one and all, as partakers of the Lord Christ, and all his treasures and gifts, shall share in one fellowship.[a] Second, that each one ought to know that he is obliged to use his gifts freely and with joy for the benefit and welfare of other members.[b]

a. 1 Cor. 1:9. God is faithful, by whom you were called into the fellowship of his Son, Jesus Christ our Lord.
1 Cor. 12:4-7, 12-13. There are varieties of gifts, but the same Spirit; and there are varieties of service, but the same Lord; and there are varieties of working, but it is the same God who inspires them all in everyone. To each is given the manifestation of the Spirit for the common good. . . . For just as the body is one and has many members, and all the members of the body, though many, are one body, so it is with Christ. For by one Spirit we were all baptized into one body—Jews or Greeks, slaves or free —and all were made to drink of one Spirit.

b. 1 Cor. 12:14, 21, 26-27. The body does not consist of one member but of many. . . . The eye cannot say to the hand, "I have no need of you," nor again the head to the feet, "I have no need of you." . . . If one member suffers, all suffer together; if one member is honored, all rejoice together. Now you are the body of Christ and individually members of it.
1 Cor. 13:4-5. Love is patient and kind; love is not jealous or boastful; it is not arrogant or rude. Love does not insist on its own way; it is not irritable or resentful.
Cf. Phil. 2:1-11; 1 Cor. 12—13.

The Holy Spirit brings men together in fellowship; he does not isolate them in a selfish enjoyment or in a proud admiration of what they could consider a completely personal honor. When a man withdraws from the church because he has "received the Holy Spirit" he shows by that very action that he does not believe in the Holy Spirit but in another power or simply in himself, his own spirit.

The Holy Spirit, God the Spirit, brings men together in a common acknowledgment of his mercy shown in Jesus Christ. Thus it is that the church, according to the Hebrew and Greek etymology of the word, *is a gathered congregation.* It is God himself who takes the initiative in this calling and this gathering. If this divine initiative is no longer recognized and believed as such, the church becomes no more than a human society under the form of a free association of goodwill, just an ecclesiastical institution.

The church manifests the work of God himself among men, whatever form they may give to it.

The church is *holy* in this sense, that she is *set apart* by God. So it is that she is *gathered, protected, and preserved* "by his Spirit and his Word, in the unity of the true faith."

The holiness of the church does not consist of any other privilege than the one of living solely by the forgiving power of God. Thus, the church for her part cannot make any claim or have any pride about it. Her holiness is not a quality that she possesses by or in herself; it is a gift of God.

The church is *Christian* because like the believer himself she is closely bound to Christ. Every time in history that this relationship has been allowed to become lax the church has fallen into one form or another of infidelity. It is important therefore that the Christian community should always be brought back to the object of its faith. The role of God's Word and of the Holy Spirit is to make possible the church's return to the truth of Jesus Christ.

The church is *universal.* She is not limited by human decision and is not the possession of one class or of one race. She proclaims the forgiveness of God throughout the entire world and to all mankind. When the church ceases to be universal, she shows that she is sick. On this point, it is clear that although the universal church cannot be limited by human decisions, she is limited nonetheless by the decision of God in Jesus Christ even as the Holy Spirit has made known to us.

The church is *the community* that *the Son of God* chooses and calls together, protects and watches over by *his Spirit and his Word in the unity of the true faith.* It is thus that we can believe in the *communion of saints.* The Latin term *sanctorum* can be understood either as a neuter or as a masculine genitive. Thus it could mean either the communion of holy things or the communion of holy persons.

When we say "I believe in the communion of saints" we confess our participation in all the treasures and all the gifts of Jesus Christ. The believer is a man who receives and accepts Christ's holiness.

Believing in the communion of saints also means believing in the communication of the gifts of God to each member of the church. The mission of the church consists essentially in *service* in the form of mutual help to the brethren within the Christian community as well as the proclamation of the gospel outside of it.

The existence of the Christian can be understood only in and through the Christian community. That is what we believe when we say "I believe in the communion of saints." The true faith that the Holy Spirit gives is not a private affair but a joyous receiving in common of the gift of God in Jesus Christ. Let us add that the church is always *lowly* and *exalted* at the same time. Since her members are participants of Jesus Christ, their community life expresses the true humanity and true divinity of the one who is the Head of the church (Ephesians 1:22).

❡ QUESTION 56. *What do you believe concerning "the forgiveness of sins"?*

That, for the sake of Christ's reconciling work,[a] God will no more remember my sins or the sinfulness with which I have to struggle all my life long;[b] but that he graciously imparts to me the righteousness of Christ so that I may never come into condemnation.[c]

a. 2 Cor. 5:19, 21. God was in Christ reconciling the world to himself, not counting their trespasses against them, and entrusting to us the message of reconciliation. . . . For our sake he made him to be sin who knew no sin, so that in him we might become the righteousness of God.
   Cf. 1 John 1:7; 2:2.
b. Jer. 31:34. "No longer shall each man teach his neighbor and each his brother, saying, 'Know the Lord,' for they shall all know me, from the least of them to the greatest, says the Lord; for I

will forgive their iniquity, and I will remember their sin no more."
Cf. Ps. 103.

Rom. 8:1-2. There is therefore now no condemnation for those who are in Christ Jesus. For the law of the Spirit of life in Christ Jesus has set me free from the law of sin and death.

c. John 3:17-18. God sent the Son into the world, not to condemn the world, but that the world might be saved through him. He who believes in him is not condemned.

The message of the church which the members of the community must tell one another and which they must proclaim to the world is fully expressed in this proposition: *I believe in the forgiveness of sins.*

The preaching, the liturgy, the life, and the confession of faith of the Christian church consist essentially in the proclamation of the forgiveness, the mercy, the benevolence, and the grace of God manifested in Jesus Christ and attested by the Holy Spirit.

The key words of this question are these: NO MORE! They ought to be triple-starred to mark the heart of the gospel promise. "For the sake of Christ's reconciling work, God will *no more* remember my sins or my sinfulness." Such is the good news of grace which we ourselves are to receive and proclaim to others. On account of this "no more" authenticated and actualized by Jesus Christ, we are no longer preoccupied with the past, however burdensome it may appear to us, nor with the future, except for rejoicing in it.

In Jesus Christ God changes places with us. We were like a child who, having taken his father's car, is forced to drive it but does not know how to drive. God says to us, "Let's change places, let me take the wheel, let me get you out of this mortal danger in which you placed yourself because of your not knowing how to drive!" The apostle Paul said, "It is no longer I who live; but Christ who lives in me" (Gal. 2:20).

That is what the Holy Spirit reveals to us. Because I believe in the Holy Spirit, God's righteousness becomes mine. We can now be sure that God will no more remember our sins; he no longer remembers the wretchedness of our actual life, our "reckless driving"; on the contrary, he teaches us to drive; he takes over the wheel and straightens it, he prevents us from falling over the precipices that border the road.

This is the certitude that motivates evangelical morality into doing something which puts joy into life. We are no longer afraid, we let God guide us. Thus the opposition is found definitely reduced between *faith* and *works:* our deeds express this new reality, knowing that from now on God directs us. As Paul puts it, Christ lives in us. We no longer believe in our works, but in the grace of God in Jesus Christ. The forgiveness of sins is not a theoretical notion but the assurance of a new possibility of living through Jesus Christ and the Holy Spirit.

❶ QUESTION 57. *What comfort does "the resurrection of the body" give you?*

That after this life my soul shall be immediately taken up to Christ, its Head,[a] and that this flesh of mine, raised by the power of Christ, shall be reunited with my soul, and be conformed to the glorious body of Christ.[b]

a. Luke 23:43. [Jesus] said to him, "Truly, I say to you, today you will be with me in Paradise."
   Phil. 1:21. For me to live is Christ, and to die is gain.
b. 1 Cor. 15:20, 42-46, 54. In fact Christ has been raised from the dead, the first fruits of those who have fallen asleep. . . . So is it with the resurrection of the dead. What is sown is perishable, what is raised is imperishable. It is sown in dishonor, it is raised in glory. It is sown in weakness, it is raised in power. It is sown a physical body, it is raised a spiritual body. If there is a physical body, there is also a spiritual body. Thus it is written, "The first man Adam became a living being"; the last Adam became a life-giving spirit. But it is not the spiritual which is first but the physical, and then the spiritual. . . . When the perishable puts on the imperishable, and the mortal puts on immortality, then shall come to pass the saying that is written: "Death is swallowed up in victory."
   Job 19:25. "I know that my Redeemer lives, and at last he will stand upon the earth."
   1 John 3:2. Beloved, we are God's children now; it does not yet appear what we shall be, but we know that when he appears we shall be like him, for we shall see him as he is.
   Phil. 3:21. [The Lord Jesus Christ] will change our lowly body to be like his glorious body, by the power which enables him even to subject all things to himself.

¶ QUESTION 58. *What comfort does the article concerning "the life everlasting" give you?*

That, since I now feel in my heart the beginning of eternal joy,[a] I shall possess, after this life, perfect blessedness, which no eye has seen, nor ear heard, nor the heart of man conceived,[b] and thereby praise God forever.[c]

a. Rom. 14:17. The kingdom of God does not mean food and drink but righteousness and peace and joy in the Holy Spirit.
b. 1 Cor. 2:9. As it is written, "What no eye has seen, nor ear heard, nor the heart of man conceived, what God has prepared for those who love him," God has revealed to us through the Spirit.
c. John 17:3. "This is eternal life, that they know thee the only true God, and Jesus Christ whom thou hast sent."

The Holy Spirit enables me to believe that Jesus Christ has conquered death and that he makes me a participant in his victory.

To confess, "I believe in the resurrection of the body," means "I believe that it will really be I—all of me, just as I am—who will be raised." This precision is necessary to forestall all purely spiritual or physical conceptions of the resurrection. It will not be our spirit or soul alone which will be restored to life; nor will we survive because of our deeds, or in the memory or thoughts of others. We actually will live again. We do not believe in a higher life, an eternity sheltering beings without substance; we believe in a new life according to the kind that Christ himself has offered us in his resurrection. We do not have to invent a theory destined to support our hope of last things; we believe what God shows us himself of these things in his revelation through Jesus Christ.

We are no longer able to accept today the duality that the Heidelberg Catechism postulates between "the soul" and "the flesh" (Question 57) nor, therefore, the reunion of the one with the other which it describes. Some recent studies bearing on biblical anthropology have shown that, for the Scriptures, man forms a whole; the expression "the flesh" particularly serves to designate man in his role as creature and more exactly a fallen creature (Isaiah 40:5-6), destined to be redeemed (Joel 2:28; cf. Acts 2:17).

It is that man—that "flesh"—who is promised resurrection, it is he who will be conformed to the glorious body of Jesus Christ (1 Corinthians 15:20, 42-44).

Notice that the Creed speaks further of *life everlasting*. The Greek term that is translated "everlasting" does not mean first and foremost "what never ends," but "what belongs to the world to come," that is, to the kingdom of God. The accent does not fall upon the eternity of this life, but on the fact that it will be lived with God and in his presence, in the communion that Jesus Christ has permitted us to share. That ought to assure us regarding the fears that we could have of "being bored" in the kingdom! No, although boredom is a prominent part of life in this world, it will be absent from the world to come, and likewise some other inconveniences that we have known on this earth. Let us note also that the new life is already beginning today, and it is the Holy Spirit who gives us the "guarantee" (2 Cor. 1:22; 5:5).

Here we have reached the end of the study of the Apostles' Creed according to the Heidelberg Catechism.

Calvin already called attention to the fact that the Creed does not speak at length about hell nor about eternal death. He believed, so far as he was concerned, that we should see in this a sign of gentleness and of a certain good-naturedness.

One ought to give a more adequate theological explanation of this phenomenon. The Apostles' Creed invites us to confess our faith. But we can only confess what is a matter of faith. The Creed indicates to us what we ought to believe: the forgiveness of God the Father manifest in Jesus Christ and attested for each one of us by the Holy Spirit, the resurrection, and everlasting life, all of which are the result of this faith. As for the others— hell, Satan, sin, and death—we are not invited to believe in these realities. The only thing that is asked of us is to believe in Jesus Christ who has conquered death.

9 / TRUE FAITH

❰ QUESTION 59. *But how does it help you now that you believe all this?*

That I am righteous in Christ before God, and an heir of eternal life.ᵃ

a. Rom. 1:17. [In the gospel] the righteousness of God is revealed through faith for faith; as it is written, "He who through faith is righteous shall live."
Cf. Hab. 2:4.
Rom. 5:1. Since we are justified by faith, we have peace with God through our Lord Jesus Christ.
John 3:36. He who believes in the Son has eternal life.

Notice immediately the words: "But how does it help you. . ." The Catechism constantly insists upon the practical use of faith (see also the formula "What benefit do we receive" which recurs several times in the preceding questions).

Faith ought to serve some end. Christianity is a piece of good news about life. Our faith concerns the actual, practical, and daily arena of human existence. The knowledge that faith gives, produces confidence that in turn makes life possible.

Such is the doctrine of *justification by faith alone* that we are going to deal with now. Faith receives the assurance of *our vindication* "in Christ before God." In Christ God gives the believer his very own righteousness and it is through faith that this acquisition takes place (Romans 4:1-5). The role of faith is decisive; it *lays hold* of the righteousness that God gives us in Christ.

According to scripture, "none is righteous, no, not one" (Rom. 3:10; see also Psalm 14:1-3; Ecclesiastes 7:20). Righteousness which is perfection according to God (Matthew 5:48; Colossians 1:28; Philippians 3:15) cannot be a quality of man; it is a gift of the one who possesses all the perfections; it is through love that God gives to men his righteousness in Jesus Christ.

To be vindicated in Christ before God means to receive a new status, the new condition that God, through his love, gives us in Jesus Christ.

Calvin said: "If a perfect man were found, he could be called righteous; but since we are all wretched sinners, we must look for our righteousness elsewhere than in ourselves, in order to endure the judgment of God."

And Luther: "I will never preach about man's righteousness or praise his works, but only thy work, that nothing is greater than thy righteousness, by which all the righteous are justified and without which all others are sinners. For if thou dost not justify, no one will be righteous by his own works. It is called thy right-

eousness because thou grantest it out of grace, and we do not receive it by works" *(The Seven Penitential Psalms, 1517, Ps. 51:
Weimar I, p. 192; Luther's Works, Vol. 14, p. 173).*

It is because of this righteousness that the believer can be
assured of being *the heir of eternal life.* We could have no certainty in this realm if we had to rely upon our works and our
merits. The newness of the gospel consists in this fact that our
assurance rests entirely in a gift of God and no longer on human
achievement. Our life and its unrighteousness entitle us to nothing but death, but the righteousness which God gives us through
Jesus Christ and in which the Holy Spirit empowers us to believe,
is the pledge for us of our eternal life. The one who lives in faith
is no longer judged on his work but on what God has done in
Jesus Christ (John 15:4; 1 Corinthians 4:4). Such is the assurance
of the man who receives justification by God in Jesus Christ
through his faith.

❡ QUESTION 60. *How are you righteous before God?*

Only by true faith in Jesus Christ.[a] In spite of the fact that my
conscience accuses me that I have grievously sinned against all
the commandments of God, and have not kept any one of them,[b]
and that I am still ever prone to all this is evil,[c] nevertheless, God,
without any merit of my own,[d] out of pure grace,[e] grants me the
benefits of the perfect expiation of Christ,[f] imputing to me his
righteousness and holiness[g] as if I had never committed a single
sin or had ever been sinful, having fulfilled myself all the obedience which Christ has carried out for me,[h] if only I accept such
favor with a trusting heart.[i]

a. Rom. 3:21-22. The righteousness of God has been manifested . . .
through faith in Jesus Christ for all who believe.
Cf. Phil. 3:8-11.

b. Rom. 3:9-10. What then? Are we Jews any better off? No, not at
all; for I have already charged that all men, both Jews and Greeks,
are under the power of sin, as it is written: "None is righteous,
no, not one."

c. Rom. 7:23. I see in my members another law at war with the law of my mind and making me captive to the law of sin which dwells in my members.

d. Titus 3:5. He saved us, not because of deeds done by us in righteousness, but in virtue of his own mercy.

e. Eph. 2:8. By grace you have been saved through faith; and this is not your own doing, it is the gift of God.

Cf. Rom. 3:24.

f. 1 John 2:1-2. We have an advocate with the Father, Jesus Christ the righteous, and he is the expiation of our sins.

g. Rom. 4:3-5. Abraham believed God, and it was reckoned to him as righteousness. Now to one who works, his wages are not reckoned as a gift but as his due. And to one who does not work but trusts him who justifies the ungodly, his faith is reckoned as righteousness.

h. Rom. 4:24. It will be reckoned to us who believe in him that raised from the dead Jesus our Lord.

Cf. 2 Cor. 5:21.

i. Rom. 3:24-25. [We] are justified by [God's] grace as a gift, through the redemption which is in Christ Jesus, whom God put forward as an expiation by his blood, to be received by faith. This was to show God's righteousness, because in his divine forbearance he had passed over former sins.

Note the words *by true faith* and remember that faith is always, according to the definition of Question 21, a "certain knowledge" and a "wholehearted trust." The faith that justifies is faith *in Jesus Christ;* he alone can give us *the righteousness of God.* Thus the means of justification is in the witness which the scripture renders to Jesus Christ and in the Holy Spirit who authenticates it.

The Catechism makes clear at this point that, if we can know this freedom, this true relief from all feeling of guilt, it is because of the "perfect expiation" and perfect obedience of Jesus Christ. The righteousness of God could not be given to man unless these requirements had been fulfilled. Jesus Christ as true God reveals the righteousness of God to us; Jesus Christ as true man accomplishes all that his righteousness demands of man in such a way that God can be satisfied with man.

Such is the doctrine of justification through faith. God himself, in Jesus Christ, accomplishes the work of perfect righteousness which alone can please him. His being made man is precisely to make us share in the fullness of this achievement (Questions 16, 17, 18). "All this comes from the fact that God loves us freely and that he does not want to remember our sins" (Calvin).

Therefore, when I believe in Jesus Christ I am sure of my vindication; I am righteous in the sight of God. "Your life is hid with Christ in God" said Paul in Colossians (3:3). The believers are "saints in Christ" (Phil. 1:1), they are "mature" (Phil. 3:15); there is "now no condemnation for those who are in Christ Jesus" (Rom. 8:1). This is the new situation of man who has been vindicated through faith in Jesus Christ. Here rests all our assurance for this age and forevermore.

❡ QUESTION 61. *Why do you say that you are righteous by faith alone?*

Not because I please God by virtue of the worthiness of my faith, but because the satisfaction, righteousness, and holiness of Christ alone are my righteousness before God,[a] and because I can accept it and make it mine in no other way than by faith alone.

a. 1 Cor. 1:30; 2:2. He is the source of your life in Christ Jesus, whom God made our wisdom, our righteousness and sanctification and redemption. . . . I decided to know nothing among you except Jesus Christ and him crucified.

❡ QUESTION 62. *But why cannot our good works be our righteousness before God, or at least a part of it?*

Because the righteousness which can stand before the judgment of God must be absolutely perfect and wholly in conformity with the divine Law.[a] But even our best works in this life are all imperfect and defiled with sin.[b]

a. Gal. 3:10. All who rely on works of the law are under a curse; for it is written, "Cursed be everyone who does not abide by all things written in the book of the law, and do them."
Cf. Deut. 27:26.
b. Isa. 64:6. We have all become like one who is unclean, and all our righteous deeds are like a polluted garment. We all fade like a leaf, and our iniquities, like the wind, take us away.

❡ QUESTION 63. *Will our good works merit nothing, even when it is God's purpose to reward them in this life, and in the future life as well?*

This reward is not given because of merit, but out of grace.[a]

a. Luke 17:10. When you have done all that is commanded you, say, "We are unworthy servants; we have only done what was our duty."

❡ QUESTION 64. *But does not this teaching make people careless and sinful?*

No, for it is impossible for those who are ingrafted into Christ by true faith not to bring forth the fruit of gratitude.[a]

a. Matt. 7:16-17. You will know them by their fruits. Are grapes gathered from thorns, or figs from thistles? So, every sound tree bears good fruit, but the bad tree bears evil fruit.
John 15:5. "I am the vine, you are the branches. He who abides in me, and I in him, he it is that bears much fruit, for apart from me you can do nothing."

Can we not receive being justified by faith in Jesus Christ alone, without any participation on our part? This is the great question with which the apostles (Romans 6:1-2) and the reformers have already had to occupy themselves. The newness of the gospel regarding our vindication through faith is so new that it runs counter to all that the religions had proposed to man. Therefore, we ought not be astonished to find it difficult to grasp it and to live in it. In the same degree that we are not yet freed from all feeling of guilt toward God, we always think that we must do something to propitiate him toward us. We cannot tolerate that an opportunity of redeeming ourselves be lost to us. Rather than believe in the gift of righteousness that God makes us, we prefer to give ourselves the false assurance of doing something ourselves for our salvation, and it is there that our unrighteousness is manifest. If the righteousness of man consists in accepting what God gives him in Jesus Christ, unrighteousness lies in the refusal of God's righteousness.

The fundamental tragedy of our condition shows up in the fact that we cannot and do not want to accept being simply forgiven sinners. We wish to offer to God something other than our wretchedness, and it is exactly in this way that "we increase our debt each day" (Question 13).

Summary

1. God does not vindicate man out of consideration for the good that he can do. We have already seen that even if man saves an appreciable number of his faculties after the fall, the use that he can make of them is nonetheless corrupted. Man through himself alone can only hate God and his neighbor (Question 5). Therefore, in justifying man, God could not make use of the capacities that, up to now, man has directed against him.

Thus our good works cannot be our righteousness before God, nor even "a part of it" (Question 62). God would not be satisfied with a few efforts of man or a little goodwill on his part; he demands "perfect righteousness."

2. Reasoning could be made more subtle; I might declare that it is on account of "the worthiness of my faith" (Question 61) that God vindicates me. If faith could be considered as an act of man, then the argument (reasoning) would hold, but if faith comprises a response from man, it is then a work of God through the Holy Spirit.

3. Finally, one could ask, does not God reward our good deeds "in this life and in the future life as well" (Question 63) and is not this the proof that he takes them into consideration? In other words, should we think that God waits for us to produce works of faith in order to vindicate us? In this way man would entrust himself to God and live in this new life and God would vindicate him in order to reward him for this very life. Once again, such reasoning falls on account of this basic objection: God requires righteousness which "must be absolutely perfect and wholly in conformity with the divine Law" (Question 62). Whatever may be the quality of the newness in the life of man, it will never be "perfect righteousness." We are "perfect" before God through Jesus Christ, but we still remain sinners.

We see now that all attempts we make to soften the doctrine of justification by faith alone are thrown back. It is not in consideration of the natural goodness of man that God vindicates him, nor on account of the worthiness of his faith, nor because of his "good works" that he can accomplish as a believer, but *solely* because of the righteousness of Jesus Christ which is imputed to the believer. Jesus Christ is the only worthy one and he merits everything. The believing man can receive this merit only from Jesus Christ, that is, from his righteousness.

In the final analysis it is not man's faith that vindicates him "but the object and content of his faith, God in Jesus Christ." One can never insist strongly enough: *it is God himself who vindicates man.* His faith is the only means that enables him to receive this righteousness.

A main conduit is indispensable for making the waterfall turn a turbine, but no one would imagine that the force did not come from the water.

Faith is indispensable but it does not save; this is the work of God in Jesus Christ and the Holy Spirit.

A right understanding of the doctrine of justification through faith alone allows the avoidance of the following deviations:

1. The *Roman Catholic* concept of salvation: justification is a function of the works of the faithful person and the merits that he has acquired on earth.

"Besides faith, other acts of virtue are required of an adult for justification; faith alone does not justify" (Bartmann: *Op. cit.,* Tome II, p. 107). And again: "The righteous merit by their good works the increase of grace, eternal life, and the increase of glory" (*Ibid.,* p. 140).

2. *Revivalism* in all its forms: faith becomes a method of salvation; conversion marks a radical change in the life of man. He can say, "Recently I was a sinner; today I am no longer one." Whence the moralism and the legalism which characterizes these groups.

Such also is the puritanical notion of salvation.

3. *Pietism:* justification is a function of sanctification. Whence the accumulation of prayer meetings, biblical studies, and all that can be considered as a means of sanctification and finally as a possibility given to man to make him worthy of God's pardon.

Let us say in conclusion that God takes us where we are and as we are. That is why the gospel of Jesus Christ is good news.

God does not wait for us to be righteous in order to vindicate ourselves. He justifies sinners; he gives freely the righteousness of Jesus Christ to me a sinner: "At once justified but still a sinner" *(simul peccator et simul justus)*, according to the formula of Luther.

We do not have to be fogged in by sin or perpetually caught up in a vain effort to eliminate it from our lives. Before everything else, we must be thankful for the vindication that God gives us through Jesus Christ. With respect to sin, it will give way, in the very degree that we will live in true gratitude. We will have no complacency toward sin but neither will we have the foolish presumption of wanting to uproot the tares before the harvest.

10 / THE HOLY SACRAMENTS

❰ QUESTION 65. *Since, then, faith alone makes us share in Christ and all his benefits, where does such faith originate?*

The Holy Spirit creates it in our hearts[a] by the preaching of the holy gospel,[b] and confirms it by the use of the holy Sacraments.

a. Eph. 2:8. By grace you have been saved through faith; and this is not your own doing, it is the gift of God.
   Cf. John 3:5.
b. 1 Peter 1:23, 25. You have been born anew, not of perishable seed but of imperishable, through the living and abiding word of God. . . . That word is the good news which was preached to you.
   Cf. Matt. 28:19-20.

When the Catechism deals with the doctrine of the sacraments, it does not begin with a general statement; it simply replies to the question, Where does faith come from? The reply: Faith comes from the Holy Spirit who "creates it in our hearts by the preaching of the holy gospel and confirms it by the use of the holy sacraments."

Remember that the sacraments concern faith; they are tied to preaching and therefore to the Word of God and the Holy Spirit. According to the definition of Paul, "faith comes from what is heard, and what is heard comes by the preaching of Christ" (Rom. 10:17).

The Holy Spirit *brings forth* faith by means of the preaching of the Word of God, and also *confirms* this faith by use of the sacraments.

Thus (a) the action of the sacrament is not identical with that of preaching; and (b) the sacrament cannot replace preaching.

Such then is the specific character of the Reformed doctrine of the sacraments. Sacraments must not be separated from the Word. "Thus we see that the sacrament is never without God's Word going before" (Calvin: *Institutes,* Book IV, Ch. XIV. Cf. English translation, Vol. 2, pp. 1276-1303).

Preaching and the sacraments are in effect two *complementary* acts of the Holy Spirit, that is, two of God's ways of working.

A right understanding of the Reformed doctrine of the sacraments keeps us from falling into two forms of deviation: spiritualism, which considers their use superfluous and even backward, according to a "developed" Christianity; sacramental mysticism, which is very close for certain Protestants to the Roman Catholic notion of *"opus operatum"*—the communication of grace by the sacrament itself.

❡ QUESTION 66. *What are the Sacraments?*

They are visible, holy signs and seals[a] instituted by God in order that by their use he may the more fully disclose and seal to us the promise of the gospel, namely, that because of the one sacrifice of Christ accomplished on the cross he graciously grants us the forgiveness of sins and eternal life.[b]

a. Rom. 4:11. Abraham received circumcision as a sign or seal of the righteousness which he had by faith while he was still uncircumcised. The purpose was to make him the father of all who . . . thus have righteousness reckoned to them.
   Cf. Gen. 17:11; Deut. 30:6.
b. Acts 2:38; 22:16. Peter said to them, "Repent, and be baptized every one of you in the name of Jesus Christ for the forgiveness of your sins; and you shall receive the gift of the Holy Spirit. . . . Now why do you wait? Rise and be baptized, and wash away your sins, calling on his name."

Matt. 26:28. "This is my blood of the covenant, which is poured out for many for the forgiveness of sins."
Cf. Heb. 9.

The word sacrament translates the Latin *sacramentum* and is used to designate on the one hand a "mystery," and on the other hand an "oath." Taking such an oath is the kind of act by which a soldier used to swear loyalty to the emperor. The *signum* (sign), a metal disc or a lead seal worn around the neck, was the pledge of this oath.

From the second century onward, the concepts of "mystery," "pledge," and "sign" became the key ideas when the sacraments were spoken of within the church.

Augustine said: "The sacrament is a visible sign of an invisible grace, having been established for our justification."

Calvin in his Catechism gives the following definition: "A sacrament is an outward attestation of the grace of God which, by a visible sign represents spiritual things to imprint the promises of God more firmly in our hearts, and to make us more sure of them" (No. 310).

Let us repeat the formula of the Heidelberg Catechism: "They are visible, holy signs and seals instituted by God in order that by their use he may the more fully (*literally*—so much the better) disclose and seal to us the promise of the gospel."

The use of the notion of "sign" is universal. This term, however, presents certain dangers: these signs can become mere symbols powerless to sustain and strengthen faith.

One must not, however, put the sign in opposition to the reality to such a degree that they become irreconcilable and end by making the sacrament meaningless. If, by definition, matter itself becomes an obstacle to the Spirit, it is impossible for God to use material stuff to confirm our faith by the Holy Spirit.

The sacrament is not only an object, a thing, a material reality, but an *action*. The work of God in Jesus Christ, attested by the scripture, is confirmed by the sacrament and it consists essentially in the repetition of an act. The sacrament has a *dynamic* meaning: something happens before the Christian community; the sacraments are a veritable *representation* of our salvation.

The sacrament is intended for the whole community. Private celebration is unlawful, and could only be permitted in exceptional cases. Rites celebrated outside of the regular hours, and not accompanied by preaching, fall also in the category of private administration of the sacrament. It is in the very bosom of the community assembled for public worship, and after the Word of God has been preached, that the sacrament must be administered. Paul said, "For as often as you eat this bread and drink the cup, you *proclaim* the Lord's death until he comes" (1 Cor. 11:26). This proclamation must be public in order to be a real confirmation of the faith.

Let us reaffirm clearly that the material stuff of the sacrament attests to the very reality of the incarnation. We are not mere spirits (souls) and, insofar as the Word of God allows our intelligence to grasp the work of God in Jesus Christ, the sacraments themselves confirm this "good work" (Phil. 1:6) for our senses. "For surely it is not with angels that he is concerned but with the descendants of Abraham" (Heb. 2:16).

Calvin declares: "If we were spiritual by nature, like the angels, we could behold God and his graces. But since we are bound up with our bodies, it is needful for us that God should make use of figures to represent to us spiritual and heavenly things; for otherwise we could not comprehend them. At the same time, it is expedient for us to have all our senses exercised in his holy promises in order to confirm us in them" (*Geneva Catechism,* No. 314).

Since it can happen that "the Word beats upon our ears in vain" (Calvin), God makes his Word known to us also by means of a concrete act.

Let us remember that God invites us to an *active* participation. This is the sense in which we say that the sacrament confirms preaching: Baptism which saves is the *pledge* of a good conscience before God (1 Peter 3:21). In participating in the sacrament, the believer attests that he believes and that he desires to believe, even as he takes part with the other members of the community in the struggle of faith. The sacrament becomes the visible and concrete, practical means of our *confession of faith* before God and men.

The proof of a confessing church is in her participation in the sacraments. This confession must be corporate and public. The community of persons celebrating the sacrament does not do it for itself alone but for the world. Nor would this act ever cloak itself in such a mysterious form that it should appear to be reserved only for the initiated few. The liturgy of the celebration must be sufficiently clear and well balanced for all those who participate in this act to be able to grasp the meaning of it through faith.

❡ QUESTION 67. *Are both the Word and the Sacraments designed to direct our faith to the one sacrifice of Jesus Christ on the cross as the only ground of our salvation?*

Yes, indeed, for the Holy Spirit teaches in the gospel and confirms by the holy Sacraments that our whole salvation is rooted in the one sacrifice of Christ offered for us on the cross.[a]

a. Rom. 6:3. Do you not know that all of us who have been baptized into Christ Jesus were baptized into his death?
   Gal. 3:27. As many of you as were baptized into Christ have put on Christ.
   1 Cor. 11:26. As often as you eat this bread and drink the cup, you proclaim the Lord's death until he comes.

This question restates precisely the purpose of the sacraments and the manner in which they should operate. The purpose is to lead us to the cross of Jesus Christ; the sacraments announce "the death of the Lord until he comes," and the means: the gospel and the Holy Spirit.

Thus we can overcome certain false interpretations that are sometimes given regarding the efficacy of the sacraments. They do not work *by themselves, ex opere operato,* without reference to the gospel and the Holy Spirit, that is to say, apart from the freedom of God himself. We quote here a "Pastoral Letter of the General Synod of the Reformed Church of the Netherlands": "According to the Roman view, true sanctifying grace is communicated to us by the sacraments which, for this reason, constitute the framework which defines and coordinates the whole Roman Catholic life. Besides the sacraments the preached Word has only a secondary value; it has only to proclaim what the sacraments alone can actually give" (*Revue Réformée,* Nos. 11-12, p. 46, 1952).

For the Reformed doctrine the sacraments do not bestow *a grace superior* to that which has been given by the Holy Spirit in preaching. They are able only to confirm the grace offered to man by the sacrifice of Jesus Christ. Nothing more than man's justification is involved.

Grace is not communicated through the material *elements* of bread and wine, but grace is received through the faith of the community by means of the confirmation which these elements convey. By this confirmation of his benevolence toward men attested by the sacraments, God *creates* and *renews* the Christian community. The Holy Spirit is not bound, however, by these forms but acts through them. So it is that through the sacraments "he may the more fully disclose and seal to us the promise of the gospel."

With regard to what God himself has instituted, we are not free. God alone is free. As for us, we are bound by what he himself tells us, does for us, and institutes for our salvation.

It is therefore not without danger that one deprives oneself of the sacraments. Vinet said: "Negligence of the means of grace is nearer than one believes to the scorn of grace." And Calvin: "Whoever abstains voluntarily from the practice of the sacraments, thinking that he does not need them, scorns Christ, rejects his grace, and snuffs out his Holy Spirit."

❡ QUESTION 68. *How many Sacraments has Christ instituted in the New Testament?*

Two, holy Baptism and the holy Supper.

The Reformed Church recognizes only two sacraments: Baptism and the Lord's Supper, those which have been instituted by Jesus Christ. The Lutheran Church has three of them: "The genuine sacraments are baptism, the Lord's Supper, and absolution (which is the sacrament of penitence), for these rites have the commandment of God and the promise of grace, which is the heart of the New Testament" (Melanchthon: *Apology of the Augsburg Confession*, Article XIII, 4).

Calvin hesitated to include ordination and the laying on of hands.

The Roman Catholic Church recognizes seven sacraments, while admitting that certain of them are more important than the others. We cite the Council of Trent: "The Catholic Church recognizes only seven sacraments: this number is established by the Holy Scripture, by the tradition of the Fathers, and by the authority of the councils. . . . Baptism, confirmation, the eucharist (Lord's Supper), penance, extreme unction, holy orders (ordination), matrimony. . . . They are, however, neither equally necessary nor of equal value nor equally significant" (*Canons and Decrees*, Session VII, Canons on Sacraments in General).

The Council insists that the Roman Catholic Church counts "only seven sacraments" because the number of them has varied in the course of the centuries; certain theologians in earlier times counted a dozen of them, such as foot washing.

Let us note again that the two sacraments of Baptism and the Lord's Supper are the only ones which are indispensable to the birth and renewal of the Christian community.

11 / HOLY BAPTISM

❡ QUESTION 69. *How does holy Baptism remind and assure you that the one sacrifice of Christ on the cross avails for you?*

In this way: Christ has instituted this external washing with water[a] and by it has promised[b] that I am as certainly washed with his blood and Spirit from the uncleanness of my soul and from all my sins, as I am washed externally with water which is used to remove the dirt from my body.[c]

a. Matt. 28:19. "Go therefore and make disciples of all nations, baptizing them in the name of the Father and of the Son and of the Holy Spirit."
Cf. Acts 2:38.

b. Matt. 3:11. "I baptize you with water for repentance, but he who is coming after me is mightier than I, whose sandals I am not worthy to carry; he will baptize you with the Holy Spirit and with fire."
Cf. Rom. 6:3-10.

c. 1 Peter 3:21. Baptism, which corresponds to this, now saves you, not as a removal of dirt from the body but as an appeal to God for a clear conscience, through the resurrection of Jesus Christ.

❧ QUESTION 70.   *What does it mean to be washed with the blood and Spirit of Christ?*

It means to have the forgiveness of sins from God, through grace, for the sake of Christ's blood which he shed for us in his sacrifice on the cross,[a] and also to be renewed by the Holy Spirit and sanctified as members of Christ, so that we may more and more die unto sin and live in a consecrated and blameless way.[b]

a. Eph. 1:7. In [Jesus Christ] we have redemption through his blood, the forgiveness of our trespasses, according to the riches of his grace.
Cf. Heb. 12:24; 1 Peter 1:2; Rev. 1:5-6.
b. 1 Cor. 6:11. You were washed, you were sanctified, you were justified in the name of the Lord Jesus Christ and in the Spirit of our God.
Rom. 6:4. We were buried therefore with him by baptism into death, so that as Christ was raised from the dead by the glory of the Father, we too might walk in newness of life.
Cf. John 1:33; Col. 2:12.

We have seen that the sacrament is a pledge given to strengthen our faith. Baptism gives us the assurance of our justification. By accepting baptism, Jesus shows that he is coming "to fulfill all righteousness" (Matt. 3:15). He is the servant of the Lord who takes the sins of the people upon himself (Isaiah 42:1; 53). The baptism with which Jesus Christ must be baptized is his *death on the cross* (Mark 10:38).

Our baptism is a *dying with Christ* (Romans 6:3), a confirmation which is given us of our sharing the benefits of Christ's work for us. We are buried and we are *raised from the dead with him* (Romans 6:4). Baptism is a sign of our new life; we are "washed" of our sins; our old self is dead and the new self begins to live.

The water of baptism signifies not only this purification and the burying of our sinful being, but also *the gift of the Holy Spirit* (Acts 2:38); the new man is born of "water and the Spirit" (John 3:5). We are sanctified (made holy). Baptism and water do not produce eternal life, but the Holy Spirit intimates it to us and brings it to fruition in us. For this reason Baptism becomes a sacrament which strengthens faith.

"The beginning of our regeneration and its end is our becoming new creatures, through the Spirit of God. Therefore the water is poured on the head as a sign of death, but in such a way that our resurrection is also represented, for instead of being drowned in water, what happens to us is only for a moment" (Calvin: *Geneva Catechism*, No. 326).

❡ QUESTION 71. *Where has Christ promised that we are as certainly washed with his blood and Spirit as with the water of baptism?*

In the institution of Baptism which runs thus: "GO THEREFORE AND MAKE DISCIPLES OF ALL NATIONS, BAPTIZING THEM IN THE NAME OF THE FATHER AND OF THE SON AND THE HOLY SPIRIT."[a] "HE WHO BELIEVES AND IS BAPTIZED WILL BE SAVED: BUT HE WHO DOES NOT BELIEVE WILL BE CONDEMNED."[b] This promise is also repeated where the Scriptures call baptism "the water of rebirth"[c] and the washing away of sins.[d]

a. Matt. 28:19.
b. Mark 16:16.
c. Titus 3:5. [God] saved us through the water of rebirth and the renewing power of the Holy Spirit (N.E.B.).
d. Acts 22:16. "Rise and be baptized, and wash away your sins."

Baptism is not a matter of take it or leave it; we cannot decide for ourselves either to accept it or do without it. We must submit to it if we wish to be faithful to the ordinance that God has instituted for our salvation.

The willingness of Jesus himself to submit to baptism makes clear to us the value which he attached to this sign. Just as he cannot save us according to the will of God without passing through this baptism, that is to say, this death, we in turn must take to ourselves this sign of our death, burial, and resurrection with Christ. Our baptism means our *repentance,* that is, our renunciation of the old order where man wants to be king and our submission to the new order where God alone is Lord.

⟨ QUESTION 72. *Does merely the outward washing with water itself wash away sins?*

No;[a] for only the blood of Jesus Christ and the Holy Spirit cleanse us from all sins.[b]

a. Matt. 3:11. "I baptize you with water for repentance, but he who is coming after me is mightier than I, whose sandals I am not worthy to carry; he will baptize you with the Holy Spirit and with fire."

Eph. 5:25b-26. Christ loved the church and gave himself up for her, that he might sanctify her, having cleansed her by the washing of water with the word.

Cf. 1 Peter 3:21.

b. 1 John 1:7. If we walk in the light, as he is in the light, we have fellowship with one another, and the blood of Jesus his Son cleanses us from all sin.

1 Cor. 6:11. You were washed, you were sanctified, you were justified in the name of the Lord Jesus Christ and in the Spirit of our God.

⟨ QUESTION 73. *Then why does the Holy Spirit call baptism the water of rebirth and the washing away of sins?*

God does not speak in this way except for a strong reason. Not only does he teach us by Baptism that just as the dirt of the body is taken away by water, so our sins are removed by the blood and Spirit of Christ;[a] but more important still, by the divine pledge and sign he wishes to assure us that we are just as truly washed from our sins spiritually as our bodies are washed with water.[b]

a. Rev. 7:14. And [one of the elders] said to me, "These are they who have come out of the great tribulation; they have washed their robes and made them white in the blood of the Lamb."

Cf. 1 Cor. 6:11.

b. Gal. 3:27. As many of you as were baptized into Christ have put on Christ.

What are the relationships between the water of baptism and the reality of the washing away of sins? It is not the water which cleanses but "the blood of Jesus Christ and the Holy Spirit." The use of water, however, ought to convince us of the reality of this cleansing. Just as certainly as water washes away dirt from the body, so does the death of Christ, of which the water of baptism is the sign, cleanse us of all sin. "God does not promise us anything in vain. Accordingly it is certain that in baptism the forgiveness of sins is offered to us and we receive it" (Calvin: *Geneva Catechism*, No. 328).

Notice, in Question 73, the words: *"not only* does he teach us, . . . *but more* important still, by the divine pledge and sign he wishes . . . "

The sacraments are not arbitrary symbols or figurative representations but efficacious signs, through the power of God.

❡ QUESTION 74. *Are infants also to be baptized?*

Yes, because they, as well as their parents, are included in the covenant and belong to the people of God.[a] Since both redemption from sin through the blood of Christ and the gift of faith from the Holy Spirit are promised to these children no less than to their parents,[b] infants are also by baptism, as a sign of the covenant, to be incorporated into the Christian church and distinguished from the children of unbelievers.[c] This was done in the Old Covenant by circumcision.[d] In the New Covenant Baptism has been instituted to take its place.[e]

a. Gen. 17:7. I will establish my covenant between me and you and your descendants after you throughout their generations for an everlasting covenant, to be God to you and to your descendants after you.

   Matt. 19:14. Jesus said, "Let the children come to me, and do not hinder them; for to such belongs the kingdom of heaven."

b. Acts 2:38-39. "Repent and be baptized every one of you in the name of Jesus Christ for the forgiveness of your sins; and you shall receive the gift of the Holy Spirit."

   Cf. Isa. 44:1-3; Luke 1:15.

c. Acts 10:47. "Can anyone forbid water for baptizing these people who have received the Holy Spirit just as we have?"

   1 Cor. 7:14. The unbelieving husband is consecrated through his wife, and the unbelieving wife is consecrated through her husband. Otherwise, your children would be unclean, but as it is they are holy.

d. Cf. Gen. 17:9-14.

e. Col. 2:11-13. In him also you were circumcised with a circumcision made without hands, by putting off the body of flesh in the circumcision of Christ; and you were buried with him in baptism, in which you were also raised with him through faith in the working of God, who raised him from the dead. And you, who were dead in trespasses and the uncircumcision of your flesh, God made alive together with him, having forgiven us all our trespasses.

We deal here with a controversial question which has aroused numerous debates in recent years: Is it necessary to baptize children or only adults?

One is surprised that to the question "Are infants also to be baptized?" the Heidelberg Catechism, after what it has taught us up to this point about the doctrine of the sacraments and specifically about Baptism, replies without hesitation: Yes!

If being baptized confirms faith, it can hardly be seen how this confirmation could happen in the case of the newborn. Besides, is it normal that a man's response to this confirmation should have to wait for fifteen years or so?

The problem is complex and deserves to be examined thoroughly. Let us note that a certain hesitation seems to have prevailed in the primitive church herself as well as in Judaism. The Jews baptized the proselytes (pagans converted to Judaism) and their children, but they circumcised the proselytes' children who were born after the conversion of their parents.

In the early church, the gift of the Holy Spirit seems sometimes to have preceded, sometimes to have followed, the administration of baptism (Cf. Acts 8:12, 14f; and Acts 10:44). Water baptism and the baptism of the Spirit could be administered by different hands (see also Acts 19:1-7). Let us never forget the disputes of Paul with those who presumed to circumcise believers. Moreover, the scriptural records do not permit us to know absolutely whether the early church baptized children or not.

Let us begin by setting forth the point of view of a partisan of adult baptism. We will then examine the position of a defender of infant baptism and try to draw the conclusions to which we are led today.

Karl Barth has repeatedly stated his position, but in a very specific and complete manner in his work entitled *The Teaching of the Church Regarding Baptism* (German edition, 1943; English translation, 1948). Here, in short, are the reasons which according to him, militate in favor of *adult baptism*. (They follow the outline of Barth's argument [Question 74] as found in his commentary on the Heidelberg Catechism, published in German in 1948, and in English in 1963).

Barth begins by pointing out that the manner in which reformers defended the baptism of infants was ill founded; they themselves were not faithful to their teaching about the sacraments, since they postulated that the sacrament was to confirm faith.

He then takes note of the three points of Question 74 which appeared to him true and yet false, by the conclusions that are drawn from them.

1. It is correct to say that little children as well as adults belong to the covenant of God and that they receive the forgiveness of sins and the Holy Spirit, but it does not mean that those who do not yet believe actually belong to the community which must bear witness to its faith.

2. It is right to say that the children of believers are distinguished from the others, but that does not imply the necessity of baptizing them.

3. It is correct to say that baptism replaces circumcision, but circumcision was used to distinguish Israel from other peoples while the baptism of little children ends by creating an almost complete confusion between the church and the world. So it is that one comes to speak of a "Christian people" and even "the Christian West."

If, says Barth, one were to demand a personal decision for each baptism, only a few men and women would ask for it. The result would be a very small church and this is what the partisans of infant baptism fear the most.

The consequences of the practice of infant baptism are on the one hand a devaluation of baptism itself, through the introduction of the rite of *confirmation*. Baptism which ought to be wholly sufficient must be completed by something else and from this fact loses its force. On the other hand, the "established" churches, practicing infant baptism, are composed mostly of men and women of whom no one demands anything and who remain dependent, passive, and uninvolved.

In a word, the argument of those who defend adult baptism comes back to this: baptism ought to confirm a previous *knowledge* of God's work for man; it assumes that faith cannot be demanded of a little child. It is the one baptized who must himself be *responsible* for the faith that he confesses. For the Baptists (defenders of adult baptism) "baptism is an inspiration, and experience which involves the one who benefits from it. It is an event which affects his whole life and which calls for a corresponding decision on the part of the baptized" (Jacques de Senarclens: *L' Homme libre,* September 1955).

What do the supporters of infant baptism (the paido-baptists) reply? Let us outline the argument of Professor Oscar Cullmann ("Baptism in the New Testament," published in *Studies in Biblical Theology,* 1950).

1. For Jesus himself, "to be baptized" means "to die" for mankind (Mark 10:38; Luke 12:50). Jesus' death on the cross has therefore the sense of a "general baptism" of every man. "It belongs to the essence of this general baptism, effected by Jesus, that it is offered in entire independence of the faith and the understanding of those who benefit from it. Baptismal grace has its foundation here, and it is in the strictest sense of the word 'prevenient grace' " (p. 20). God loves us before we have known him and before we ourselves have loved him (1 John 4:19).

2. Baptism is an incorporation into the body of Christ. By the death of Christ upon the cross, the grace of God is given to *all* men; moreover, baptism means entrance into the church, Christ's earthly body. Baptism establishes, therefore, a distinction between a general "reign of Christ" and this specific "body of Christ."

3. Although faith must be required of an adult asking for baptism, it is not necessary for a child born of Christian parents. The faith of the parents, or even that of one of them, is a sufficient guarantee of the subsequent faith of the child (1 Corinthians 7:14).

4. Circumcision is not only the sign of the entry into a natural community, namely, the Jewish people; it is also "from the time of its institution the seal of a covenant which is available to all" (p. 61). According to Romans 4:11, the sign of circumcision is given to Abraham "as a seal of the righteousness that he had by faith." Paul even says that "real circumcision is a matter of the

heart, spiritual and not literal" (Rom. 2:29). In short, the apostle ties circumcision and baptism very tightly together: "You were circumcised · . . . in the circumcision of Christ; and you were buried with him in baptism" (Col. 2:11-12).

Let us summarize the argument of Oscar Cullmann: "By his death and resurrection, and independent of men, Christ has accomplished for them all, a *general baptism*. By the act . . . of baptism . . . God places the baptized in the Christian community, *united in the body of Christ,* by making him share in a special way in the once-for-all saving event. Faith as the human response to this grace of God is decisive. . . . Baptism is the completion of *Jewish circumcision* and the proselyte baptism connected with it" (p. 70).

Let us note that an ancient document dating from the years 90-120, the *Didache* or "The Teaching of the Twelve Apostles," says this with respect to baptism: "Now concerning baptism thus you shall baptize. Having first recited all these things (namely the Christian teaching recorded in the *Didache* itself), baptize in the name of the Father, and of the Son, and of the Holy Spirit, in running water. But if you have no running water, baptize in other water; and if you cannot in cold, then in warm. But if you have neither, pour water upon the head three times, in the name of the Father and Son and Holy Spirit. *But before the baptism let the baptizer and the baptized fast, and whatever others can; but the baptized you shall commend to fast for two or three days before"* (J. B. Lightfoot: *The Apostolic Fathers,* p. 232).

It is evident that these instructions can only concern *adults.*

In practice, therefore, we will have:

1. Some churches that recognize infant baptism only. This was the case of almost all the churches of the Calvinistic tradition until recent times.

2. Some churches that permit the baptism of adults only. Such is the case with the Baptist churches, in Anglo-Saxon countries especially.

3. Some churches that acknowledge two forms of procedure. In general these are the free churches and many churches of the Calvinist type that recognize both infant baptism and adult baptism as well.

It seems to us inadequate to leave the choice to the sole discretion of the parents, without explaining to them the reasons that would argue for the practice of the one way rather than the other.

If the baptism of children has ultimately been justified (often very laboriously) by the reformers, it is on the ground that it was one of the pillars of the Christian state. According to the principle *cuius regio, eius religio* (whose region, his religion), each state ought to have its own confession, namely, that of its sovereign or of the majority of the citizens. Baptism became a guarantee of "the true religion" and had to be forcibly administered to all. The church has had the opportunity to observe in the last decades the error and the dangers inherent in the very idea of a Christian state. Today we are again being called to become *the confessing church,* as it was in the first centuries, before Christianity was proclaimed the official religion. In place of a Christian state, or at any rate one that pretends to be so, in which there is an established but weak church made up of people who are for the most part indifferent, it would be more desirable for us today to have *a confessing church in a secular state;* a church which, without being hostile to the state, renders it the service of openly confessing the Christian faith in such a way that the state can be enlightened by her witness.

The practice of adult baptism is closely tied to the structure of the confessing church. We do not claim, of course, that a baptized child cannot become a responsible citizen, but simply that the danger of making people indifferent is greater in the one case than in the other.

12 / THE LORD'S SUPPER—HOLY COMMUNION

⊈ QUESTION 75. *How are you reminded and assured in the holy Supper that you participate in the one sacrifice of Christ on the cross and in all his benefits?*

In this way: Christ has commanded me and all believers to eat of this broken bread, and to drink of this cup in remembrance of him. He has thereby promised[a] that his body was offered and broken on the cross for me, and his blood was shed for me, as surely as I see with my eyes that the bread of the Lord is broken for me, and that the cup is shared with me. Also, he has promised that he himself as certainly feeds and nourishes my soul to everlasting life with his crucified body and shed blood as I receive from the hand of the minister and actually taste the bread and the cup of the Lord which are given to me as sure signs of the body and blood of Christ.

a. See Question 77 below.

Let us point out at the outset that the sacrament of the Lord's Supper is established by *a command of Christ:* "Jesus Christ has commanded me, like all believers, to eat this broken bread and to drink of this cup in memory of him." No longer can we hide from the command of preaching; no longer ought we to be able to hide from the holy Supper. Each time that the Word is preached, the sacrament ought to be celebrated. In order to be faithful to the command of Christ, we ought to take communion every Sunday: "It is for historical reasons and not a matter of doctrine that holy Communion is not celebrated each Sunday and that it is often separated from the service by a specific benediction that seems to permit the faithful not to participate at all. These historical reasons reveal the wretchedness of the church; but they do not justify this wretchedness" (Pierre Maury: *Les Sacrements,* p. 60).

The command of Christ is suited to *the promise:*

1. The broken bread and the shared cup attest to us that the body of Christ has been broken and his blood shed for us. We can observe it with our own eyes. What happens at the communion table is as assured for us as what happened on the cross, and vice versa.

2. The bread and the wine which I receive from the hand of the minister (that is from "the servant" and not only from the pastor) certify to me that Christ himself nourishes me and quenches my thirst. It is Christ who gives me life; it is through him that I can and must live.

Because Christ has instituted the Lord's Supper and has given the command to repeat this act, we are assured that his promise is fulfilled each time that we are reunited around the holy table: Jesus Christ himself announces his death for us and gives us his life.

It is in this way also that Jesus fulfilled the Jewish Passover (Exodus 12; Matthew 26:17-29). He identifies himself with the paschal lamb whose blood saves from death (Hebrews 9:20). It is thus that he fulfills *the new covenant* (Exodus 24:6-8). Paul says of Christ that he is "our Passover" (1 Cor. 5:8).

The command and the promise of the holy Communion are therefore true to God's own purpose. What Christ accomplishes is exactly what God wills for our salvation.

◖ QUESTION 76. *What does it mean to eat the crucified body of Christ and to drink his shed blood?*

It is not only to embrace with a trusting heart the whole passion and death of Christ, and by it to receive the forgiveness of sins and eternal life.[a] In addition, it is to be so united more and more to his blessed body by the Holy Spirit dwelling both in Christ and in us[b] that, although he is in heaven[c] and we are on earth, we are nevertheless flesh of his flesh and bone of his bone,[d] always living and being governed by one Spirit, as the members of our bodies are governed by one soul.[e]

a. John 6:35, 40. Jesus said to them, "I am the bread of life; he who comes to me shall not hunger, and he who believes in me shall never thirst. . . . This is the will of my Father, that everyone who sees the Son and believes in him should have eternal life."
   John 6:53-54. Jesus said to them, "Truly, truly, I say to you, unless you eat the flesh of the Son of man and drink his blood, you have no life in you; he who eats my flesh and drinks my blood has eternal life, and I will raise him up at the last day."
b. John 6:56. "He who eats my flesh and drinks my blood abides in me and I in him."
c. Acts 3:20-21. May [the Lord] send the Christ appointed for you, Jesus, whom heaven must receive until the time for establishing all that God spoke by the mouth of his holy prophets from of old. Cf. Acts 1:9-11; 1 Cor. 11:26.
d. Eph. 5:30. We are members of his body.
   Cf. 1 Cor. 6:15, 17, 19.
e. 1 John 3:24b. By this we know that he abides in us, by the Spirit which he has given us.
   Eph. 4:15-16. We are to grow up in every way into him who is the head, into Christ, from whom the whole body, joined and knit

together by every joint with which it is supplied, when each part is working properly, makes bodily growth and upbuilds itself in love.

Cf. John 6:56-58; 15:1-6.

This question deals with the mystery of *our true communion* with the glorified Christ. We share in the life of Christ through the sacrament; we are joined to his glorified body in such a way that we become "flesh of his flesh and bone of his bone."

Recall the reply to Question 49: "What benefit do we receive from Christ's ascension into heaven?" "First, that he is our Advocate in the presence of his Father in heaven. Second, that *we have our flesh in heaven.*"

The sacrament of the holy Communion makes effective the promise contained in Christ's ascension.

Let us summarize two points:

1. It is the Holy Spirit, "dwelling both in Christ and in us," who bestows this communion. The Spirit of Christ which has been given to us "governs" us and gives us life. This is henceforth our "common denominator," with Christ and among us.

2. This communion through the Holy Spirit is, however, strictly bound to participation in the Lord's Supper. This communion is given to us because we "eat the crucified body of Christ" and we drink "his shed blood." This is sacramental realism.

The resurrected and exalted Christ keeps his promise of not leaving us desolate (John 14:18). We live with him as long as he is at the right hand of God, the Father. Through our participation in the holy Communion the exalted and glorified Christ gives us his strength and makes us share in his power. It is also in this way that he asserts his lordship in the world by means of his believers. The authority of the church can never be other than Christ's own, being revealed in and through men whom he summons to the table in order to invest them with his authority. Participation in the sacraments not only involves the sanctification of the individual believer but also the church being disciplined for her witness in the world.

Perseverance in "the apostles' teaching" and "the breaking of bread" is the condition that Christ has set forth for the extension of his church on earth (Acts 2:42-47).

❡ QUESTION 77. *Where has Christ promised that he will feed and nourish believers with his body and blood just as surely as they eat of this broken bread and drink of this cup?*

In the institution of the holy Supper which reads: THE LORD JESUS ON THE NIGHT WHEN HE WAS BETRAYED TOOK BREAD, AND WHEN HE HAD GIVEN THANKS, HE BROKE IT, AND SAID, "THIS IS MY BODY WHICH IS FOR YOU. DO THIS IN REMEMBRANCE OF ME." IN THE SAME WAY ALSO THE CUP, AFTER SUPPER, SAYING, "THIS CUP IS THE NEW COVENANT IN MY BLOOD. DO THIS, AS OFTEN AS YOU DRINK IT, IN REMEMBRANCE OF ME." FOR AS OFTEN AS YOU EAT THIS BREAD AND DRINK THE CUP, YOU PROCLAIM THE LORD'S DEATH UNTIL HE COMES.[a] This promise is also repeated by the apostle Paul: WHEN WE BLESS "THE CUP OF BLESSING," IS IT NOT A MEANS OF SHARING IN THE BLOOD OF CHRIST? WHEN WE BREAK THE BREAD, IS IT NOT A MEANS OF SHARING THE BODY OF CHRIST? BECAUSE THERE IS ONE LOAF, WE, MANY AS WE ARE, ARE ONE BODY; FOR IT IS ONE LOAF OF WHICH WE ALL PARTAKE.[b]

a. 1 Cor. 11:23-26.
   Cf. Matt. 26:26-28; Mark 14:22-24; Luke 22:19.
b. 1 Cor. 10:16-17 (N.E.B.).

All that we have said up to this point rests directly upon the fact that the holy Supper was instituted by Christ himself. Here we depend upon a *command* and a *promise* of Christ. The sacrament of the Lord's Supper is not a symbol, more or less explicit or more or less impressive, one that could be dispensed with if necessary; nor a ceremony that the church must gather around with greater pomp in order to attract crowds who would be enticed by the esthetic, thrilling, or awe-inspiring aspect of the thing. No, it is a matter of a *relationship* which Christ himself has established. Wherever the holy Communion is celebrated, Christ is present; the bread and the wine of the Lord's Supper become the elements which attest the reality of his work for us and our participation in his benefits. "Seeing that Jesus Christ is the Truth, there can be no doubt that the promises which he made at the Supper are actually fulfilled in it, and that what he figures in it is made true. Thus in accordance with what he promises and represents in the sacraments, I do not doubt that he makes us *partakers*

of his very essence, in order to unite us with himself in one life"
(Calvin: *Geneva Catechism,* No. 353).

❡ QUESTION 78. *Do the bread and wine become the very body and blood of Christ?*

No, for as the water in baptism is not changed into the blood of Christ, nor becomes the washing away of sins by itself, but is only a divine sign and confirmation of it, so also in the Lord's Supper[a] the sacred bread does not become the body of Christ itself,[b] although, in accordance with the nature and usage of sacraments,[c] it is called the body of Christ.

a. Matt. 26:26-29. As they were eating, Jesus took bread, and blessed, and broke it, and gave it to the disciples and said, "Take, eat; this is my body." And he took a cup, and when he had given thanks he gave it to them, saying, "Drink of it, all of you; for this is my blood of the covenant, which is poured out for many for the forgiveness of sins. I tell you I shall not drink again of this fruit of of the vine until that day when I drink it new with you in my Father's kingdom."

b. 1 Cor. 11:26-28. As often as you eat this bread and drink the cup, you proclaim the Lord's death until he comes. Whoever, therefore, eats the bread or drinks the cup of the Lord in an unworthy manner will be guilty of profaning the body and blood of the Lord. Let a man examine himself, and so eat of the bread and drink of the cup.

c. 1 Cor. 10:1-4. I want you to know, brethren, that our fathers were all under the cloud, and all passed through the sea, and all were baptized into Moses in the cloud and in the sea, and all ate the same spiritual food and all drank the same spiritual drink. For they drank from the spiritual Rock which followed them, and the Rock was Christ.
Cf. Gen. 17:10-19; Exod. 12:27, 43, 48.

❡ QUESTION 79. *Then why does Christ call the bread his body, and the cup his blood, or the New Covenant in his blood, and why does the apostle Paul call the Supper "a means of sharing" in the body and blood of Christ?*

132

Christ does not speak in this way except for a strong reason. He wishes to teach us by it that as bread and wine sustain this temporal life so his crucified body and shed blood are the true food and drink of our souls for eternal life.[a] Even more, he wishes to assure us by this visible sign and pledge that we come to share in his true body and blood through the working of the Holy Spirit as surely as we receive with our mouth these holy tokens in remembrance of him,[b] and that all his sufferings and his death are our own as certainly as if we had ourselves suffered and rendered satisfaction in our own persons.

a. John 6:51, 55. I am the living bread which came down from heaven; if anyone eats of this bread, he will live forever; and the bread which I shall give for the life of the world is my flesh. . . . For my flesh is food indeed, and my blood is drink indeed.

b. 1 Cor. 10:16-17. When we bless "the cup of blessing," is it not a means of sharing in the blood of Christ? When we break the bread, is it not a means of sharing in the body of Christ? Because there is one loaf, we, many as we are, are one body; for it is one loaf of which we all partake (N.E.B.).

In what way does Christ manifest his presence to the community assembled around the holy table?

Let us recall the different interpretations which have been given in the course of history:

1. For the *Roman Catholic Church,* Christ is materially present in the elements of bread and wine. The words of consecration "this is my body" pronounced by the priest effect the miracle of a transformation of the bread and the wine into the body and blood of Jesus Christ. We quote the Catechism of the Council of Trent: "The Catholic faith teaches us that there are specifically three wholly marvelous things which are performed in this sacrament, by the words of the consecration: the first is that the actual body of our Lord Jesus Christ, that same body which was born of the Virgin Mary and which is seated in heaven at the right of the eternal Father, is contained in this sacrament. The second, that nothing of the substance of which the bread and wine are composed remains. . . . Not only is Jesus Christ in his entirety contained within each element but even within the least part of either element. . . . So it is with a great deal of significance that this

marvelous change is called *transubstantiation* by the Catholic Church" (Ch. IV, Questions xxvi, xxxiv, xl).

2. Without going as far, Luther saw in these words, "this *is* my body," the pledge of *a real presence* of Christ. Bread remains bread; wine is no longer transformed. Christ, however, has bound the mystery of his presence to these very elements; such is the teaching of *consubstantiation*. Calvin does not deny the real presence, but he insists less on the material localization of this presence in these elements than on the action of the Holy Spirit, without going so far as to allow the presence of Christ to become purely spiritual, as has sometimes been believed. Witness this quotation from the *Institutes:* "But if it is true that a visible sign is given us to seal the gift of a thing invisible, when we have received the symbol of the body, let us no less surely trust that the body itself is also given to us" (Book IV, Ch. XVII. Cf. English translation, p. 1371).

3. Zwingli, taking a position against Luther whose interpretation he judges as being too materialistic, ended, accordingly, by going too far the other way. Bread and wine are no more than *symbols;* they are meant to remind us of the sacrifice of Christ on on the cross. According to this teaching, the holy Supper is above all a commemoration of the death of the Savior, a ceremony "in memoriam" as it were; Christ is present in the memory of those who participate in this act. Such however was not the whole thought of Zwingli who also says that the supper is "an act of the grace of God with us." Face to face with Luther, however, he defended his purely symbolic and commemorative conception of the Supper and it is this which is attributed to him even today.

It is necessary to set aside the extreme interpretations, the Roman Catholic *materialism* and Zwinglian *spiritualism* and to remember that the words "this *is* my body" are indeed the pledge of *a real presence*. The *is* refers us to the incarnation, to the "Word made flesh," to the "true God and true man"; it reminds us that God through Christ has assumed flesh similar to ours. This "is" confirms the witness of the prophets and the apostles with respect to the reality of the presence of God himself among men. In instituting the holy Supper, Jesus attests to the continuity of this bodily presence.

Since the ascension, however, the body of Christ is at the right hand of God. The bread and wine are the signs of this twofold reality of the incarnate and exalted Christ. They allow us to await him in reality, since, according to the promise connected with the event of the ascension: "This Jesus who was taken up from you into heaven will come *in the same way* as you saw him go into heaven" (Acts 1:11).

"Just as in the upper room he offered to his disciples the material signs of his life sacrificed for them, so too around the holy table. It is he, the living presence, faithful to this invisible meeting place which he has fixed with his own, who designates by means of bread and wine the sacrifice which he has fulfilled for the believer, namely, his mighty act. It is he who is actually there, not the matter of a dead body or of shed blood. *The sign does not designate things, but Someone*" (Maury: *Op. cit.,* p. 66).

So then, instead of concentrating upon the elements themselves as, for example, the men of the sixteenth century did, seeking to find out how it is possible for the bread and the wine "to be," "to become," "to mean," or "to represent" the body and blood of Christ, we should pay attention to *the act* that the Christian community fulfills. Some men and women are gathered around a table. One of them breaks bread and distributes it, he raises the cup and has it passed among his brothers and sisters. Then the whole community prays and sings a hymn. It is in this very act that Christ manifests his presence, as he manifested it the first time among his disciples and as he will manifest it anew in the midst of his own in his Father's kingdom (Matthew 26:29). *Thus the holy Communion actualizes the event, past and future, of the Christ who has come and will come again, of the Christ incarnate and glorified.* According to his promise, Jesus Christ is present in the midst of the community which shares in the meal of the holy Supper as he was present in the midst of the disciples in the upper room and as he will be again in his kingdom. The material signs of bread and wine are the visible pledges that the invisible Christ gives to the community in the time which elapses between his first bodily manifestation among men and the second which is still to come.

In resumé, the bread and wine of the holy Communion attest to us that Christ has come, that he is living, and that he will come again. Thus we are assured of his birth, his death, his exaltation, and the promise of his return. The community gathered around the table prays: "Come, Lord Jesus, be our host and bless that which thou hast given" (liturgical form quoted by Karl Barth).

❡ QUESTION 80. *What difference is there between the Lord's Supper and the papal Mass?*

The Lord's Supper testifies to us that we have complete forgiveness of all our sins through the one sacrifice of Jesus Christ which he himself has accomplished on the cross once for all;[a] (and that through the Holy Spirit we are incorporated into Christ,[b] who is now in heaven with his true body at the right hand of the Father[c] and is there to be worshiped.[d]) But the Mass teaches that the living and the dead do not have forgiveness of sins through the sufferings of Christ unless Christ is again offered for them daily by the priests (and that Christ is bodily under the form of bread and wine and is therefore to be worshiped in them). Therefore the Mass is fundamentally a complete denial of the once for all sacrifice and passion of Jesus Christ[e] (and as such an idolatry to be condemned).

NOTE: This question first appeared in part in the second edition. The sections in parentheses were added in the third.

a. Heb. 7:27; 9:12, 25-28. He has no need, like those high priests, to offer sacrifices daily, first for his own sins and then for those of the people; he did this once for all when he offered up himself. . . . He entered once for all into the Holy Place, taking not the blood of goats and calves but his own blood, thus securing an eternal redemption. . . . Nor was it to offer himself repeatedly, as the high priest enters the Holy Place yearly with blood not his own; for then he would have had to suffer repeatedly since the foundation of the world. But as it is, he has appeared once for all at the end of the age to put away sin by the sacrifice of himself. And just as it is appointed for men to die once, and after that comes judgment, so Christ, having been offered once to bear the sins of many, will appear a second time, not to deal with sin but to save those who are eagerly waiting for him.
Cf. Heb. 10:10-18.

b. 1 Cor. 6:17. He who is united to the Lord becomes one spirit with him.

c. Heb. 1:3; 8:1. When he had made purification for sins, he sat down at the right hand of the Majesty on high. . . . The point in what we are saying is this: we have such a high priest, one who is seated at the right hand of the throne of the Majesty in heaven.

d. John 20:17. I have not yet ascended to the Father; but go to my brethren and say to them, I am ascending to my Father and your Father, to my God and your God.

Acts 7:55-56. He, full of the Holy Spirit, gazed into heaven and saw the glory of God, and Jesus standing at the right hand of God; and he said, "Behold, I see the heavens opened, and the Son of man standing at the right hand of God."

Col. 3:1. If then you have been raised with Christ, seek the things that are above, where Christ is, seated at the right hand of God. Cf. John 4:21-24; Phil. 3:20; 1 Thess. 1:10.

e. Heb. 9:25-26; 10:11-14. Nor was it to offer himself repeatedly, as the high priest enters the Holy Place yearly with blood not his own; for then he would have had to suffer repeatedly since the foundation of the world. But as it is, he has appeared once for all at the end of the age to put away sin by the sacrifice of himself. . . . Every priest stands daily at his service, offering repeatedly the same sacrifices, which can never take away sins. But when Christ had offered for all time a single sacrifice for sins, he sat down at the right hand of God, then to wait until his enemies should be made a stool for his feet. For by a single offering he has perfected for all time those who are sanctified.

We have already seen what determines the fundamental content of the Roman Catholic doctrine of the Mass, namely, the transubstantiation of the elements of bread and wine through the words of consecration.

Let us say, in addition, that in the Roman Church, only a priest, set apart by the sacrament of ordination, is entitled to pronounce these words by which the act of transformation of the elements is effected. "The form to be used in the consecration of the bread follows next to be treated of, not however with a view that the faithful people should be taught these mysteries, unless necessity requires it (for those who have not been initiated into holy orders, it is unnecessary to instruct touching these matters)" (*Catechism of the Council of Trent*, Ch. IV, Question xix).

This doctrine leads to the following abuses against which the Heidelberg Catechism protests:

137

1. The Mass considered as *a perpetual sacrifice,* the priest slaying Christ each day on the altar; that position leads to a denial of the effectiveness of the unique sacrifice of Christ which he himself offered *once for all* (Hebrews 9:28). Either this sacrifice is unique and it frees us from the burden of our sins, from condemnation and death, or else this sacrifice must be repeated and is no more the work of Christ, Emmanuel, God with us and for us. Indeed, it appears that Roman Catholic doctrine may be interpreted otherwise. Bartmann explains that, according to the Catechism of the Council of Trent, "the sacrifice of the Mass is the real performance of the sacrifice of the cross, that is to say, the sacrifice of the cross which having been only once accomplished historically is made mysteriously actual in *a sacramental manner.* This performance happens, it is true, under the symbolic signs of the sacrificial death of Christ; but it still happens in a real manner in that the Christ is truly present under these signs, and present in his capacity as victim and sacrificing priest" (Bartmann: *Op. cit.,* Tome II, p. 381; italics by Bartmann). But who is able to follow Roman Catholic theology in such subtle distinctions?

2. The Mass considered as *a manifestation of Christ* in the elements of bread and wine in such a way that the most holy sacrament must be worshiped, since "Christ, whole and entire, is contained not only under each species, but also in each particle of either species" *(Catechism of the Council of Trent,* Ch. IV, Question xxxiv).

Either Jesus is the *only Savior* and *his sacrifice is unique,* as *unique as the authority of the scripture* which bears witness to it, or else we recognize *another authority* and so need *other sacrifices* and *other saviors.*

The table of the Lord is the place where God's eternal truth is apportioned to men.

13 / CHURCH DISCIPLINE

❦ QUESTION 81. *Who ought to come to the table of the Lord?*

Those who are displeased with themselves for their sins,[a] and who nevertheless trust that these sins have been forgiven them and that their remaining weakness is covered by the passion and death of

Christ,[b] and who also desire more and more to strengthen their faith and improve their life.[c] The impenitent and hypocrites, however, eat and drink judgment to themselves.[d]

a. Matt. 5:3. "Blessed are the poor in spirit, for theirs is the kingdom of heaven."
b. Ps. 103:2-3. Bless the Lord, O my soul, and forget not all his benefits, who forgives all your iniquity, who heals all your diseases. Eph. 1:7. In [Jesus Christ] we have redemption through his blood, the forgiveness of our trespasses, according to the riches of his grace.
c. Matt. 5:5. "Blessed are the meek, for they shall inherit the earth." Ps. 116:12-14. What shall I render to the Lord for all his bounty to me? I will lift up the cup of salvation and call on the name of the Lord, I will pay my vows to the Lord in the presence of all his people.
d. 1 Cor. 10:21; 11:28. You cannot drink the cup of the Lord and the cup of demons. You cannot partake of the table of the Lord and the table of demons. . . . Let a man examine himself, and so eat of the bread and drink of the cup.

Questions 81-85 bring us to the problem of church discipline. The preaching of the gospel and its confirmation by the Holy Spirit in the sacraments of Baptism and the Lord's Supper allow the Christian community to test its faith as to its goal, on the one hand, and in regard to practical decisions which this faith implies for the life of the individual believer as well as that of the community, on the other.

In other words, the Word of God and the sacraments exercise a purifying influence upon the church's confession of faith. It is this very purification that is called "church discipline."

It is significant that the authors of the Catechism have placed the question of church discipline under the doctrine of the sacraments and particularly the doctrine of the Lord's Supper and that they have not attempted to treat this problem separately.

"Who ought to come to the table of the Lord?"

1. *Those who are displeased with themselves:* those who are penitent, those who are entirely obedient to the grace of Jesus Christ, through the Holy Spirit's power. In other words, those who count upon no one but God and his steadfast love and not at all upon themselves and their works.

But what does the famous text of the first letter to the Corinthians mean: "Whoever eats the bread or drinks the cup of the Lord in *an unworthy manner* will be guilty of profaning the body and blood of the Lord" (11:27)? Formerly it was thought that the believer must have attained moral worth and a certain degree of perfection in order to dare to present himself without danger at the table of the Lord. This interpretation is responsible for the fear that many have experienced upon approaching the communion table as well as for their general disaffection for the importance of the sacrament of the Lord's Supper: one scarcely would dare to accept an invitation associated with such threats.

It could not be a question, in this text, of a worthy life being required of the communicant or of the quality of his faith. If the sacrament is given to us to confirm and put new life into our faith, it is clear that a faith that is already perfect and absolutely deserving of its object, could not be expected of us.

No, nothing is asked of us other than that we be displeased with ourselves, that is, that we *repent*. "I would be the most wretched of men, Christ having instituted the sacraments of my salvation, if I had failed to furnish myself with the preliminary conditions so that grace might be bestowed upon me at the very instant in which I partake of the Lord's Supper! God invites us there not because we love Jesus Christ but in order that we may learn to love him" (Pierre Lestringant, in *Les Sacrements,* p. 81).

2. *Those who also desire more and more to strengthen their faith and improve their life,* that is, those who depend upon God's mercy and power alone for advancement in the Christian life and who recognize in the sacrament of the holy Communion an effective means established by Jesus Christ himself for the progress of his church on earth.

Hypocrites and those who are not willing to be changed must abstain from the communion; that is, those who, no longer believing in it, think that they must "practice" it for the fear of public opinion or even to conceal from men those acts which they know God condemns. These can also be calloused persons who, being familiar with God's way for the salvation of men, refuse really to get involved in it. Then again, their participation in the holy Supper serves to veil their real inner feelings, that is, their refusal of God's forgiveness.

Notice that hypocrisy can be unconscious. The function of Word and sacrament consists precisely in laying our hypocrisy bare to us.

In short, the only condition set forth for a real and beneficial participation in the Lord's Supper is repentance. "Communion is an act of grace upon a sin for which one repents" (de Saussure: *Op. cit.*, p. 25).

The community that is gathered around the table of the Lord, to whom he responds in his mercy, can only be that of men and women who depend upon him and his grace for everything. Furthermore, they are themselves sinners and know its wretched consequences; they have no worth in themselves. Around the communion table all are in the same situation and no one can avail himself of any privilege. "Now, if we feel disgust at being associated by Baptism and the Lord's Supper with vile men, and regard our connection with them as a sort of stain upon us, we ought immediately to descend into ourselves, and to search without flattery our own evils. Such an examination will make us willingly allow ourselves to be washed in the same fountain with the most impure, and will keep us from rejecting the righteousness which he offers indiscriminately to all the ungodly, the life which he offers to the dead, and the salvation which he offers to the lost" (Calvin: *Commentary on a Harmony of the Evangelists*, Matthew 9:12, pp. 402-403).

❡ QUESTION 82. *Should those who show themselves to be unbelievers and enemies of God by their confession and life be admitted to this Supper?*

No, for then the covenant of God would be profaned and his wrath provoked against the whole congregation.[a] According to the ordinance of Christ and his apostles, therefore, the Christian church is under obligation, by the office of the keys, to exclude such persons until they amend their lives.

a. 1 Cor. 11:20, 26-29, 34. When you meet together, it is not the Lord's Supper that you eat. . . . For as often as you eat this bread and drink the cup, you proclaim the Lord's death until he comes. Whoever, therefore, eats the bread or drinks the cup of the Lord in an unworthy manner will be guilty of profaning the body and blood of the Lord. Let a man examine himself, and

so eat of the bread and drink of the cup. For anyone who eats and drinks without discerning the body eats and drinks judgment upon himself. . . . If anyone is hungry, let him eat at home—lest you come together to be condemned.
Cf. Isa. 1:11-15; 66:3; Ps. 50:16.

€ QUESTION 83. *What is the office of the keys?*

The preaching of the holy gospel and Christian discipline. By these two means the kingdom of heaven is opened to believers and shut against unbelievers.[a]

a. Matt. 16:19. "I will give you the keys of the kingdom of heaven, and whatever you bind on earth shall be bound in heaven, and whatever you loose on earth shall be loosed in heaven."
John 20:23. "If you forgive the sins of any, they are forgiven; if you retain the sins of any, they are retained."

In regard to "the office of the keys," observe that the German text employs the expression *"Amt der Schlüssel,"* that is, the "duty," the "office," the "service." It is under the influence of the Roman Catholic teaching that *Amt* has been translated "power."

The New Testament contains a twofold promise of Jesus to Peter: "You are Peter, and on this rock I will build my church" and "I will give you the keys of the kingdom of heaven" (Matt. 16:18-19).

It is known that the Roman Catholic Church bases on this text the doctrine of the primacy of Peter and of the apostolic succession, according to which the church is an institution of salvation represented by the pope, the successor of Saint Peter. For the Catholic Church the power of "binding and loosening" consists in the privilege that has been entrusted to the ecclesiastical hierarchy of forgiving sins by the sacrament of penance. It is the church that absolves what has been *confessed* to her and for which she has prescribed an adequate *penance*. Such is "the power of the keys" in the Roman conception.

"The power which the church has to forgive sins extends to all sins without exception" (Bartmann: *Op. cit.,* Tome II, p. 408). And again: "The form of the sacrament of penance is the absolution of the priest. This absolution is sanctifying and effects pardon; it is not declarative, in the sense that it would simply announce that God has pardoned the sin" (*Ibid.*, p. 413).

Let us note that the Protestant interpretation of this text went too far when it claimed that only Peter's faith was taken into account. It is also a question of his person, but in his capacity as an *apostle*. The church is built upon "the foundation of the apostles and prophets, Christ Jesus himself being the chief cornerstone" (Eph. 2:20). There was, to be sure, the explicit promise of Christ to Peter, but it is improper to want to extend the benefit of this promise to his "successors."

As to "the keys of the kingdom of heaven," a study of the texts of the New Testament which speak of the ministry of the church (Ephesians 4:12; 2 Corinthians 2:14-16; Matthew 10:13-15; Acts 3:19-26) indicates that the first duty of this ministry consists in *the preaching of grace;* it is the Word of God preached and received by men in repentance and faith that "binds" or "loosens," because the gospel of Jesus Christ is the "power of God for salvation to everyone who has faith" (Rom. 1:16); it has the power of revealing to men their hardness of heart, or, on the contrary, of freeing them from it.

"The church founded by Jesus on the apostle Peter is not an institution of priests commissioned to exercise a kind of jurisdiction over souls. It is as witnesses and confessors of Christ, as messengers of the Word, that the apostles shall exercise their ministry. The authority and effectiveness of this ministry originates in no other power than in the Word which they will preach" (Hébert Roux: *L'Evangile du Royaume*, pp. 192-193).

The power of the keys is not a human power, but that of God himself who alone can "bind and loose." It is the Word of God, that is, Jesus Christ who is *the key.*

When the church finds herself constrained to exclude by "the office of the keys" (Question 82), it does so by preaching in such a way that the "unbelievers and enemies of God" may be fore-warned. The exclusion from the Lord's Supper by the office of the keys is not final; it is conditioned by the improvement of life, that is, by repentance.

Such is the first aspect of church discipline. In its second aspect it will rightly turn to "remonstrance" or "brotherly warning," that is, "the cure" of the individual soul.

¶ QUESTION 84. *How is the kingdom of heaven opened and shut by the preaching of the holy gospel?*

In this way: The kingdom of heaven is opened when it is proclaimed and openly testified to believers, one and all, according to the command of Christ, that as often as they accept the promise of the gospel with true faith all their sins are truly forgiven them by God for the sake of Christ's gracious work. On the contrary, the wrath of God and eternal condemnation fall upon all unbelievers and hypocrites as long as they do not repent.[a] It is according to this witness of the gospel that God will judge the one and the other in this life and in the life to come.

a. Matt. 28:19. "Go therefore and make disciples of all nations, baptizing them in the name of the Father and of the Son and of the Holy Spirit."

John 20:21-23. Jesus said to them again, "Peace be with you. As the Father has sent me, even so I send you." And when he had said this, he breathed on them, and said to them, "Receive the Holy Spirit. If you forgive the sins of any, they are forgiven; if you retain the sins of any, they are retained."

Matt. 16:19. "I will give you the keys of the kingdom of heaven, and whatever you bind on earth shall be bound in heaven, and whatever you loose on earth shall be loosed in heaven."

Cf. John 3:18-36; Rom. 2:2-17.

¶ QUESTION 85. *How is the kingdom of heaven shut and opened by Christian discipline?*

In this way: Christ commanded that those who bear the Christian name in an unchristian way either in doctrine or in life should be given brotherly admonition. If they do not give up their errors or evil ways, notification is given to the church or to those ordained for this by the church. Then, if they do not change after this warning, they are forbidden to partake of the holy Sacraments and are thus excluded from the communion of the church and by God himself from the kingdom of Christ.[a] However, if they promise and show real amendment, they are received again as members of Christ and of the church.[b]

a. Matt. 18:15-18. "If your brother sins against you, go and tell him his fault, between you and him alone. If he listens to you, you have gained your brother. But if he does not listen, take one or two others along with you, that every word may be confirmed by the evidence of two or three witnesses. If he refuses to listen to them, tell it to the church; and if he refuses to listen even to the church, let him be to you as a Gentile and a tax collector. Truly, I say to you, whatever you bind on earth shall be bound in heaven, and whatever you loose on earth shall be loosed in heaven."

1 Cor. 5:11-13. I wrote to you not to associate with anyone who bears the name of brother if he is guilty of immorality or greed, or is an idolator, reviler, drunkard, or robber—not even to eat with such a one. For what have I to do with judging outsiders? Is it not those inside the church whom you are to judge? God judges those outside. Drive out the wicked person from among you.

Cf. 2 Thess. 3:14; 2 John 10-11.

b. Luke 15:18. "I will arise and go to my father, and I will say to him, 'Father, I have sinned against heaven and before you.' "

Cf. 2 Cor. 2:6-11.

If the preaching of the gospel can "open" or "shut" the kingdom of heaven, the church has to be on guard, making certain that it is really the gospel which is being proclaimed and "openly testified to believers, one and all." The later Helvetic Confession, in the French text of 1566, says: "It is required that church assemblies be public and well attended and not done secretly or out of sight. . . . It is necessary that the places in which the faithful assemble be proper and fitting to the church of God. Let one choose, therefore, ample and spacious church houses" (Ch. xxii).

The preaching in the service of worship, and in private for those who cannot participate, constitutes the essential element of "the office of the keys" and consequently of "church discipline." A Christian community that is aware of its responsibility with respect to all mankind will take care that this office can be exercised under the best possible conditions. The people of God will pay particular attention to the content of the preaching in order to be assured that it is in accord with the gospel itself.

If God judges "the one and the other in this life and in the life to come," "according to this witness of the gospel," the discipline of the church will have to take special care that this witness can be heard. The community must exercise over itself, and in the highest degree over its preachers, a watchful control in order that the preaching be rigorously evangelical. If church discipline were better understood and applied, it would be impossible for the sermon to be transformed into moral, social, philosophical, artistic, or religious lectures. If the church gives out *anything other* than the gospel of Jesus Christ, it runs the risk of closing the very doors of the kingdom of heaven to men. It is on this "anything other" in preaching that church discipline must bear down. It is regrettable that we have come to treat this as merely a question of good manners, whereas it must be considered essentially a matter of good preaching, namely, fidelity to the gospel of Jesus Christ. "If anyone comes to you and does not bring this doctrine, do not receive him into the house or give him any greetings; for he who greets him shares his wicked work" (2 John 1:10-11).

The exercise of church discipline with respect to preaching is not above all else a responsibility of the authorities of the church, but first of all that of the community itself. Every adult believer, that is, every member properly informed by the Word of God, must exercise discipline in respect to those who are commissioned to preach in the church. The renewal of the church is in large part a function of the conscientious exercise of this responsibility by the members of the Christian community.

Let us be quite clear that only those who are a part of the community are subject to church discipline, that is, those who have been baptized and share in the holy Communion. The discipline of the church could not claim to exercise authority over those who did not even acknowledge being members. The "consistory" of Calvin was in this regard an error imputable to the inherently false notion of a Christian state. Difficulties with church discipline are multiplied, we must admit, in an "established" church. (Cf. Peter Berger: *The Noise of Solemn Assemblies,* Ch. II.)

Man's Gratitude and Obedience—New Life
Through the Holy Spirit

We come to the third part of the Catechism entitled "Man's Gratitude and Obedience." The Heidelberg Catechism is original in this sense, that the Law is no longer considered as a policeman, blocking the approach to the domain which God has reserved. On the contrary, it is the expression of a new possibility of life that God gives us in the gospel and through the Holy Spirit. It is true, according to Luther's expression, that it is "impossible to keep the Law in any way without God's grace." The newness is that we are enabled to do it precisely by this grace.

We shall develop in the paragraphs which follow what has already been outlined in Question 3 regarding the relationship of the gospel and law. We insist that the gospel and law must never be separated, that it ought never come to pass that the Law be reduced merely to ethics or that the gospel be treated as a theory irrelevant to life. "All grace is obedience and all obedience is grace" (de Pury, *et. al.: L'Ordre de Dieu,* p. 10).

14 / DISCIPLESHIP AND GOOD WORKS

❡ QUESTION 86. *Since we are redeemed from our sin and its wretched consequences by grace through Christ without any merit of our own, why must we do good works?*

Because just as Christ has redeemed us with his blood he also renews us through his Holy Spirit according to his own image, so that with our whole life we may show ourselves grateful to God

for his goodness[a] and that he may be glorified through us;[b] and
further, so that we ourselves may be assured of our faith by its
fruits[c] and by our reverent behavior may win our neighbors to
Christ.[d]

a. Rom. 6:13; 12:1. Do not yield your members to sin as instruments
of wickedness, but yield yourselves to God as men who have
been brought from death to life, and your members to God as instruments of righteousness. . . . I appeal to you therefore, brethren, by the mercies of God, to present your bodies as a living
sacrifice, holy and acceptable to God, which is your spiritual
worship.
Cf. 1 Peter 2:5-10.

b. Matt. 5:16. Let your light so shine before men, that they may see
your good works and give glory to your Father who is in heaven.
1 Cor. 6:19-20. Do you not know that your body is a temple of
the Holy Spirit within you, which you have from God? You are
not your own; you were bought with a price. So glorify God in
your body.
Cf. 1 Peter 2:12.

c. Matt. 7:17. Every sound tree bears good fruit, but the bad tree
bears evil fruit.
Cf. Luke 13:6-9.
Gal. 5:22-24. The fruit of the Spirit is love, joy, peace, patience,
kindness, goodness, faithfulness, gentleness, self-control; against
such there is no law. And those who belong to Christ Jesus have
crucified the flesh with its passions and desires.

d. 1 Peter 3:1-2. You women must accept the authority of your husbands, so that if there are any of them who disbelieve the gospel
they may be won over, without a word being said, by observing
the chaste and reverent behavior of their wives (N.E.B.).

The answer to Question 64 said: "It is *impossible* for those who
are ingrafted into Christ by true faith not to bring forth the fruit
of gratitude." Thus, although works are not at all necessary for
our salvation, they are, nevertheless, the expression of our new
life. "The gospel of grace does not excuse us from works; it changes
the motive of them" (de Saussure: *Op. cit.*, p. 29). We never do
works *in order* to be saved but *because* we are already saved.

Works play a threefold role in the new life:

1. They enable us *to express to God our gratitude and to glorify him.* "I appeal to you," said Paul, "by the mercies of God, to

148

present your bodies as a living sacrifice, holy and acceptable to God, which is your spiritual worship" (Rom. 12:1).

2. Works *encourage us in our faith*. We need a confirmation of the objective truth of our salvation; God grants it to us in the works of faith. One judges the tree by its fruit (Matthew 7:17-20; Luke 13:6-9).

3. Works are *a witness to our neighbors*. Our works should speak of Christ to others. It should be a permanent criterion that our words and our deeds bespeak not ourselves, but Christ. "Works illumined by the Christian witness preach Christianity; the silent deed preaches Rousseauism" (de Saussure: *Op. cit.*, p. 31).

Such is the threefold form of the witness of works of faith. Thus it is that the church must *confess its faith through obedience*. "This is the *work* of God, that you *believe* in him whom he has sent" (John 6:29).

❡ QUESTION 87. *Can those who do not turn to God from their ungrateful, impenitent life be saved?*

Certainly not! Scripture says, "Surely you know that the unjust will never come into possession of the kingdom of God. Make no mistake: no fornicator or idolater, none who are guilty either of adultery or of homosexual perversion, no thieves or grabbers or drunkards or slanderers or swindlers, will possess the kingdom of God."[a]

a. 1 Cor. 6:9-10 (N.E.B.).
   Cf. Gal. 5:19-21; Eph. 5:5-33; 1 John 3:14-24.

❡ QUESTION 88. *How many parts are there to the true repentance or conversion of man?*

Two: the dying of the old self and the birth of the new.[a]

a. Rom. 6:4-6. We were buried therefore with him by baptism into death, so that as Christ was raised from the dead by the glory of the Father, we too might walk in newness of life. For if we have been united with him in a death like his, we shall certainly be united with him in a resurrection like his. We know that our old self was crucified with him so that the sinful body might be destroyed, and we might no longer be enslaved to sin.

2 Cor. 5:17. Therefore, if anyone is in Christ, he is a new creation, the old has passed away, behold the new has come.

Cf. Eph. 4:22-24; Col. 3:5-10; 1 Cor. 5:7.

❲ QUESTION 89. *What is the dying of the old self?*

Sincere sorrow over our sins and more and more to hate them and to flee from them.[a]

a. Rom. 8:13. If you live according to the flesh you will die, but if by the Spirit you put to death the deeds of the body you will live.

2 Cor. 7:10. Godly grief produces a repentance that leads to salvation and brings no regret, but worldly grief produces death.

Cf. Joel 2:13; Ps. 51:3, 8, 17.

❲ QUESTION 90. *What is the birth of the new self?*

Complete joy in God through Christ[a] and a strong desire to live according to the will of God in all good works.[b]

a. Rom. 5:1. Since we are justified by faith, we have peace with God through our Lord Jesus Christ.

Cf. Rom. 14:17; Isa. 57:15.

b. Gal. 2:20. I have been crucified with Christ; it is no longer I who live, but Christ who lives in me; and the life I now live in the flesh I live by faith in the Son of God, who loved me and gave himself for me.

Cf. Rom. 6:10-11.

Notice the categorical answer "Certainly not" to Question 87. The one who does not glorify God in his works shows that he does not truly believe in Jesus Christ and that he has not truly died and risen with him. It is on the basis of works that the reality of the new life is verified. "Although we may not be saved *by* works, we are not saved *without* works" (de Saussure: *Ibid.*).

It is a falsification of the question to put a versus between *faith* and *life,* between *theology* and *action,* between *practical faith* and *intellectual faith.* There are not two opposing or even complementary realities in faith and works, for they are one and the same reality: God's work of redemption which bestirs our faith in Jesus Christ produces the corresponding works in us. It is necessary to say, therefore, that where these works are not found, true faith is also absent.

"The good law and that in which one lives is the love of God, spread abroad in our hearts by the Holy Spirit" (Luther: *Disputation Against Scholastic Theology,* 1517: Weimar I, p. 228; *Luther's Works,* Vol. 31, p. 15).

As to *conversion* or *repentance,* the term which the New Testament employs to designate this reality means literally "to think afterward, to change one's mind," and so also "to change direction." The one who repents or is converted acknowledges, by the grace of God, that he has taken a wrong road; he regrets, he detests his former way; he pledges himself to the new way by a complete reorientation of his entire being. Conversion or repentance always entails a negative and a positive aspect. The believer is not called upon to sink into an everlasting remorse or regret. The man who repents must rise up and go forward (2 Samuel 12:20; Matthew 9:5; Philippians 3:14). "Godly grief produces a repentance that leads to salvation and brings no regret; but worldly grief produces death" (2 Cor. 7:10).

Again, more precisely, repentance is *the first fruit of faith* (Acts 2:37-38). Besides, the Christian life is impossible unless faith has produced this first fruit of repentance and conversion. "Except for this being turned inside out our most impressive advancements are only toward perdition" (de Saussure: *Op cit.,* p. 33).

Conversion implies not only a change of life, an improvement, but, in the most literal sense a death and a resurrection (Romans 6). "The new man is not a superman, but another man. To repent does not mean to become better, but to become entirely another person" (*Ibid.*).

Be it noted that conversion is not the result of man's initiative but of God's (Acts 9:1-9). Moreover, even though the conversion of a man is fully complete once for all, there is always need to renew confidence in the efficacy of the sacrifice of Jesus Christ. "Original sin is like a beard," said Farel; "it is necessary to shave it every day."

Practically, a man's conversion consists in:

1. A real *grief* about his sin (Luke 22:62).

2. A sincere *confession* of his faults that one can make to a brother in the faith (1 John 1:9; Matt. 3:6).

3. A *reparation* for these faults, in so far as this is possible (Luke 19:8).

4. Finally, a true *joy* induced by the grace received (Luke 10:20) and a genuine *love* of God expressing itself in the practice of the works of faith (1 John 5:1-5).

❡ QUESTION 91. *But what are good works?*

Only those which are done out of true faith,[a] in accordance with the Law of God,[b] and for his glory,[c] and not those based on our own opinion or on the traditions of men.[d]

a. Rom. 14:20b, 22b-23. Everything is indeed clean, but it is wrong for anyone to make others fall by what he eats . . . happy is he who has no reason to judge himself for what he approves. But he who has doubts is condemned, if he eats, because he does not act from faith; for whatever does not proceed from faith is sin.

b. 1 Sam. 15:22. Samuel said, "Has the Lord as great delight in burnt offerings and sacrifices, as in obeying the voice of the Lord? Behold, to obey is better than sacrifice, and to hearken than the fat of rams."
   Cf. Eph. 2:10.

c. 1 Cor. 10:31. Whether you eat or drink, or whatever you do, do all to the glory of God.

d. Deut. 12:32. "Everything that I command you you shall be careful to do; you shall not add to it or take from it."
   Matt. 15:9. "In vain do they worship me, teaching as doctrines the precepts of men."
   Cf. Isa. 29:13; Ezek. 20:18-19.

❡ QUESTION 92. *What is the Law of God?*

God spoke all these words saying:

First Commandment
"I AM THE LORD YOUR GOD, WHO BROUGHT YOU OUT OF THE LAND OF EGYPT, OUT OF THE HOUSE OF BONDAGE. YOU SHALL HAVE NO OTHER GODS BEFORE ME."

Second Commandment

"YOU SHALL NOT MAKE YOURSELF A GRAVEN IMAGE, OR ANY LIKENESS OF ANYTHING THAT IS IN HEAVEN ABOVE, OR THAT IS IN THE EARTH BENEATH, OR THAT IS IN THE WATER UNDER THE EARTH; YOU SHALL NOT BOW DOWN TO THEM OR SERVE THEM; FOR I THE LORD YOUR GOD AM A JEALOUS GOD, VISITING THE INIQUITY OF THE FATHERS UPON THE CHILDREN TO THE THIRD AND FOURTH GENERATION OF THOSE WHO HATE ME, BUT SHOWING STEADFAST LOVE TO THOUSANDS OF THOSE WHO LOVE ME AND KEEP MY COMMANDMENTS."

Third Commandment

"YOU SHALL NOT TAKE THE NAME OF THE LORD YOUR GOD IN VAIN; FOR THE LORD WILL NOT HOLD HIM GUILTLESS WHO TAKES HIS NAME IN VAIN."

Fourth Commandment

"REMEMBER THE SABBATH DAY, TO KEEP IT HOLY. SIX DAYS YOU SHALL LABOR, AND DO ALL YOUR WORK; BUT THE SEVENTH DAY IS A SABBATH TO THE LORD YOUR GOD; IN IT YOU SHALL NOT DO ANY WORK, YOU, OR YOUR SON, OR YOUR DAUGHTER, YOUR MANSERVANT, OR YOUR MAIDSERVANT, OR YOUR CATTLE, OR THE SOJOURNER WHO IS WITHIN YOUR GATES; FOR IN SIX DAYS THE LORD MADE HEAVEN AND EARTH, THE SEA, AND ALL THAT IS IN THEM, AND RESTED THE SEVENTH DAY; THEREFORE THE LORD BLESSED THE SABBATH DAY AND HALLOWED IT."

Fifth Commandment

"HONOR YOUR FATHER AND YOUR MOTHER, THAT YOUR DAYS MAY BE LONG IN THE LAND WHICH THE LORD YOUR GOD GIVES YOU."

Sixth Commandment

"YOU SHALL NOT KILL."

Seventh Commandment

"YOU SHALL NOT COMMIT ADULTERY."

Eighth Commandment

"YOU SHALL NOT STEAL."

Ninth Commandment

"YOU SHALL NOT BEAR FALSE WITNESS AGAINST YOUR NEIGHBOR."

Tenth Commandment

"YOU SHALL NOT COVET YOUR NEIGHBOR'S HOUSE; YOU SHALL NOT
COVET YOUR NEIGHBOR'S WIFE, OR HIS MANSERVANT, OR HIS MAID-
SERVANT, OR HIS OX, OR HIS ASS, OR ANYTHING THAT IS YOUR NEIGH-
BOR'S."[a]

a. Exod. 20:1-7.
   Cf. Deut. 5:6-21.

¶ QUESTION 93. *How are these commandments divided?*

Into two tables,[a] the first of which teaches us in four commandments how we ought to live in relation to God; the other, in six
commandments, what we owe to our neighbor.[b]

a. Exod. 34:28-29. He was there with the Lord forty days and forty
   nights; he neither ate bread nor drank water. And he wrote upon
   the tables the words of the covenant, the ten commandments.
   When Moses came down from Mount Sinai, with the two tables
   of the testimony in his hand as he came down from the moun-
   tain, Moses did not know that the skin of his face shone because
   he had been talking with God.
   Cf. Deut. 4:13; 10:3.
b. Matt. 22:37-39. [Jesus] said to him, "You shall love the Lord your
   God with all your heart, and with all your soul, and with all
   your mind. This is the great and first commandment. And a
   second is like it, You shall love your neighbor as yourself."

Not all works are good, only those which proceed from faith
and are, consequently, in accordance with the Law of God. "God
will not be served according to our imagination, but in the way
that pleases him" (Calvin: *Geneva Catechism,* No. 130).

"The grace of God is given for the purpose of directing the will,
lest it err even in loving God" (Luther: *Op. cit.:* Weimar I, p.
228; *Luther's Works,* Vol. 31, p. 15).

The criterion of what constitutes the will of God is never in
ourselves but outside of us, in the Law, that is in the entire scripture which bears witness to the will of God both for men and
against them.

The Decalog or *Ten Commandments* is an epitome of the

Law of God contained in the whole scripture. It is important to stress that the Law does not proclaim anything other than what the whole scripture affirms.

We have a second epitome of God's will in *the Sermon on the Mount*. Neither one should ever be separated from the unity of God's revelation. These are not documents having a value in themselves which one could study for themselves.

The Sermon on the Mount does not make the Decalog null and void. Jesus does not proclaim a "higher morality" than that of Moses; he does not come "to destroy" but "to fulfill" (Matt. 5:17). In delivering us from the slavery of sin, Jesus himself gives us the possibility of fulfilling the Law. "If the Ten Commandments tell where man may and ought to stand before and with God, then the Sermon on the Mount tells us that he has really been placed there by God's act" (Quoted in *Karl Barth's Church Dogmatics*, p. 112, by Otto Weber).

Jesus proclaims the commandment in such a way that it is no longer possible to turn away from it; since he is himself the grace of God whereby we are empowered to keep the absolute demands of the Law, he wants us to ask for this grace. It is he who enables us to live in peace, in confidence, and in the joy of the new life (Matthew 5:21-22, 27-28, 38-39, 43-44).

Thus the Law makes us aware of the will of God; the Sermon on the Mount shows us that this will is absolute and does not allow any compromise; Jesus Christ fulfilled this Law and because he frees us, he makes us, in our turn, capable of fulfilling it.

The Law is thus the guide of regenerated man.

It is regrettable that the Reformed tradition has most often reduced the Law to nothing other than detector of human sin. The place which we assign to it in our worship is significant in this respect: the Law leads to humiliation and the confession of sins. We do not deny that this is clearly one of the roles which the Law is called upon to play; when we are put over against the revelation of the holiness of God, we can only humble ourselves.

The Law, however, ought not to appear to us only as the revelation of the will of God which we cannot do. It ought also to be the indicator of the new possibility given to us in Jesus Christ. By the grace of God, the Law becomes something which we can actually and joyously do, *in gratitude.*

An order of worship which is concerned to express the whole evangelical truth ought to make a place for the Law after the assurance of pardon as well as before.

The two tables of the Law have been epitomized by Jesus in the *summary* of the Law (Matthew 22:37-39). The word "table" is derived from the Latin *tabula* which means a board, then a register, a document, a contract, a testament. The "tables of the Law" contain the very terms of the covenant which God has made with the men he has called (Deuteronomy 4:13-23).

The first and greatest commandment, "You shall love the Lord your God with all your heart, and with all your soul, and with all your mind," defines the first table; it reminds us "how we ought to live in relation to God." The second commandment, "You shall love your neighbor as yourself," sums up the second table, that is, it teaches us "what we owe to our neighbor."

Notice that the second commandment is "like the first." The second table must not be separated from the first. The Christian life can be lived only in obedience to the two tables. We cannot love God alone, which would lead us into *pietism,* nor our neighbor alone, which is what *humanitarianism* claims. True faith consists in faithful obedience to the two commandments: the love of God and of the neighbor. The works of faith must serve at once the glory of God and the welfare of man.

Keep in mind that the Law is given by love and for the purpose of making us capable of loving. If it detects sin, it is not itself sinful (Romans 7:7). The disapproval of Paul is directed against man, the sinner, but not as was sometimes understood, against the Law itself (Romans 7:14). We must not fear the Law as if it could do nothing but bring about evil. On the contrary we should rejoice each time that we are reminded of it for, guided by the Law, we are enabled to serve God in gratitude, through works conformable to his will.

Luther said: "The Law is not to be shunned; but without the theology of the cross man misuses the best in the worst manner" *(Heidelberg Disputation,* 1518: Weimar I, p. 354; *Luther's Works,* Vol. 31, p. 40).

The "theology of the cross" makes a piece of good news of the Law. Only through the cross does God give us by his grace the possibility of not using the Law in a pernicious manner.

15 / LOVE AND HONOR TO GOD—
THE FIRST TABLE OF THE LAW

❡ QUESTION 94. *What does the Lord require in the first commandment?*

That I must avoid and flee all idolatry,[a] sorcery, enchantments,[b] invocation of saints or other creatures[c] because of the risk of losing my salvation. Indeed, I ought properly to acknowledge the only true God,[d] trust in him alone,[e] in humility[f] and patience[g] expect all good from him only,[h] and love,[i] fear,[j] and honor[k] him with my whole heart. In short, I should rather turn my back on all creatures than do the least thing against his will.[l]

a. 1 Cor. 10:5-14. With most of [our fathers] God was not pleased; for they were overthrown in the wilderness. Now these things are warnings to us, not to desire evil as they did. Do not be idolators as some of them were. . . . We must not indulge in immorality as some of them did. . . . We must not put the Lord to the test . . . nor grumble. . . . Now these things happened as a warning, but they are written down for our instruction. . . . Therefore, let anyone who thinks that he stands take heed lest he fall. . . . My beloved, shun the worship of idols.
Cf. 1 Cor. 6:9-10.

b. Lev. 19:31. "Do not turn to mediums or wizards; do not seek them out, to be defiled by them: I am the Lord your God."
Cf. Deut. 18:10-12.

c. Matt. 4:10. Jesus said to him, "Begone, Satan! for it is written, 'You shall worship the Lord your God and him only shall you serve.' "
Cf. Rev. 19:10; 22:8-9.

d. John 17:3. "This is eternal life, that they know thee the only true God, and Jesus Christ whom thou hast sent."

e. Jer. 17:5, 7. Thus says the Lord: "Cursed is the man who trusts in man and makes flesh his arm, whose heart turns away from the Lord. . . . Blessed is the man who trusts in the Lord, whose trust is the Lord."

f. 1 Peter 5:5-6. You that are younger be subject to the elders. Clothe yourselves, all of you, with humility toward one another, for "God opposes the proud, but gives grace to the humble."

g. Heb. 10:36. You have need of endurance, so that you may do the will of God and receive what is promised.
Cf. Rom. 5:3-4; Phil. 2:14; Col. 1:11-12.

h. James 1:17. Every good endowment and every perfect gift is from above, coming down from the Father of lights with whom there is no variation or shadow due to change.
Cf. Ps. 104:27-28.

i. Deut. 6:5. You shall love the Lord your God with all your heart, and with all your soul, and with all your might.
Cf. Matt. 22:37.

j. Deut. 6:2. Fear the Lord your God, you and your son and your son's son, by keeping all his statutes and his commandments, which I command you, all the days of your life.
Cf. Ps. 111:10; Prov. 1:7; 9:10; Matt. 10:28.

k. Rev. 5:13. I heard every creature in heaven and on earth and under the earth and in the sea, and all therein, saying, "To him who sits upon the throne and to the Lamb be blessing and honor and glory and might forever and ever!"

l. Matt. 10:37. "He who loves father or mother more than me is not worthy of me; and he who loves son or daughter more than me is not worthy of me."
Cf. Matt. 5:29-30; Acts 5:29.

℄ QUESTION 95. *What is idolatry?*

It is to imagine or possess something in which to put one's trust in place of or beside the one true God who has revealed himself in his Word.[a]

a. Gal. 4:8-9. Formerly, when you did not know God, you were in bondage to beings that by nature are no gods; but now that you have come to know God, or rather to be known by God, how can you turn back again to the weak and beggarly elemental spirits, whose slaves you want to be once more?
Cf. 1 Chron. 16:26; 2 Chron. 16:12; Phil. 3:18-19; Eph. 2:12; 2 John 1:9.

Questions 94-103 treat of the first table of the Law, namely, of the love and honor that we owe to God.

Before telling us what he expects of us, God begins by telling us *who he is and what he has done for us:* "I am the Lord your God, who brought you out of the land of Egypt, out of the house of bondage. You shall have no other gods before me."

The God who requires of us the obedience of faith is not a principle, an impersonal force, an idea; he is not "something beyond us." The true God, the one whom we must worship and serve, *reveals* himself by acquainting us with his name: "I am," in Hebrew *Jahweh* (Exodus 3). "It is still a question whether the reply that God gives to Moses is a revelation or a concealment; in the first case, it would be translated: 'I am the one who is,' in the second case: 'I am who I am,' that is to say, 'that is none of your business.' There is probably a partial truth in each of these interpretations . . . the formula's deliberate ambiguity is intended to safeguard the mystery which remains complete in spite of the revelation" (*Vocabulaire biblique,* ed. Jacob, p. 69).

It is like the meaning of the event of the burning bush. God reveals himself but at the same time he says, "Do not come near" (Exod. 3:5). We cannot capture God, subjugate him to ourselves and reduce him to a formula. God is God and he intends to remain so. This is the meaning of "I am."

The God whom we must serve is first of all introduced to us as one who is different from us; he governs us by his holiness (Exodus 3:5), and sets a limit between man and himself that the creature must not overstep. God is not in us; he is outside of us. That is why we are able to worship and serve him.

But the one who says, "I am," tells us at the same time, "I am the Lord *your* God." He is made known as the God of mercy who is truly for man. However, he keeps the initiative and decides that he will come near to man; Jesus Christ is God coming to us.

There is always in God this twofold reality: on the one side, he is hidden, he escapes the control of man; he is "the other," the holy God; but on the other side, he wants to be for man. "I am the Lord your God, *who brought you out of the land of Egypt, out of the house of bondage.*" God reveals himself as the one who is concerned about man, who frees him and saves him. We are no longer in slavery, no longer slaves of false gods; we are free, having been set free so that we may serve the one true God.

The commandment not to have "any other gods" must be considered less as a command than as an impossibility. It is not possible for those who have been freed by the true God, and who are free from now on to serve him alone, to be able to worship other gods again. "No one *can* serve two masters" (Matt. 6:24). The first commandment serves thus as the criterion for our faith. God is saying to us: "Do you believe in the liberation that I have given you? Do you really have confidence in me?"

The first commandment is not presented to us as a completely outward obligation, something that we must absolutely do under penalty of displeasing God. No, it is a reminder of the gospel of God in Jesus Christ: God is the one who comes to liberate us so that we can serve him. Still it is necessary that we believe in him.

"If we doubt or do not think that God is merciful, and that we are acceptable to him, or, worse than that, if we claim to be acceptable to him on account of our own works, we are engaged in pure hypocrisy. On the outside one is venerating God; inwardly, he is setting up an idol within himself" (Luther: *Good Works,* 1520: Weimar VI, p. 211; *Luther's Works,* Vol. 44).

We cannot put our trust anywhere else than in the true God if we really want to serve him. Luther says, "That to which you defer and surrender your heart is properly your God."

With respect to the words *before me,* Calvin states: "Since he who sees and knows all is the Judge of the secret thoughts of men, it means that he wants to be worshiped as God, not only by outward confession, but also in pure trust and affection of heart" *(Geneva Catechism,* No. 142).

In a word, the first commandment reaffirms for our faith that God has loved us. It is by virtue of this initiative that we can in our turn love and serve him.

To obey the Law means: to love God with all my heart, with all my strength, with all my soul, and with all my mind. Practically that means listening to him, putting all our trust in him, worshiping him and praying to him. We do all that, knowing that he will never abandon us because he is the true God who sets men free.

❡ QUESTION 96. *What does God require in the second commandment?*

That we should not represent[a] him or worship him in any other manner than he has commanded in his Word.[b]

a. Acts 17:29. Being then God's offspring, we ought not to think that the Deity is like gold, or silver, or stone, a representation by the art and imagination of man.

Cf. Deut. 4:15-19; Isa. 40:18-25; Rom. 1:23.

b. 1 Sam. 15:23. "Rebellion is as the sin of divination, and stubbornness is as iniquity and idolatry. Because you have rejected the word of the Lord, he has also rejected you from being king."
Cf. Deut. 12:30-32; Matt. 15:9.

❡ QUESTION 97. *Should we, then, not make any images at all?*

God cannot and should not be pictured in any way. As for creatures, although they may indeed be portrayed, God forbids making or having any likeness of them in order to worship them, or to use them to serve him.[a]

a. Exod. 23:24; 34:13-14. You shall not bow down to their gods, nor serve them, nor do according to their works, but you shall utterly overthrow them and break their pillars in pieces. You shall tear down their altars and break their pillars, and cut down their Ashérim (for you shall worship no other god, for the Lord, whose name is Jealous, is a jealous God).
Cf. Num. 33:52; Deut. 4:15-16; 7:5; 12:3-4; 2 Kings 18:3-4.

❡ QUESTION 98. *But may not pictures be tolerated in churches in place of books for unlearned people?*

No, for we must not try to be wiser than God who does not want his people to be taught by means of lifeless idols,[a] but through the living preaching of his Word.[b]

a. Hab. 2:18-20. What profit is an idol when its maker has shaped it, a metal image, a teacher of lies? For the workman trusts in his own creation when he makes dumb idols! Woe to him who says to a wooden thing, Awake; to a dumb stone, Arise! Can this give revelation? Behold, it is overlaid with gold and silver, and there is no breath at all in it. But the Lord is in his holy temple; let all the earth keep silence before him.
Cf. Jer. 10:8.

b. 2 Tim. 3:16-17. All scripture is inspired by God and profitable for teaching, for reproof, for corrections, and for training in righteousness, that the man of God may be complete, equipped for every good work.
Cf. 2 Peter 1:19.

We are prone not only to worship false gods but even to make for ourselves a false image of the true God. "Paganism is the worship of false gods, whereas idolatry is the false worship of God" (de Saussure: *Op. cit.,* p. 39).

We note that the Roman Catholic Church has dropped the second commandment. "The biblical explorer who arrives at the chapter giving the Ten Commandments is not a little surprised to see that the sacred text does not correspond to the catechism that he learned as a child: the second commandment has been completely omitted. On the other hand, the tenth commandment has been cut in two. The sixth and ninth are nearly alike and placed under the same rubric. What is more serious is that the whole order of the sacred code has been upset" (Claudel, quoted by de Saussure: *Op. cit.,* p. 42).

Still let us not imagine that the second commandment embarrasses Catholics only! We Protestants are also capable of making images of God, images which are much more dangerous because they are more subtle. Can we truly say that we do not "represent" God in any way and that we do not "worship him in any other manner than he has commanded in his Word"?

The second commandment asks the question: Which is the God whom we serve? The true God or a dream, a figment of the imagination, an ideal that we have invented, if not by our hands at least in our minds? Do we really believe what God tells us of himself in his Word, and everything that he tells us, or do we rather seek to mold him to our liking? Do we accept being judged by him or do we rather claim that we ourselves can judge him? Are we believers who receive in faith what God allows us to know of him or rather nonbelievers who want to make themselves a god that goes before them (Exodus 32:1)?

In the second commandment God himself wishes to keep us from going astray from him. "He shows us the correct form of worship in order that he may draw us away from all superstitions, and carnal ceremonies" (Calvin: *Geneva Catechism,* No. 149).

For the sake of our salvation, God reminds us that he is *a jealous God.* It is not without danger that one withdraws from him; it is not with impunity that one disdains his Word, the revelation which God gives of himself. Here is posed a question of *life* and *death* for us: "See, I have set before you life and good, death and evil. Because I command you this day to love the Lord your God, to walk in his ways and to keep his commandments and his statutes and ordinances so that you may live . . . choose life and you shall live!" (See Deuteronomy 30:15-20.)

So great is God's love for us that he prevents us from living in error and delusion with relation to him. God does not wish to let us die apart from him in ignorance of this truth. When, however, he reveals his truth to us, he expects that we shall walk in it.

If, contrary to what the Word of God tells us, we insist on looking for God in ourselves, in nature, in our imagination, in our minds, or anywhere else than in the place where he really is and is actually revealed for us, then we should not be surprised at the deadly sterility of our works and of those of the church as well.

To obey the second commandment means, therefore, to believe in the revelation of God in Jesus Christ, his Word made flesh (John 1:14), "the image of the invisible God" (Col. 1:15), the one in whom "the whole fullness of deity dwells bodily" (Col. 2:9).

We cannot make for ourselves any other picture of God than that which he gives us of himself in Jesus Christ. The one who obeys the second commandment accepts the witness of the prophets and the apostles concerning Christ, the whole scripture of the Old and the New Testaments. He listens also to the preaching of this Word of God as it is being brought to life today by the Holy Spirit and is being confirmed for us through the sacraments.

"Why," asks the Catechism of Calvin, "does God mention here *a thousand* generations, and in regard to punishment mention only three or four? To signify that it is his nature to exercise kindness and gentleness much more than strictness or severity, as he testifies when he says that he is ready to show mercy, but slow to anger" (No. 158).

It is necessary to underscore this reminder of the infinite mercy of God accompanying the declaration of the fact that he is a jealous God. It is to save us that God loves us and because he loves us he cannot bear to see us prefer someone else to him. "God," says Calvin, "cannot allow any associate-gods" (No. 152).

We have already seen this with respect to the doctrine of *the Trinity*. It is the very truth of the revelation that makes every representation of God impossible. One cannot represent a God who reveals himself in three different ways without ceasing to be the same God. Such will always be the question that faith must ask of Christian art. We do not dispute its legitimacy, we simply demand that it be well understood that human art will never be able to represent but one form of the being of God, namely, his humanity. Let us hope that it will faithfully represent this humanity and not pretend to picture his divinity also! One does not communicate God in producing a suave Christ!

Once again, the only representation of God is in his Word which announces to us who he is and all that he does for man as Father, Son, and Holy Spirit.

¶ QUESTION 99. *What is required in the third commandment?*

That we must not profane or abuse the name of God by cursing,[a] by perjury,[b] or by unnecessary oaths.[c] Nor are we to participate in such horrible sins by keeping quiet and thus giving silent consent. In a word, we must not use the holy name of God except with fear and reverence[d] so that he may be rightly confessed[e] and addressed[f] by us, and be glorified in all our words and works.[g]

a. Lev. 24:11, 13, 16. The Israelite woman's son blasphemed the Name, and cursed. And they brought him to Moses. . . . And the Lord said to Moses, . . . "He who blasphemes the name of the Lord shall be put to death; the sojourner as well as the native, when he blasphemes the Name, shall be put to death."

b. Lev. 19:12. "You shall not swear by my name falsely, and so profane the name of your God: I am the Lord."

c. Matt. 5:37. "Let what you say be simply 'Yes' or 'No'; anything more than this comes from evil."
Cf. James 5:12.

d. Ps. 99:3. Let them praise thy great and terrible name! Holy is he! Deut. 28:58. "Fear this glorious and awful name, the Lord your God."

e. Matt. 10:32. "Everyone who acknowledges me before men, I also will acknowledge before my Father who is in heaven."

f. 1 Tim. 2:8. I desire then that in every place the men should pray, lifting holy hands without anger or quarreling.

g. Col. 3:17. Whatever you do, in word or deed, do everything in the name of the Lord Jesus, giving thanks to God the Father through him.
Cf. Rom. 2:24; 1 Tim. 6:1.

¶ QUESTION 100. *Is it, therefore, so great a sin to blaspheme God's name by cursing and swearing that God is also angry with those who do not try to prevent and forbid it as much as they can?*

Yes, indeed;[a] for no sin is greater or provokes his wrath more than the profaning of his name. That is why he commanded it to be punished with death.[b]

a. Lev. 5:1. "If anyone sins in that he hears a public adjuration to testify and though he is a witness, whether he has seen or come to know the matter, yet does not speak, he shall bear his iniquity."
b. Lev. 24:15-16. "Say to the people of Israel, Whoever curses his God shall bear his sin. He who blasphemes the name of the Lord shall be put to death."

¶ QUESTION 101. *But may we not swear oaths by the name of God in a devout manner?*

Yes, when the civil authorities require it of their subjects, or when it is otherwise needed to maintain and promote fidelity and truth, to the glory of God and the welfare of our neighbor. Such oath-taking is grounded in God's Word[a] and has therefore been rightly used by God's people under the Old and New Covenants.[b]

a. Deut. 6:13. You shall fear the Lord your God; you shall serve him, and swear by his name.
   Cf. Deut. 10:20; Isa. 48:1; Heb. 6:16.
b. Cf. Gen. 21:24; 31:53-54; Josh. 9:15, 19; 1 Sam. 24:22; 2 Sam. 3:35; 1 Kings 1:28-30; Rom. 1:9; 2 Cor. 1:23.

¶ QUESTION 102. *May we also swear by the saints or other creatures?*

No; for a lawful oath is a calling upon God, as the only searcher of hearts, to bear witness to the truth, and to punish me if I swear falsely.[a] No creature deserves such honor.[b]

a. 2 Cor. 1:23. I call God to witness against me—it was to spare you that I refrained from coming to Corinth.
b. Matt. 5:34-35. I say to you, Do not swear at all, either by heaven, for

165

it is the throne of God, or by the earth, for it is his footstool, or by Jerusalem, for it is the city of the great King.

You shall not take the name of the Lord your God in vain. The transgression of this commandment does not generally appear too serious to us; it is only a matter of words! In our perspective, it is primarily acts that count! The truth is that a name is intimately linked with a person. For example, we do not like to see our own name distorted. We resent that as a personal affront.

The name of God reveals his very person and it is the name which saves us. To take the name of God in vain, in one way or another, is not to take God the Savior seriously. This finally comes around to not believing that he is God, the only true God, the one who has made himself known in Jesus Christ and to whom he has given his name. Jesus Christ is "Lord, to the glory of God the Father" (Phil. 2:11). "Of the Son he says: 'Thy throne, O God, is for ever and ever' " (Heb. 1:8). There is a real *presence* of God among men in Jesus Christ, through the Word, and the Holy Spirit who bears witness to it. To take the name of God in vain means not to take this presence seriously, to speak in this world as if God had never come and as if he were no longer present. Finally, it is not to believe in the resurrection which makes "all things new."

First of all, salvation influences our speech. The third commandment protects us:

1. From making use of the threefold holy name of God as a compost heap for our anger. That is to fall into the despair of the man who believes himself abandoned by God. The man who swears either wishes to avenge himself upon God or to wheedle God's power for his own use by uttering his name as a blasphemy.

2. From swearing an oath before God without his being truly present; in particular, in the commitments which we are called upon to take at the moment of our baptism or of our marriage, or again in the response that we have to give to God at the time in which he calls us to a particular service in the church, or in the state. In a general way, it concerns all the occasions in which we have to confess our faith in public or in the bosom of the Christian community.

3. From speaking of God falsely or loosely, in such a way that we have his name constantly on our lips and that we claim to be

166

able to explain everything that happens to us or others as if we ourselves were in such intimacy with God that we are familiar with his most secret plans.

4. From praying otherwise than before God as a creature before his creator, that is, from praying before men to glorify oneself. One of the rules of Christian prayer is that we must cultivate objectivity and sobriety. Therefore, we do not risk praying "in order to be seen by men."

5. From being inattentive at the time of the reading of the Word of God or of the preaching of this Word, as if we could dispense with listening to God himself in order to think of something "more important"!

The consequences of disobedience to the third commandment are serious (Leviticus 24:15), because they bear witness to our infidelity. The one who takes God's name in vain does not believe that it is God who saves; he is not vindicated by faith; he is not free from the burden of the curse that weighs upon man.

¶ QUESTION 103. *What does God require in the fourth commandment?*

First, that the ministry of the gospel and Christian education be maintained,[a] and that I diligently attend church, especially on the Lord's day,[b] to hear the Word of God,[c] to participate in the holy Sacraments,[d] to call publicly upon the Lord,[e] and to give Christian service to those in need.[f] Second, that I cease from my evil works all the days of my life, allow the Lord to work in me through his Spirit, and thus begin in this life the eternal Sabbath.[g]

a. 2 Tim. 2:2; 3:15. What you have heard from me before many witnesses entrust to faithful men who will be able to teach others also. . . . From childhood you have been acquainted with the sacred writings which are able to instruct you for salvation through faith in Christ Jesus.

Cf. 1 Tim. 4:13-16; 5:17; 1 Cor. 9:13-14.

b. Lev. 23:3. Six days shall work be done; but on the seventh day is a sabbath of solemn rest, a holy convocation; you shall do no work; it is a sabbath to the Lord in all your dwellings.

Acts 2:42, 46. They devoted themselves to the apostles' teaching and fellowship, to the breaking of bread and the prayers. . . . And day by day, attending the temple together and breaking bread in their homes, they partook of food with glad and generous hearts.

Cf. Ps. 68:26.

c. Rom. 10:17. Faith comes from what is heard, and what is heard comes by the preaching of Christ.

1 Cor. 14:19. In church I would rather speak five words with my mind, in order to instruct others, than ten thousand words in a tongue.

Cf. 1 Cor. 14:29, 31.

d. 1 Cor. 11:24. The Lord Jesus said, "Do this in remembrance of me."

e. 1 Tim. 2:1. First of all, then, I urge that supplications, prayers, intercessions, and thanksgivings be made for all men.

f. 1 Cor. 16:2. On the first day of every week, each of you is to put something aside and store it up, as he may prosper, so that contributions need not be made when I come.

g. Isa. 66:23. "From new moon to new moon, and from sabbath to sabbath, all flesh shall come to worship before me," says the Lord.

Remember the sabbath day, to keep it holy. Six days you shall labor, and do all your work; but the seventh day is a sabbath to the Lord your God.

The fourth commandment speaks of rest and of work. Notice first of all that rest is mentioned before work. Man's work is seen only in connection with the hallowing of the Lord's day.

The purpose of the fourth commandment is not simply to assure a necessary alternation between work and rest. There is no question in the Bible of man's right to rest or to have leisure time. It is not man who demands the sabbath but God who gives it to him as a grace.

The sabbath certifies a community of life between God and his people; it is the sign of the covenant (Exodus 31:16-17). The day of rest reminds Israel that he is not abandoned, left to himself, but that God has wished to bind his destiny to that of his people. They share the same conditions of life.

The day of rest recalls God's mighty deed for men, namely, *the creation.* By the same token, the Christian church has chosen Sunday, because this day commemorates the resurrection of Christ; Sunday recalls the creation and announces the new creation, the kingdom of God, the new heaven and the new earth. Sunday is the mark of the final sabbath in which man, finally liberated, will be able to live in the communion which was his with God before the fall.

The fourth commandment nourishes and quickens our faith in the risen Christ who is himself for us the promise of the kingdom. It is necessary that we *hallow* Sunday by the means that God himself puts at our disposal, that is, by meditating together upon his Word and by participating in the sacraments. No more than we shall be alone and deprived of the blessings of God in the kingdom can we be so today. Sharing in the worship of the church is not an obligation but a means which God, in his grace, gives us in order to enable us to receive in faith the full and complete communion of the kingdom. There is a resemblance and a continuity between the community assembled around Christ and that which gathers on Sunday to announce and prefigure the community of the kingdom.

Moreover, the day of rest bears witness that we consider ourselves "incapable of any good," unable to save ourselves, of living, of giving meaning to our life. In instituting a day of rest, God asks us to put an end to all work, and all empty meaningless activity so that we may know the one who "is at work in [us], both to will and to work" (Phil. 2:13). Calvin said: "It is utterly necessary for us to rest in order that God work in us; we must yield our will, resign our heart, renounce all the desires of our flesh. In short, we must refrain from everything that rests upon our own judgment; since we have God working in us, we yield to him" (Quoted by Visser't Hooft: *L'Ordre de Dieu*, p. 56).

This is perhaps one of the aspects of the hallowing of Sunday which we forget most often: we mean the demonstration of our own inability, in favor of a true gratitude for the power of God's work for us. Each Sunday we confess that by grace we are saved through faith (Ephesians 2:8).

One has asked now and then with more or less anxiety what "to hallow," that is, to keep Sunday holy, means in a practical way. We do not think there can be any strict rule in this sphere. What truly matters is that we live this day in the presence of God, in the full acknowledgment of his love for us.

All one can say is that not being able to share in the worship of the community should always be felt as a painful loss. We endanger ourselves by not using these means which God gives us to renew his grace within us, of no longer being able to spend this day gratefully in the presence of God. We condemn ourselves to the "gloomy Sundays" that a song of the pre-war period had unhappily made famous!

As to work, from a free expression of man's life, as it was meant to be before the fall, it has become slavery. It is no longer a service rendered to God but has become an attempt of man to make himself equal to God and even to take his place.

In recalling us to the real meaning of our life, the day of rest frees us from the terrible routine that never ends and from the haunting feeling of not having done enough. We do not have to satisfy God by our labor since he freely gives us of his grace. Thus we can work in freedom, joy, and gratitude because we have this day of rest which completely renews our life and gives the entire week its right perspective.

The gracious gift of Sunday is much more than a mere opportunity to rest from our weariness. The fourth commandment reminds us that God has given us the opportunity to live in faith as free men.

Calvin rightly emphasized that "God never required obedience to any precept more strictly than to this one." In the Law of God, it is not a question of morals, of obligation, or of duty, but of the very possibility of life through faith.

The four commandments of the first table remind us that God is Lord of our life and we can put our trust in none other than in him alone.

16 / LOVE AND SERVICE OF THE NEIGHBOR— THE SECOND TABLE OF THE LAW

❮ QUESTION 104. *What does God require in the fifth commandment?*

That I show honor, love, and faithfulness to my father and mother and to all who are set in authority over me; that I submit myself with respectful obedience to all their careful instruction and discipline;[a] and that I also bear patiently their failures,[b] since it is God's will to govern us by their hand.[c]

a. Eph. 6:1-4. Children, obey your parents in the Lord, for this is right. "Honor your father and mother" (this is the first commandment with a promise), "that it may be well with you and that you may live long on the earth." Fathers, do not provoke your children to anger, but bring them up in the discipline and instruction of the Lord.

Rom. 13:1-2. Let every person be subject to the governing authorities. For there is no authority except from God, and those that exist have been instituted by God. Therefore he who resists the authorities resists what God has appointed, and those who resist will incur judgment.

Cf. Prov. 1:8; 4; 20:20; Deut. 6:6-9.

b. Prov. 23:22. Hearken to your father who begot you, and do not despise your mother when she is old.

1 Peter 2:18. Servants, be submissive to your masters with all respect, not only to the kind and gentle but also to the overbearing.

c. Col. 3:18-21. Wives, be subject to your husbands, as is fitting in the Lord. Husbands, love your wives, and do not be harsh with them. Children, obey your parents in everything for this pleases the Lord. Fathers, do not provoke your children, lest they become discouraged.

Cf. Eph. 6:1-9; Rom. 13:1-8; Matt. 22:21.

Honor your father and your mother that your days may be long in the land which the Lord your God gives you. The authority of parents is the sign of God's authority. We are not autonomous beings; we have a father and a mother; we are subject to authorities. Each of them reminds us, sometimes in a very critical manner and in the encounter of faith, of the very authority of God who is our Father.

The fifth commandment asks us not only to love our parents but also *to honor* them. This emphasis should prevent us from thinking that we can obey this command naturally. "Some people are so perverse by nature that they are ashamed of their parents, perhaps on account of their poverty, their plebian condition, their deformity, or even their dishonor. They let themselves be moved more by such things than by the commandment of God who is above all things and has given them such parents according to his wise benevolence, that he might train them and test them by his law" (Luther: *Op. cit.:* Weimar VI, p. 251; *Luther's Works,* Vol. 44). Here again the Law brings us back to the gospel: only man liberated by Jesus Christ can honor his parents as God asks him and in such a way that this respect is a sign of the honor that the believer owes to God.

This commandment is associated with *a promise:* "that your days may be long in the land which the Lord your God gives you." Calvin understood it literally: "God will give long life to those who honor their fathers and mothers as they ought" *(Geneva Catechism,* No. 188).

Luther also: "For the scripture, to have a long life means not only to live a long time but to have all that belongs to life, health in particular, a wife and children, food, peace, good company, and so on—all those things without which one cannot happily enjoy life, nor endure its length. If you do not want to obey your father and mother and let them guide you, you will starve and die" (Quoted by de Quervain: *L'Ordre de Dieu,* pp. 78-79).

Others have thought that one must see here an indication of God's patience with regard to man. The promise would mean that in our world threatened by the disorder of sin God upholds those conditions of life for which submission to authorities and particularly to parents becomes the instrument. Thus, he who obeys the fifth commandment, contributes to the sustaining of the rule of God on the earth. Moreover, the faithfulness of the believer justifies God's patience in sustaining the world and consequently prolonging its existence.

We do not believe, however, that the fifth commandment teaches us that natural submission is all that is necessary for the maintenance of good order. Rather, it reminds us that we can and must put our trust in the righteous and merciful Lord.

Now it is in this perspective that we can understand the ministry of parents and in a more general way, the responsibility of the teacher. Since God is the Lord of grace and intends that we should always be grateful for his lordship, he gives us the family as a gift. If it is possible for children to love and honor their parents only in the faith, their parents will be able to educate their children only in the assurance that they do not own them. Parents do not have to want what they themselves want or what their children want, but what God wishes for both of them.

"There is a . . . dishonor to parents . . . which is given the noble appearance of real honor; such is the case when the child always has his own way and the parents by earthly love authorize it. Here, one is honored, another is loved, and on all sides it is a delightful thing; the father and mother please the child and in turn the child pleases the parent. All this brings out the fact that the parents, being blind, do not acknowledge or honor God according to the first three commandments; that is why they cannot see at all what produces delinquency in children and how they should instruct and discipline them" (Luther: *Op. cit.*: Weimar VI, p. 252; *Luther's Works,* Vol. 44).

It is not necessary to enumerate at length the consequences of this disorder. We measure them each day. Today there is great anguish among teachers and parents who harvest with tears what they have sown in ignorance or in the conviction of doing good. It appears more and more clearly that we have taken a wrong road and that the goal of education is not the "happiness" of the child, understood as an ideal value and having its purpose within itself. Neither is it the honor of the parents, conceived in a purely egotistical way, but the glory of God alone. Here again all the rest is "a gift from above" if the intention is right.

The father is basically *the one to whom the question is put* (Deuteronomy 6:20-25). He answers this question with the authority that God has given him. The word of instruction must be the Word of God, a confession of faith in the Lord who has delivered his people from "the house of bondage." The father must represent the one who liberates but he should not claim to be the one who does it himself. There is an order of instruction which one must respect. Moreover, the child is *the one who dares to ask the question* (Deuteronomy 32:7). True education can only be a dialog, nourished by God's great work for his people. It can be developed only in the context of *the covenant of grace.*

So it is that *the parents are the hands of God* (Kohlbrügge, quoted by de Quervain: *Op. cit.*, p. 74). We must emphasize that this is valid only within the community of faith, inside the covenant of grace itself. That is, practically, in the degree to which parents recognize themselves as invested with such a ministry, to that extent they are not opposed to what God would do through their hands.

Thus, the fifth commandment leads us into the dialectic of *obedience* and *disobedience*. We are always in a critical position in relation to our parents and our children. Jesus declares, "He who loves father and mother more than me is not worthy of me" (Matt. 10:37). We live the fifth commandment within the crisis induced by sin. Family relationships do not escape suffering; they make us share in the drama of the cross.

Naturally in the crisis of sin the family can only deserve the famous apostrophe: "Families with closed hearths, I hate you!"

Family relationships must be lived in covenant so that they may be constantly purified anew by the cross of Jesus Christ. If such is the case, we will be able to share the enthusiasm of Luther: "What opportunity for good works you parents have in your home, in regard to your child whose needs are like those of the soul that is hungry and thirsty, is naked, poor, imprisoned and sick! Ah, what a happy marriage, and what a happy home that would be, blessed with such parents! In truth, it would be a true church, a choice fellowship, indeed even a paradise!" (*Op. cit.:* Weimar VI, p. 254; *Luther's Works,* Vol. 44).

❡ QUESTION 105.   *What does God require in the sixth commandment?*

That I am not to abuse, hate, injure, or kill my neighbor, either with thought, or by word or gesture, much less by deed, whether by myself or through another,[a] but to lay aside all desire for revenge;[b] and that I do not harm myself or willfully expose myself to danger.[c] This is why the authorities are armed with the means to prevent murder.[d]

a. Matt. 5:21-22. "You have heard that it was said to the men of old, 'You shall not kill; and whoever kills shall be liable to judgment.' But I say to you that everyone who is angry with his brother shall be liable to judgment; whoever insults his brother shall be liable to the council, and whoever says, 'You fool!' shall be liable to the hell of fire."

b. Rom. 12:19. Beloved, never avenge yourselves, but leave it to the wrath of God; for it is written, "Vengeance is mine, I will repay, says the Lord."

Cf. Eph. 4:26; Matt. 5:25, 39-40; 18:35.

c. Matt. 4:7. "You shall not tempt the Lord your God."
d. Rom. 13:4. The [governing authority] is God's servant for your good. But if you do wrong, be afraid, for he does not bear the sword in vain; he is the servant of God to execute his wrath on the wrongdoer.
Cf. Gen. 9:6; Matt. 26:52.

❡ QUESTION 106. *But does this commandment speak only of killing?*

In forbidding murder God means to teach us that he abhors the root of murder, which is envy,[a] hatred,[b] anger, and desire for revenge,[c] and that he regards all these as hidden murder.[d]

a. Gal. 5:19-21. The works of the flesh are plain . . . enmity, strife, jealousy, anger, selfishness, dissension, party spirit, envy. . . . I warn you, as I warned you before, that those who do such things shall not inherit the kingdom of God.
Cf. Rom. 1:29.
b. 1 John 2:9. He who says he is in the light and hates his brother is in the darkness still.
c. Rom. 12:19. Beloved, never avenge yourselves, but leave it to the wrath of God; for it is written, "Vengeance is mine, I will repay, says the Lord."
d. 1 John 3:15. Anyone who hates his brother is a murderer, and you know that no murderer has eternal life abiding in him.

❡ QUESTION 107. *Is it enough, then, if we do not kill our neighbor in any of these ways?*

No; for when God condemns envy, hatred, and anger, he requires us to love our neighbor as ourselves,[a] to show patience, peace, gentleness,[b] mercy,[c] and friendliness[d] toward him, to prevent injury to him as much as we can,[e] also to do good to our enemies.[f]

a. Matt. 22:39. "You shall love your neighbor as yourself."
Matt. 7:12. "Whatever you wish that men would do to you, do so to them; for this is the law and the prophets."
b. Rom. 12:10. Love one another with brotherly affection; outdo one another in showing honor.
Cf. Eph. 4:2; Gal. 6:1-2; Matt. 5:5.

175

c. Matt. 5:7. "Blessed are the merciful, for they shall obtain mercy." Cf. Luke 6:36.

d. Rom. 12:15-18. Rejoice with those who rejoice, weep with those who weep. Live in harmony with one another; do not be haughty, but associate with the lowly; never be conceited. Repay no one evil for evil, but take thought for what is noble in the sight of all. If possible, so far as it depends upon you, live peaceably with all.

e. Matt. 5:45. "Be sons of your Father who is in heaven; for he makes his sun rise on the evil and on the good, and sends rain on the just and on the unjust."

f. Matt. 5:44. "I say to you, Love your enemies and pray for those who persecute you."

Rom. 12:20-21. It is written, "If your enemy is hungry, feed him; if he is thirsty, give him drink; for by so doing you will heap burning coals upon his head." Do not be overcome by evil, but overcome evil with good.

You shall not kill. One could say of all the commandments of the Law that they remind us that nothing rightly belongs to us. That is particularly true of the sixth; in killing a man, we lay our hands upon a life that belongs only to God.

God created man in his own image. Each being, whatever may be his fallen state, is a reflection of this image. Neither in his own right nor by exercising the authority which God has entrusted to him can man do away with another man and thus reduce the image of God on earth to dimensions which appear to him expedient.

Moreover, every human being, no matter who he is, is a man whom God wants to save; each man whom God has called into being is destined to know and receive his grace in Jesus Christ.

Such are the basic reasons which absolutely forbid man to kill. The sixth commandment reminds us that God is the Lord and Master of life.

To the same extent that he stops confessing his faith in the Lord of life, man will have the pretension to arrogate to himself the right to kill "for just motives." One can never affirm it sharply enough: in God's order, there can be no just motives which would warrant taking the life of a man. Each time a human being is wiped out, witness is borne to the disorder of sin and not to the order of God and his grace.

One could not, therefore, agree with the Catechism of the Council of Trent that it is "certain that God does not oppose all kinds of killing since he does not forbid us to kill dumb animals. . . . Authorities are permitted to condemn even men to death. . . . For the same reason soldiers who kill their enemies in a just war are not guilty of homicide, because they do it in defense of their country" (Ch. VI, Questions iii, iv, v).

The very concepts of just wars and just motives have all now been seriously called into question again and will be all the more as the Christian church rediscovers the meaning of her absolute loyalty to the gospel of Jesus Christ. There arise in increasing numbers men who are called to bear witness against perversions to which the sixth commandment has been subject. In the degree to which they act out of a concern for absolute obedience to God, conscientious objectors must be listened to and their word must be received as a prophetic witness of the order of God in the midst of the world's disorder.

The embarrassed explanations of certain theologians trying to establish the right to kill according to the will of God indicate that the cause is indefensible. No one has the right to make an attempt upon the life of his neighbor under any circumstance.

The sixth commandment therefore, *condemns murder, capital punishment, war, and suicide.*

Thus, we cannot say with Luther: "Neither God nor the government is included in this commandment. . . . What is forbidden here applies to private individuals, not to governments" (*The Large Catechism,* p. 389; *The Book of Concord*).

No one can put himself above the commandment in order to justify his decision even if this behavior is made necessary by sin.

The responsibility of the church is to remind the state of this commandment, so that it will never forget that all life belongs to God and is for his glory.

To be sure, here again, this demand will keep the church in a state of permanent tension. She must never act as if she herself could claim to solve the crisis provoked by the rigor of evangelical witness. It was through the abuse of logic and undue anxiety to conform to the demands of the state that the reformers claimed to justify war or the death penalty, for example.

We are called upon to confess our faith in the absolute lordship of God manifested in Jesus Christ. The Christian does not yield to the temptations of worldly logicality. He does not say that war is necessary or inevitable, he proclaims *something else* in the name of Jesus Christ and of his Law.

Let us reaffirm that this commandment refers not only to murder in the bodily sense but likewise to all violence done to man and to the integrity of his person. It is thus that every *contempt of man* is already a murder.

Finally, let us never forget that Jesus likened anger to murder (Matthew 5:22).

We are *responsible* for the life of our neighbor. Not only must we allow him to live, but we must also help him live. The neighbor is the one who fell among robbers (Luke 10:30).

In the very extent to which he allows us to exercise mercy toward him, he reminds us that we too live only by virtue of this mercy. The neighbor in his very distress becomes a sign of God's mercy for us. This is essentially what creates the respect we owe to another's life: the neighbor is a Word of God for us.

"You shall love your neighbor as yourself." This commandment sums up the entire second table of the law.

❡ QUESTION 108. *What does the seventh commandment teach us?*

That all unchastity is condemned by God,[a] and that we should therefore detest it from the heart,[b] and live chaste and disciplined lives,[c] whether in holy wedlock or in single life.[d]

a. Gal. 5:19-21. The works of the flesh are plain: immorality, impurity, licentiousness. . . . I warn you, as I warned you before, that those who do such things shall not inherit the kingdom of God.
b. Jude 23. Save some, by snatching them out of the fire; on some have mercy with fear, hating even the garment spotted by the flesh.
c. 1 Thess. 4:3-4. This is the will of God, that you should be holy: you must abstain from fornication; each one of you must learn to gain mastery over his body, to hallow and honor it (N.E.B.).
d. Heb. 13:4. Let marriage be held in honor among all, and let the marriage bed be undefiled; for God will judge the immoral and adulterous.
   Cf. 1 Cor. 7:1-9, 25-28.

¶ QUESTION 109. *Does God forbid nothing more than adultery and such gross sins in this commandment?*

Since both our body and soul are a temple of the Holy Spirit, it is his will that we keep both pure and holy. Therefore he forbids all unchaste actions, gestures, words,[a] thoughts, desires,[b] and whatever may excite another person to them.[c]

a. Eph. 5:3-4. Fornication and indecency of any kind, or ruthless greed, must not be so much as mentioned among you, as befits the people of God. No coarse, stupid, or flippant talk; these things are out of place; you should rather be thanking God (N.E.B.).
Cf. 1 Cor. 6:18-20.
b. Matt. 5:27-29. "You have heard that it was said, 'You shall not commit adultery.' But I say to you that everyone who looks at a woman lustfully has already committed adultery with her in his heart. If your right eye causes you to sin, pluck it out and throw it away; it is better that you lose one of your members than that your whole body be thrown into hell."
c. Eph. 5:18. Do not get drunk with wine, for that is debauchery; but be filled with the Spirit.
Cf. 1 Cor. 15:33.

You shall not commit adultery. Marriage has been willed by God to put an end to the *loneliness* of man. In the order of creation, the union of man and woman is such that they are completely fulfilled in each other; they have no need of anything else. Man and woman are together in the most perfect *communion*. The institution of marriage is a sign of God's love for his people (Ephesians 5:21-33; Isaiah 62:5). As long as a man and a woman live in the communion of God, the marriage does not suffer any damage.

Temptation has always consisted of a promise of something better. Satan proposes to the man and the woman to withdraw from the order of God so that they may know something else. This is how disorder in the relationship of man with God is born and consequently in the relationships between man and woman. "The devil can make all the promises of God but he cannot keep them" (de Pury: *L'Ordre de Dieu*, p. 113).

Seduced by Satan, the man wanted another God and consequently another wife and the woman another husband. Formerly together in *communion*, they are now together in *separation*.

We quote Ramuz: "He says to himself: 'That's the curse.' He figures. They were now one and one, he and she. One and one, that makes two. But that's the curse, because one and one right now makes two but *at first* it made only one. . . . He sees that they are separated, and we are separated. He sees that they are estranged, and we are estranged" *(Adam and Eve)*.

Such is the actuality of Paradise Lost. The relationships between man and woman are the first to suffer from the separation of man from God. If God is no longer the Lord of man, there is no longer any possible communion between man and woman; not being faithful to God, they cannot be faithful to each other. In spite of all their efforts, man and woman cannot find communion again; being together becomes an irksome chore. The man, whose loneliness God wished to break, is alone again and involves the woman in an affliction similar to his own.

Adultery is therefore the desperate means of getting out of the infernal circle of being in solitude together. Madam Bovary is not frivolous; she is desperate. She believes there is something better and she is looking for it.

Nonetheless, even though man is unfaithful to God and as a result to his wife, God is faithful to him. He reveals to us in Jesus Christ that he forgives us even in our unfaithfulness.

It is from this forgiveness that conjugal life again becomes possible. Because God forgives me, I can forgive my mate. No more shall I say, It is her (his) fault! But it is my fault, it is our fault! I no longer look at my mate as a culprit and a perpetual offender while wrapping myself up in the morose contemplation of my broken happiness. I do not harp on my own righteousness. We both know that we are miserable and incapable of any good. We both know what we really are because God himself revealed our situation to us in Jesus Christ. We no longer have any illusions about each other; we do not put our trust in ourselves, in our own capabilities, as if we ourselves could save our married life from shipwreck. We put our trust in the grace of him who, while revealing our wretchedness to us, has made known to us at the same time his infinite mercy.

The cross is the reef on which conjugal illusions come to grief but it is also the only possibility of living together in the knowledge of sin *forgiven*. The cross makes forgiveness possible between man and woman and empowers them, whatever may happen, to recover their communion.

Premarital counseling should serve to make the young husband and wife conscious of this situation so that they do not enter into married life with the illusion that they will do "better than others" or that, if some difficulties arise, they will love one another enough to be able to overcome them all alone. The drama of sin is such that it can change the most beautiful love into hate.

The Christian home is the place where a man and a woman live solely by the faithfulness of God, on his mercy alone and through it alone.

Let us not get the idea, however, that all the rocks will be removed from their pathway. The Christian home knows the same difficulties as the nonchristian. It cannot be otherwise inasmuch as we live in the conditions of this world.

Only when a married life is lived in the full confidence of the mercy of God manifested in Jesus Christ, *is nothing ever lost*. On the contrary, everything is always saved by the faithfulness of God.

"Married life," says Roland de Pury, "should be compared to a couple of ropedancers. Whether it is a question of a Christian couple or a pagan couple . . . they find themselves facing the same dangers, the same struggle to keep their balance. It can even happen that the pagan family maintains it longer and that its harmony seems greater. The difference is not in the way in which they succeed in maintaining themselves and recovering themselves. The difference shines through on the day of the fall, the day on which the balance is lost. When the pagan couple falls, it falls without anything being able to hold it back; it is smashed to the earth by the weight of its double egoism, and the conjugal union is destroyed. The believing family also falls; the sin which lives in us makes it lose the equilibrium of the common life over and over again. *But then, it falls into the net of God's faithfulness.* It is securely held there. It can make mistakes but not be destroyed by the evil. The bottomless pit is filled up and the family picks up its conjugal life, with a broken and renewed heart" (*L'Ordre de Dieu,* p. 119).

Married life is, therefore, a succession of falls and recoveries (ups and downs), and it is necessary to know it. One must say also that the size and the frequency of the movement decrease in proportion as our experience with the faithfulness of God is enriched. One falls less far and also less often. The Christian couple tends, therefore, toward a final balance of their recovered communion. Such is the grace of God; it makes us recognize the conditions necessary for the life of God's kingdom in the midst of the sinful world.

Let us say, further, that the seal of the grace of God on a couple is *the child*. Moreover, although the seal may not be indispensable for believing in this grace, it is a sign of it.

Ultimately the child is the one who makes adultery impossible. If it is already grievous and fraught with consequences for one to be unfaithful to the mate God has given us, how much more is it so to be unfaithful to the child God gives us as a sign of his mercy!

God knows the causes of infidelity both for us and for our children; he does us the favor, therefore, of giving us this precise commandment: "You shall not commit adultery." In being faithful to each other a man and a woman announce to the world the possibility of human fidelity to God. In the struggles of their married life they proclaim the struggle and final victory of God in Jesus Christ. A faithful couple is a sign of the kingdom which is coming.

❮ QUESTION 110. *What does God forbid in the eighth commandment?*

He forbids not only the theft and robbery[a] which civil authorities punish, but God also labels as theft all wicked tricks and schemes by which we seek to get for ourselves our neighbor's goods, whether by force or under the pretext of right,[b] such as false weights[c] and measures,[d] deceptive advertising or merchandising,[e] counterfeit money, exorbitant interest,[f] or any other means forbidden by God. He also forbids all greed[g] and misuse and waste of his gifts.[h]

a. 1 Cor. 6:10. Nor thieves, nor the greedy, nor drunkards, nor revilers, nor robbers will inherit the kingdom of God.
   Cf. 1 Cor. 5:9-13.
b. Luke 3:14. Soldiers also asked him, "And we, what shall we do?"

And he said to them, "Rob no one by violence or by false accusation, and be content with your wages."

Cf. 1 Thess. 4:6.

c. Prov. 11:1. A false balance is an abomination to the Lord, but a just weight is his delight.

d. Ezek. 45:10. "You shall have just balances, a just ephah, and a just bath."

Cf. Deut. 25:13-16.

e. Prov. 12:22. Lying lips are an abomination to the Lord, but those who act faithfully are his delight.

f. Luke 6:35. "Love your enemies, and do good, and lend, expecting nothing in return; and your reward will be great, and you will be sons of the Most High; for he is kind to the ungrateful and the selfish."

Cf. Ps. 15:5.

g. Luke 12:15. He said to them, "Take heed, and beware of all covetousness; for a man's life does not consist in the abundance of his possessions."

Cf. 1 Cor. 6:10.

h. Luke 16:1-2. He also said to the disciples, "There was a rich man who had a steward, and charges were brought to him that this man was wasting his goods. And he called him and said to him, 'What is this that I hear about you? Turn in the account of your stewardship, for you can no longer be steward.' "

❢ QUESTION 111. *But what does God require of you in this commandment?*

That I work for the good of my neighbor wherever I can and may, deal with him as I would have others deal with me,[a] and do my work well so that I may be able to help the poor in their need.[b]

a. Matt. 7:12. "Whatever you wish that men would do to you, do so to them; for this is the law and the prophets."

b. Eph. 4:28. Let the thief no longer steal, but rather let him labor, doing honest work with his hands, so that he may be able to give to those in need.

Cf. Phil. 2:4.

You shall not steal. The eighth commandment is dominated by the promise of God to Abraham and through him to all the people of Israel. "I will give to you, and to your descendants after you, the land of your sojournings, all the land of Canaan, for an everlasting possession; and I will be their God" (Gen. 17:8; see also Leviticus 25:38; Numbers 34:2; Deuteronomy 32:49).

God is the owner and master of all things and it is he who gives to man all the goods he needs in order to live. Man is never more than a manager, one to whom God entrusts the responsibility of oversight. Moreover, the one who possesses something is accountable to God and to the neighbor for it. Calvin pleads: "We must remember that what each person possesses did not happen to him by fortuitous chance but by the choice of the one who is sovereign Master and Lord of all. This is why one cannot defraud anyone of these bounties, lest God's purpose for him be violated" (*Institutes,* Book I, Ch. XVI, pp. 197 ff.).

The promised land, the country of Canaan, has been given to Israel as a sign of the sovereignty and love of God. God does not want his own people to lack the necessities of life, and he *gives* these things to them for their use. But he remains the owner of them all: "The earth is the Lord's and the fullness thereof, the world and those who dwell therein" (Ps. 24:1).

All the legislation of Israel aims at safeguarding this right of God. "The land shall not be sold in perpetuity, for the land is mine; for you are all strangers and sojourners with me" (Lev. 25:23). This explains the stubbornness of Naboth in his refusal to Ahab: "The Lord forbid that I should give you the inheritance of my fathers" (1 King 21:3).

Everything belongs to God: "The silver is mine and the gold is mine, says the Lord of hosts" (Hag. 2:8).

Such is the basis of the economic morality which rises out of the providence of God. God intends to retain the ownership of everything, because he wants to have everything at his disposal for all his creatures.

In this perspective, we are far removed from economic theories based upon humanism and humanitarian concern. Everything was distorted in this domain the day that man claimed a right which belonged only to God. In robbing God, man has cheated his neighbor. At such a point one could say the situation has become so flagrant that "ownership is theft." So it is whenever God is no longer recognized and confessed as the Master and Lord of all things.

On the very day when we said with Jean Jacques Rousseau that "the earth belongs to no one," there began the economic and social difficulties in which we are still entangled today. By opposing one economic system to another, men are searching, without even realizing it, for a better organization of society to compensate for the initial mistake which was to make all systems inadequate, namely, that God is no longer acknowledged as the sole owner of all goods. It is man's responsibility to bear fruit to the glory of his Lord and for the welfare of other men. We blame the systems, but it is man himself who is indicted by the Word of God.

It is not without reason that one of the most secretive, mysterious, and inscrutable sectors of man's life has always been that of money. It is preeminently the subject about which one does not speak in company, and for a very good reason!

The falsification of life is always the result of man's lie to God. The deceit without equal consists in pretending to God and to men that we are administering his goods, whereas we have actually hoarded them for ourselves (Acts 5:1-11).

Luther has called attention to the fact that the eighth commandment covers practically every facet of social life: "This commandment involves an act which produces many good works and condemns numerous vices. That act is benevolence; thereby each one, while helping himself, is desirous of helping and of being of service to others. On the other hand, it not only fights against theft and extortion but also against all the depreciation which can be practiced against other people in regard to their worldly goods, for example, greed, usury, exorbitant taxes, exploitation, making use of deceptive merchandising, false weights and measures. And who could enumerate all those things, those little, sharp, new, and clever tricks of which the number increases daily in all industry, and by which each one seeks his advantage to the detriment of others, thereby denying the law?" (*Op. cit.:* Weimar VI, p. 270; *Luther's Works,* Vol. 44).

Our Christian vocation calls us to be witnesses of the new order established in this world by the grace of God in Jesus Christ, to the end that life may be possible for all men on earth.

"You shall not steal!" is really an echo of God saying, "I am the Lord your God who brought you out of the house of bondage."

The eighth commandment invites us to respond to this revelation in such a way that nothing ever escapes from this lordship.

❡ QUESTION 112. *What is required in the ninth commandment?*

That I do not bear false witness against anyone,[a] twist anyone's words,[b] be a gossip or a slanderer,[c] or condemn anyone lightly without a hearing.[d] Rather I am required to avoid, under penalty of God's wrath, all lying and deceit as the works of the devil himself.[e] In judicial and all other matters I am to love the truth, and to speak and confess it honestly.[f] Indeed, insofar as I am able, I am to defend and promote my neighbor's good name.[g]

a. Prov. 19:5. A false witness will not go unpunished, and he who utters lies will not escape.

b. Ps. 15:3, 5. [He] who does not slander with his tongue, and does no evil to his friend, nor takes up a reproach against his neighbor . . . shall never be moved.

c. Rom. 1:29-30. They were filled with all manner of wickedness, evil, covetousness, malice. Full of envy, murder, strife, deceit, malignity, they are gossips, slanderers, haters of God, insolent, haughty, boastful, inventors of evil, disobedient to parents.

d. Matt. 7:1. "Judge not, that you be not judged."
Cf. Luke 6:37.

e. John 8:44. "You are of your father the devil, and your will is to do your father's desires. He was a murderer from the beginning, and has nothing to do with the truth, because there is no truth in him. When he lies, he speaks according to his own nature, for he is a liar and the father of lies."
Prov. 12:22; 13:5. Lying lips are an abomination to the Lord, but those who act faithfully are his delight. . . . A righteous man hates falsehood, but a wicked man acts shamefully and disgracefully.
Cf. Lev. 19:11-12.

f. Eph. 4:25. Putting away falsehood, let everyone speak the truth with his neighbor, for we are members one of another.
Cf. 1 Cor. 13:6.

g. 1 Peter 4:8. Hold unfailing your love for one another, since love covers a multitude of sins.

You shall not bear false witness against your neighbor. "This commandment appears minor, and yet it is so great that whoever intends to respect it must necessarily take a risk and pledge his body and his life, his goods, his honor, his friends and all that he possesses, and yet it does no more than restrict the operation of this little organ that we call the tongue" (Luther: *Op cit.:* Weimar VI, p. 273; *Luther's Works,* Vol. 44).

While oftentimes one tends to make out of the ninth commandment a "minor" commandment, of very limited range, namely, against slander and particularly against false testimony before a court of justice, Luther has seen that there is involved here the whole question of the integrity of our life; the ninth commandment reminds us that the Christian is a man called upon to risk everything in the confession of his faith. In the ninth commandment we are faced with the responsibility of doing our share of the work of truth in the world. It is an extremely risky action. Luther said: "If the gospel were to revive and make itself heard again, the whole world without any doubt would come alive and blossom anew; but most of the kings, princes, bishops, doctors, ecclesiastics, and all the great ones would be in conflict with it and would be enraged, as has always happened when the Word of God has appeared in broad daylight; for the world cannot endure what comes from God" (*Op. cit.:* Weimar VI, p. 274; *Luther's Works,* Vol. 44).

The bearing witness of which the ninth commandment speaks is essentially and above all the witness which we have to make to the truth of God revealed in Jesus Christ, the witness par excellence. We cannot testify without reference to that Word. If we claim to contribute in this world a word that may be of our understanding, a completely personal testimony and based upon our conception of the truth for us, our testimony would already be false by definition and all the Pilates of this world will be right in asking also, "What is the truth?" (John 18:38).

The Christian must be *a witness to the truth* and know what that involves. We quote here some extracts from one of the most disturbing pages of Kierkegaard: "A witness to the truth is a man whose life from first to last is unacquainted with everything which is called enjoyment. . . . A witness to the truth is a man who in poverty witnesses to the truth—in poverty, in lowliness, in abasement; and so is unappreciated, hated, abhorred, and then derided, insulted, mocked—the daily bread of persecution he was richly provided with every day. . . . Verily there is that which is more contrary to Christianity, and to the very essence of Christianity, than any heresy, any schism, more contrary than all heresies and all schisms combined, and that is, to *play* Christianity. But precisely in the very same sense that the child plays soldier, it is playing Christianity to take away the danger (Christianly, 'witness' and 'risk' correspond), and in place of this to introduce power (to be a danger for others), worldly goods, advantages, luxurious enjoyment of the most exquisite refinements" (*Attack upon "Christendom,"* translated by Walter Lowrie, pp. 7-8).

Now, literally "to play at Christianity" is to pretend to testify to the truth without submitting oneself completely to this very truth. Kierkegaard stands with Luther here when he describes to us the risks of the Christian witness.

It is necessary to know this and to choose between the risk of human persecution if we obey God and the threat of divine judgment if we obey only men!

The ninth commandment invites us, therefore, in the first place, to believe and to confess, according to his Word, that God is true. The Christian witness is a confession of faith in God the Father, Son, and Holy Spirit. It is only then that our words will be trustworthy.

Because I know that God judges me and is gracious to me, condemns me and forgives me, humiliates me and exalts me, puts me to death with Christ and makes me live again with him, I also know that it is the same for my neighbor. Since God judges me and reprieves me, I shall never stand before my neighbor in the position of the righteous before the sinner, but as a man justified by the grace of God; and I shall know by God's own Word that the neighbor is what I am.

In the exact case where I shall be called to bear witness for or against my neighbor in a human court of justice, I shall not give in to my personal feelings of hate or pity; I shall submit my judgment to the truth of God himself in such a way that the words which come out of my mouth say nothing less and nothing more than what God himself says to me in Jesus Christ.

The ninth commandment reminds us that we are responsible

for our brothers. This is far from being a "minor" commandment. It concerns the whole of our life in the service of God.

Finally, it is not a question here of our freedom to judge, but
of the freedom of God himself, who, by his Word, wants to be
able to bear witness against all men and at the same time for
them.

17 / THE JOY OF THE RIGHTEOUS MAN

❰ QUESTION 113. *What is required in the tenth commandment?*

That there should never enter our heart even the least inclination or thought contrary to any commandment of God, but that
we should always hate sin with our whole heart and find satisfaction and joy in all righteousness.[a]

a. Rom. 7:7. What then shall we say? That the law is sin? By no
   means! Yet, if it had not been for the law, I should not have
   known sin. I should not have known what it is to covet if the
   law had not said, "You shall not covet."

You shall not covet . . . anything that is your neighbor's. The
current interpretation tends to belittle the import of the tenth
commandment by making disobedience of this command of God
no more than a mishap, and on the whole not very serious, for
which one consoles himself easily by saying to himself that every
man is envious of his neighbor and covets one thing or another.
The tenth commandment is reduced to the rank of a moral demand that no one can live up to.

Actually it is another matter entirely. This commandment
raises the question of the very foundation of our Christian life.
Let us quote Roland de Pury: "This tenth commandment reveals to us a dreadful secret. It is the look of the judge which
penetrates to the very source of our attitudes; it is the sword
which cuts asunder the veil of our best behavior. Right in the
middle of my best efforts to organize my life: You covet! declares
the judge. In all that you do to regain my paradise, it is covetousness that motivates you to it! Wasted effort! Effort utterly wasted!
I want nothing of what you bring to me like this. You pretend to

189

do my will, and your heart is full of self-interest, jealousy, and ulterior motives" (*L'Ordre de Dieu,* p. 176).

The tenth commandment calls into question the very reality of our life as men set free by Jesus Christ; it recalls us to the order of salvation by grace through faith alone. To covet means to want something else because we are not satisfied with what God gives us, because we do not believe that Jesus Christ has "fully paid for all [our] sins" (Question 1).

Covetousness is the sin of unsatisfiedness, that is, of unbelief. The one who covets does not believe that God has given him everything *gratis;* he does not believe that God loves him and consequently, he does not love God.

Such is the root of covetousness and this sin opens the door for all the others. Man, who is not satisfied with God, seeks for compensations. His imagination undertakes to open up for him more pleasing prospects—if only he possessed the house, the wife, the style of living, the car of his neighbor, he would be perfectly happy, perfectly satisfied; then in fact, he would be able to live, what is called "really living."

The one who covets wishes *to have* something else or *to be* someone else. For example, he imagines that if he were in this or that position which he knows well, he would really be the self he ought to be, that for which he was called and which up to the present he was not able to be, not having the opportunity to become so.

The life of the one who covets is a hell.

It happens that covetousness has some very lofty ambitions. Indeed, covetousness aspires to nothing less than to possess God himself. Such is the betrayal of religion. Jesus died under the burden of this ambition of men to lay hold of God and possess him: "This is the heir; come, let us kill him and have his inheritance" (Matt. 21:38).

Besides all the other sins, covetousness engenders the most serious one of all, namely, *hypocrisy.* Because we doubt the freely given salvation that God gives us in Jesus Christ, we believe that he ought to prove himself to us. We covet the salvation which God actually gives us. Thus "all our efforts will never succeed, except to give us *the best possible air of being what we*

190

are not" (de Pury: *L'Ordre de Dieu,* p. 183). We are not satisfied with God and we give ourselves the appearance of being so, while secretly resenting what he asks of us. Our Christian life ceases being an act of joyous gratitude, becoming no more than the most tedious of obligations.

Covetousness hollows out a ditch filled with hate between the Creator and his creature. It is precisely to fill up this ditch that Jesus Christ came into the world.

When God says to us, "You shall not covet!" he does not come to feed the fire of our covetousness by laying upon us an impossible demand; he reminds us that Jesus Christ came to put an end forever to all covetousness in us by giving us the fullness of God himself. It is only a question of our believing him.

All human covetousness submits to death at the foot of the cross. When men finally believed that they were able to possess God by nailing him to the cross, God showed them that he is not a God whom men can master; Christ is risen from the dead.

We cease to covet when we believe that the event of Good Friday and Easter means the total gift which God makes of himself to men.

Therefore, we have peace, peace in the heart, peace in the imagination, peace in the senses, the total peace of a man who knows that there is nothing more to covet from anyone, since he has received all there is from God.

To do the will of God becomes a joy and no longer an irksome task which we perform in spite of ourselves. "He who looks into the perfect law," says the Letter of James, "the law of liberty, and perseveres, being no hearer that forgets but a doer that acts, *he shall be blessed in his doing"* (1:25).

There is a delight in the Law that only man freed by Jesus Christ can know. We understand now the joy that bursts forth in the Psalm 119: "Lead me in the path of thy commandments for I delight in it—I find my delight in thy commandments, which I love—Oh, how I love thy law—thy testimonies are wonderful" (35, 47, 97, 129).

Yes, that is true. It is true that the God who satisfies us perfectly prevents us from coveting anymore. It is true that he makes us capable of doing his will in joy and in gratitude.

❡ QUESTION 114. *But can those who are converted to God keep these commandments perfectly?*

No, for even the holiest of them make only a small beginning in obedience in this life.[a] Nevertheless, they begin with serious purpose to conform not only to some, but to all the commandments of God.[b]

a. 1 John 1:8. If we say we have no sin, we deceive ourselves, and the truth is not in us.

Rom. 7:14. We know that the law is spiritual; but I am carnal, sold under sin.

b. Rom. 7:22. I delight in the law of God, in my inmost self.

James 2:10. Whoever keeps the whole law but fails in one point has become guilty of all of it.

❡ QUESTION 115. *Why, then, does God have the ten commandments preached so strictly since no one can keep them in this life?*

First, that all our life long we may become increasingly aware of our sinfulness,[a] and therefore more eagerly seek forgiveness of sins and righteousness in Christ.[b] Second, that we may constantly and diligently pray to God for the grace of the Holy Spirit, so that more and more we may be renewed in the image of God, until we attain the goal of full perfection after this life.[c]

a. 1 John 1:9. If we confess our sins, [God] is faithful and just, and will forgive our sins and cleanse us from all unrighteousness.

Cf. Ps. 32:5; Rom. 3:19; 7:7.

b. Rom. 7:24-25. Wretched man that I am! Who will deliver me from this body of death? Thanks be to God through Jesus Christ our Lord!

c. 1 Cor. 9:24. Do you not know that in a race all the runners compete, but only one receives the prize? So run that you may obtain it.

Cf. Phil. 3:12-14.

These two questions state precisely the aim of the Law and the possibility of our fulfilling it. To the question of knowing whether we can "keep these commandments perfectly," the Catechism replies with a "no" tempered by a "nevertheless."

The whole problem of the Law is set between these two terms. We cannot live the Law; nevertheless we actually do begin to live it all the same.

There is a before and an after in the Christian life and it is the cross of Jesus Christ that is the dividing line. When a man has died to himself he can henceforth do the will of God.

One must not neglect this "small beginning in obedience." It is there so that we "may be assured of our faith by its fruits" (Question 86). God gives us this grace to indicate to us by our works that we are on the right road to salvation, through faith alone. It is not the purpose, of course, that we glorify ourselves anew with these works, but only that we return thanks to God for granting them to us.

The Catechism states clearly that we "begin to conform not only to some but to all the commandments of God." The new life that God gives us in Jesus Christ concerns our whole being and consequently all our works. We cannot make some distinctions within the Law and claim to live one part of the commandments and not the others. This would be a sign that we were not yet liberated by Jesus Christ. We have seen it—the Law of God forms a whole and all the commandments recall us to the cross. Each commandment is in itself a preaching of the gospel of grace so that we may be reminded that by ourselves we are not able to do the will of God.

The Law helps us "become increasingly aware of our sinfulness." It makes us "pray for the grace of the Holy Spirit."

A right understanding of the Law and its role will prevent us from clinging to the arbitrary distinction which we used to think we had to make between the gospel and the Law, as if the God who speaks to us in the Old Testament were not the same as the one who speaks to us in the New. Jesus did not come "to abolish but to fulfill" (Matt. 5:17). The gospel is a piece of good news because Jesus Christ has fulfilled the Law in such a way that we can fulfill it in our turn.

God does not abandon us to hopelessness for not being able to do his will; he enables us to do it today in anticipation of the day when we shall do it perfectly in the kingdom. The Law is our hope through the gospel of Jesus Christ.

❪ QUESTION 116. *Why is prayer necessary for Christians?*

Because it is the chief part of the gratitude which God requires of us,[a] and because God will give his grace and Holy Spirit only to those who sincerely beseech him in prayer without ceasing, and who thank him for these gifts.[b]

a. Ps. 50:14-15. Offer to God a sacrifice of thanksgiving, and pay your vows to the Most High; and call upon me in the day of trouble; I will deliver you, and you shall glorify me.
b. Matt. 7:7-8. "Ask, and it will be given you; seek and you will find; knock, and it will be opened to you. For everyone who asks receives, and he who seeks finds, and to him who knocks it will be opened."
   Cf. Luke 11:9-13.

❪ QUESTION 117. *What is contained in a prayer which pleases God and is heard by him?*

First, that we sincerely call upon the one true God, who has revealed himself to us in his Word,[a] for all that he has commanded us to ask of him.[b] Then, that we thoroughly acknowledge our need and evil condition[c] so that we may humble ourselves in the presence of his majesty.[d] Third, that we rest assured[e] that, in spite of our unworthiness, he will certainly hear our prayer for the sake of Christ our Lord, as he has promised us in his Word.[f]

a. Ps. 145:18. The Lord is near to all who call upon him, to all who call upon him in truth.
   John 4:24. "God is Spirit, and those who worship him must worship in spirit and truth."
b. 1 John 5:14. This is the confidence which we have in [the Son of God], that if we ask anything according to his will he hears us.
   Cf. James 1:5; Rom. 8:26.
c. Isa. 66:2. "All these things my hand has made, and so all these things are mine, says the Lord. But this is the man to whom I will look, he that is humble and contrite in spirit, and trembles at my word."
   Cf. 2 Chron. 20:12.
d. 2 Chron. 7:14. "If my people who are called by my name humble themselves, and pray and seek my face, and turn from their wicked

ways, then I will hear from heaven, and will forgive their sin and heal their land."

e. James 1:6. Let him ask in faith, with no doubting, for he who doubts is like a wave of the sea that is driven and tossed by the wind.

f. Matt. 7:8. "Everyone who asks receives, and he who seeks finds, and to him who knocks it will be opened."

John 14:13-14. "Whatever you ask in my name, I will do it, that the Father may be glorified in the Son; if you ask anything in my name, I will do it."

Cf. Dan. 9:17-18; Rom. 10:13.

1. *Why is prayer necessary?* Prayer makes up one part of the gratitude which we owe to God; it is the essential expression of it. A Christian is by definition a man who prays.

The Catechism states that prayer is "the chief part of the gratitude which God requires of us." We forget this too often. We seek to express to God our gratitude but we do not know how to set about it. Remember that prayer is the chief part of gratitude; prayer is therefore the first act of a saved man.

To acknowledge or to be grateful means, literally, "to know again." The man who prays knows the God who is revealed to him in Jesus Christ. His prayer expresses his faith and shows that he continues to know God as he is enabled to know him. Prayer is therefore the sign of the constancy of faith. "Every man who knows God ought to be grateful to him" (Barth).

Be quite sure that prayer, understood as an act of everlasting gratitude, is the means of receiving the abundance of God's gifts. According to the language of the Catechism, God "will give his grace and Holy Spirit only to those who sincerely beseech him in prayer without ceasing, and who thank him for these gifts."

Prayer is therefore indispensable to the Christian life; it is as necessary to the life of faith as breathing is to the body. Each time that we pray we are encouraged to remember the work of God on our behalf so that we may thank him. Prayer is the response of man to the initiative of the divine love.

But if it is an act of gratitude, prayer is also *an act of anguish.* The man who knows God in Jesus Christ also knows himself through this revelation. Jesus Christ shows us what our true situation is in the presence of God. Prayer is an appeal for help. In the distress which is his and of which he receives the full revelation, man can do nothing other than pray; he cries for help. But he does it in faith, knowing from whence his help comes, that is, from "the Lord who made heaven and earth" (Ps. 121). To pray in deepest anguish is an act of confession of faith, made possible by the mercy of God in Jesus Christ.

In every way prayer is *a gift of God*. It is a favor which he bestows upon us, enabling us to share in his work among men. It will be helpful to quote here a very beautiful text of Luther, in the Large Catechism: "This we must know, that all our shelter and protection rest in prayer alone. We are far too feeble to cope with the devil and all his power and adherents that set themselves against us. Therefore we must consider and take up those weapons with which Christians must be armed in order to stand against the devil. What do you think has won such great victories over the undertakings of our enemies, whereby the devil thought to crush us together with the gospel, except that the prayers of a few devoted people intervened like a wall of iron on our side to protect us? Our enemies may deride and mock us. We shall nevertheless be a match both for them and the devil by prayer alone, if we persevere diligently and do not become slack. For we know that when a Christian prays, 'Dear Father, let thy will be done,' God replies to him, 'Yes, dear child, it shall be so in spite of the devil and the whole world'" (Part III, Prayer, Para. 31, quoted by Barth, *Prayer*, pp. 9-10).

In short, for all these reasons prayer is *an act of obedience* to God. "Prayer," said Luther, "is an obligation which God prescribes for us. Let no one imagine that praying is of little or no importance. To pray, in accordance with the second commandment, is to call upon God in all our needs. God demands that we pray, and has not left it to our choice. If we want to be Christians we must pray" (Barth: *Op. cit.*, Para. 7).

So it is that every individual whim and every selfish extravagance is excluded from prayer. True prayer can be identified only in the context of the drama of divine-human encounter within which God's will for us is revealed. It is an act of obedience to God and not a natural inclination of the heart of man. We must ask ourselves, when we pray, whether we are praying in obedient faithfulness or in infidelity, in submission to God or in search of self-glorification. The will of God as manifested in Jesus Christ is the test.

Finally, prayer is the very act of the man whose faith makes it possible for him to live with confidence. Indeed, Jesus said, "When the Son of man comes will he find faith on earth?" (Luke 18:8). The defects of our prayer are those of our faith. We can only pray in full and complete gratitude toward the God and Father of our Lord Jesus Christ. The man who prays knows what he has received from God and that he has the right to expect everything from him. Prayer is the act of a faith that is consistent.

2. *How ought one to pray?* The reformers, like the authors of the Heidelberg Catechism, insisted that the Christian should pray *from the bottom of the heart.* Of course, they did not intend to offer a reward for sentimental debauchery. This sort of thing would have been entirely out of keeping with God and his glory.

By these words, "from the bottom of the heart," the reformers intended that the believer pray *in faith,* that is to say, in the knowledge of and in gratitude toward the one to whom he prays. This is the way in which the two greatest dangers threatening prayer may be avoided: rote and empty phrases. "The way to pray," says Luther, "is the use of few words, but with depth of meaning and conviction. The fewer the words, the better is the prayer; the more words the worse the prayer: a small number of words and depth of meaning is Christian, multiplicity of words with little meaning is pagan" (*Explanation of the Lord's Prayer,* 1519: Weimar, II, p. 81; *Luther's Works,* Vol. 42).

The believer must pray in the presence of God; he must take seriously both his anguish and the mercy of God. To the question "What kind of feeling should we have in prayer?" Calvin's Catechism replies: "First, we must feel our wretchedness and poverty, and this feeling must beget sorrow and anguish in us. Second, we must have a burning desire to obtain grace from God. This desire will also kindle our hearts, and engender in us an ardent longing to pray" (No. 243).

Let us note that the reformers make no distinction between the so-called liturgical prayer and the so-called spontaneous prayer. The question of the legitimacy of these two forms of prayer is not even asked by the one who prays "in the presence of God." It will not be a matter of choosing one manner of praying to the exclusion of the other, but of our always asking whether we are actually praying in the presence of God. Some prayers are horizontal and others are vertical. True prayer belongs to the second category, whatever its form may be. Is it necessary to add that the danger of rote practice threatens spontaneous prayer as well as liturgical prayer? Thus spontaneous prayer must tend toward objectivity and the liturgical prayer must be prayed with "affection," "from the heart," and not merely with the lips.

As to the command that the apostle Paul gives *to pray constantly* (1 Thessalonians 5:17), it can be understood in two ways: either as a recommendation to pray as often as possible, at every opportunity, or as an invitation to make one's entire life an act of prayer. Calvin said: "The tongue is not always necessary but there must always be understanding and affection" (*Geneva Catechism,* No. 240). We can pray either "verbally," that is, explicitly, by formulating for ourselves or for others the content of the prayer which we bring to God, or "in spirit," that is, implicitly in silence. Luther warns us against the dangers inherent in this latter way: "No one ought to rely on his heart alone and want to pray without words, unless he is well trained in spirit and knows, from experience, how to shut out alien thoughts; otherwise, the devil would completely seduce him and would soon have destroyed the prayer in his heart. Moreover, one must hold on to the words and be lifted up by resting back upon them, until the feathers have grown and one knows how to soar without the aid of words" (*Op. cit.:* Weimar II, p. 85; *Luther's Works,* Vol. 41).

Implicit prayer is legitimate but one must use it with discretion since inevitably it allows for distraction much more than does explicit prayer. As a general rule it is better to formulate the prayer that we are offering up to God, and to accept as a favor the fact of being able, in certain circumstances, to pray in silence.

Our whole life must be an act of prayer. There is no hiding the fact that it takes time. "As sparingly as one begins to pray, by some silent signs, by prayer at the table, by a short verse, morning and night—even these crude beginnings involve a regularity and already prayer takes up time. . . . This is not at all surprising, for prayer is a claim of God upon our life. . . . Modern man in particular has his time occupied. He views this situation as the working of blind fate. . . . But there is more than an impersonal fate involved here: there is a human fault. . . . The person who lets the time for prayer slip by, neglects time for himself. . . . Prayer, when we practice it, hinges the day together. . . . Whoever begins to conquer time by prayer, to master it by marshaling it, that man learns by what struggle he will come through. To win this war, we must 'bring forth fruit with patience' (Luke 8:15)" (Hans Asmussen: *Le Combat de la Prière*, p. 29).

The command to pray without ceasing is a constant reminder of the limits of possibility and of impossibility in our Christian life.

❡ QUESTION 118. *What has God commanded us to ask of him?*

All things necessary for soul and body[a] which Christ the Lord has included in the prayer which he himself taught us.

a. James 1:17. Every good endowment and every perfect gift is from above, coming down from the Father of lights with whom there is no variation or shadow due to change.
Matt. 6:33. Seek first [your heavenly Father's] kingdom and his righteousness, and all these things shall be yours as well.

❡ QUESTION 119. *What is the Lord's Prayer?*

"OUR FATHER WHO ART IN HEAVEN, HALLOWED BE THY NAME. THY KINGDOM COME, THY WILL BE DONE, ON EARTH AS IT IS IN HEAVEN. GIVE US THIS DAY OUR DAILY BREAD; AND FORGIVE US OUR DEBTS, AS WE ALSO HAVE FORGIVEN OUR DEBTORS; AND LEAD US NOT INTO TEMPTATION, BUT DELIVER US FROM EVIL, FOR THINE IS THE KINGDOM AND THE POWER AND THE GLORY, FOREVER. AMEN."[a]

a. Matt. 6:9-13.
Cf. Luke 11:2-4.

3. *To whom must we pray?* God manifests the extent of his steadfast love for us by teaching us himself the manner in which we must and can pray to him. We are not free to do or be what we please. *The Law* tells us what is pleasing to God and how he

wants to be served in gratitude. *The Lord's Prayer* indicates to us how God wants to be sought in gratitude.

"If we followed our own fantasy," says Calvin, "our prayers would be very badly ordered. We are so ignorant that we cannot judge what is good to ask; moreover, all our desires are so unruly that we must not give them free rein" *(Geneva Catechism,* No. 253).

The Lord's Prayer is the pattern and model of every prayer prayed in faith. This does not mean that we are limited to praying nothing but the "Our Father." Rather it means that all prayers ought to be inspired by it; the Lord's Prayer includes "all things necessary for body and soul," according to the teaching of Jesus Christ himself.

Our Lord's Prayer reveals to us who the God is to whom we ought to pray and what we can ask of him in accordance with his will. It is the prayer of Christ, the one which he has spoken for us and with us as true man in the presence of God, and which he teaches to men as true God among men. In praying the Lord's Prayer, we pray the prayer which God can accept from men since we are praying with Christ.

This prayer comprises an invocation, six petitions, and a doxology glorifying the name of God. The first three petitions concern the glory of God, the other three are related to our good. Since, however, the good which we seek from God through Jesus Christ is in accordance with his will, all six of the petitions included in the Lord's Prayer concern the glory of God.

Remember that the Lord's Prayer permits us to ask for "all things necessary for soul and body." This is the prayer of the man whose debt had been "fully paid" (Question 1) by the gift of the righteousness of God in Jesus Christ. Such is the prayer of faith; it knows that the petition is already granted.

19 / OUR LORD'S PRAYER

❑ QUESTION 120. *Why has Christ commanded us to address God: "Our Father"?*

That at the very beginning of our prayer he may awaken in us the childlike reverence and trust toward God which should be the motivation of our prayer, which is that God has become our Father through Christ and will much less deny us what we ask him in faith than our human fathers will refuse us earthly things.[a]

a. Matt. 7:9-11. "What man of you, if his son asks him for a loaf, will give him a stone? Or if he asks for a fish, will give him a serpent? If you then who are evil, know how to give good gifts to your children, how much more will your Father who is in heaven give good things to those who ask him?"
Cf. Luke 11:11-13.

❡ QUESTION 121. *Why is there added: "who art in heaven"?*

That we may have no earthly conception of the heavenly majesty of God,[a] but that we may expect from his almighty power all things that are needed for body and soul.[b]

a. Jer. 23:23-24. "Am I a God at hand, says the Lord, and not a God afar off? Can a man hide himself in secret places so that I cannot see him? says the Lord. Do I not fill heaven and earth? says the Lord."
Cf. Acts 17:24-25.
b. Rom. 8:32. He who did not spare his own Son but gave him up for us all, will he not also give us all things with him?
Cf. Rom. 10:12.

Our Father. Without the revelation of God in Jesus Christ, this *invocation* would be impossible. Actually, these words are our response to God's approach. Unaided, we cannot say to God: "Our Father." When we stand by ourselves, we feel estranged from him; we fear and hate him (Question 5). By ourselves, therefore, we cannot put our trust in "our Father who art in heaven." We persist in looking for other sources of security, whereas Jesus Christ alone can make it possible for us to say "our Father" in the full sense of the word and with full confidence in his faithfulness. According to an expression of Luther in his *Explanation of the Lord's Prayer,* Jesus Christ helps us ascend to heaven by "taking us into his skin and on his back" (Weimar II, p. 84; *Luther's Works,* Vol 41). When we say "our Father" we are literally carried by Christ. We have full confidence in the one to whom we pray and the hearing which he accords us. Jesus Christ opens for us the communion with God which alone makes prayer possible.

As to the name "Father," it is most adequate, the one which best fits God at the time when he comes to us to enable us to pray to him. "Our God gives himself a name, which suggests only gentleness and kindness, in order to take away from us all doubt and anxiety, and to give us boldness in coming to him personally" (Calvin: *Geneva Catechism*, No. 260).

On the one hand we fear God, as we must fear our father according to God's own will; but on the other hand, because we can have confidence in him we pray to him with boldness and familiarly.

Notice also that the first word that Christ teaches his followers is in the plural: *"Our* Father."* We are not alone; we pray with all those whom God invites to share the gift of his grace in Jesus Christ; we pray in the "communion of saints," with those who already pray, but also in the communion of those who do not pray as yet. God is also their Father.

"Before praying, then, I first seek the company of other men. I know that all of you are facing the same difficulties as I. Let us therefore consult with one another and mutually give what we are able. However, we cannot put our trust in fellow creatures. There may be a few men capable of telling us what we need, or at least of giving us certain indications. But the gift itself can come from God alone" (Barth: *Prayer,* pp. 19-20).

Finally, this "our" indicates the involvement of all men whose Father is God. When we say "our Father" we remind each other that we are all interdependent; we acknowledge and we confess that we are responsible for all our neighbors. Thus true prayer, prayer according to the teaching of Christ, does not isolate us. In restoring our Father to us, Jesus Christ gives us back all our brothers.

Who art in heaven. The words *in heaven* make it clear that this Father whom we can approach with boldness and personally is not, however, a God whom we can have for our own use. At the very moment that he shares with us the fatherhood of God, Jesus Christ reminds us of his sovereignty. Although he is our Father and has decided because he loves us to make us share in all the benefits of our adoption, God remains different and beyond our reach. It is on this account that he can be truly "for us" (Rom. 8:31).

Thus God is revealed as "Our Father who art in heaven," "so that," as Calvin's Catechism says, "when we call upon him, we may learn to lift up our thoughts on high, and not to have any carnal or earthly thoughts of him, not to measure him by our apprehension, nor to subject him to our will; but to adore his glorious majesty in humility. It teaches us to have more reliance on him, since he is governor and master of all" (No. 265).

This is also the basis of the doctrine of divine providence.

❡ QUESTION 122. *What is the first petition?*

"Hallowed be thy name." That is: help us first of all to know thee rightly,[a] and to hallow, glorify, and praise thee in all thy works through which there shine thine almighty power, wisdom, goodness, righteousness, mercy, and truth.[b] And so order our whole life in thought, word, and deed that thy name may never be blasphemed on our account, but may always be honored and praised.[c]

a. John 17:3. "This is eternal life, that they know thee the only true God, and Jesus Christ whom thou hast sent."
   Cf. Jer. 9:23-24; Matt. 16:17; Ps. 119:105; James 1:5.
b. Ps. 119:137. Righteous art thou, O Lord, and right are thy judgments.
   Cf. Rom. 11:33-36.
c. Pss. 71:8; 115:1. My mouth is filled with thy praise, and with thy glory all the day. . . . Not to us, O Lord, not to us, but to thy name give glory, for the sake of thy steadfast love and thy faithfulness!

Hallowed be thy name. Jesus Christ is the full and complete manifestation of the name which God had revealed to Moses. Jesus Christ himself is the name of God among men.

To hallow the name of God means in the first place "rightly to know God," the God who in Jesus Christ has given his name to men so that they know him. This hallowing could not take place in a vacuum. Luther was right in saying that "this prayer struggles against that abominable pride which forms the head, life, and innermost essence of all sinfulness" (*Op. cit.:* Weimar II, p. 95; *Luther's Works,* Vol. 41).

We are preoccupied, first of all, with our name, and concern for the name of God scarcely engages our attention. We take care of the reputation of our name, thinking, more or less consciously, that the reputation of God's name concerns him alone and that he has only to do for his name what we strive to do for ours.

Now, the incarnation of God in Jesus Christ means that the holy God renounces the isolation of his holiness in order to come and mingle with men. In Jesus Christ the holiness of God comes down to be with men who henceforth are going to be held responsible for it. A believer is a man who, since the day of his baptism, has agreed to bear the responsibility of the name of God the Father, the Son, and the Holy Spirit before men.

One must insist with more force than ever that the Christian witness in the world is bound up with the name of Jesus Christ. Neither nature, nor conscience, nor the heart of man can of themselves make the name of God known. It is not enough simply to be a man, to hallow the name of God among men. It is necessary to have been baptized into the death and resurrection of Jesus Christ so that our humanity no longer speaks of itself, in pride and vanity, but only of God's compassion and steadfast love for us. Then, and only then, can our witness to the world, as believers, truly serve to make the name of God known; and then the name of God will be hallowed on earth.

It is absolutely necessary to be clear, however, that the holy God sanctifies us himself by Jesus Christ in order that we can in our turn hallow him among men. Luther said: "Observe that the name of God is holy in itself and that it is not sanctified by us; what is more, it is he who sanctifies all things who makes us holy also" (*Op. cit.:* Weimar II, p. 87; *Luther's Works,* Vol. 41).

The question of hallowing the name of God is essentially and before everything else the concern of preaching. "Hallowed be thy name" means in the first place: "Give us excellent preaching of thy Word. Would that we might truly hear it and welcome it in such a way that thy name shall be hallowed among men."

Praying the first petition of the Lord's Prayer is actually asking God to bring about, in his church, the miracle of a true confession, a true consideration of his Word, so that it and it alone should be taken seriously. That will mean, says Barth, that "we stop leafing through the Bible instead of reading it. May we moderate a little our habit of quoting the Bible, instead of living with it and of letting it speak. May we pray that the Bible will not cease holding our attention. May the Bible not begin to make us yawn, and thy Word, in all its parts, not become a boring matter in our minds and in our mouths. May it not become a bad sermon, a bad catechism, a bad theology. All these remarks are very simple but also quite necessary. A bad sermon is the opposite of this hallowing" (*Prayer,* p. 45).

The church must live in this world out of what she has received in Jesus Christ. "May God's Word," says Barth, "become anew for us each day the Word of God. May it not be a truth, a principle, something which one places on the table, but a living person, the great mystery and the great simplicity" (*Ibid.*).

By praying thus, we ask for a true humility, that is, the capacity to accept simply what God tells us and that it is he who speaks to men and not we. By praying "Hallowed be thy name" we proclaim our will to take God quite seriously with full confidence in his faithfulness so that our lives bear the mark of authenticity, that men may know that the Word of God is true, and that Jesus Christ has come to declare the righteousness and steadfastness of God's love for us. We ask God that we may live in peace and in joy, since it would appear that life is actually possible in this world where the name of God is already hallowed by the Word, attested by Jesus Christ.

❡ QUESTION 123. *What is the second petition?*

"Thy kingdom come." That is: so govern us by thy Word and Spirit that we may more and more submit ourselves unto thee.[a] Uphold and increase thy church.[b] Destroy the works of the devil, every power that raises itself against thee, and all wicked schemes thought up against thy holy Word,[c] until the full coming of thy kingdom[d] in which thou shalt be all in all.[e]

a. Matt. 6:33. "Seek first [your heavenly Father's] kingdom and his righteousness, and all these things shall be yours as well."

Ps. 119:5. O that my ways may be steadfast in keeping thy statutes!

b. Ps. 51:18. Do good to Zion in thy good pleasure; rebuild the walls of Jerusalem.

c. 1 John 3:8. He who commits sin is of the devil; for the devil has sinned from the beginning. The reason the Son of God appeared was to destroy the works of the devil.
Cf. Rom. 16:20.

d. Rev. 22:17. The Spirit and the Bride say, "Come." And let him who hears say, "Come." And let him who is thirsty come, let him who desires take the water of life without price.
Cf. Rom. 8:22-24.

e. 1 Cor. 15:20, 28. In fact Christ has been raised from the dead, the first fruits of those who have fallen asleep. . . . When all things are subjected to him, then the Son himself will also be subjected to him who put all things under him, that God may be everything to every one.

Thy kingdom come. "By this petition, the church goes straight to the goal and does not beat around the bush. If she knew what she was asking, she would not dare to pray thus. She asks for the downfall of Babylon, the city which men build on oppression, greed, and deception, the ruin of all that men raise up for themselves, and the upbuilding of Jerusalem, the city which God founded on truth, righteousness, and love" (de Pury: *Notre Père,* p. 50).

When the church prays the second petition of the Lord's Prayer, she affirms thereby that she does not believe the kingdoms of this world are ultimate. The church believes in the kingdom of God manifested in Jesus Christ (Mark 1:15; Luke 17:21, "in the midst of you").

What the Christian church hopes for has nothing in common with a blind optimism, the kind that is always ready to change into the depths of despair. No, the church believes in the kingdom which has come and will come. Her hope is completely bound to the person of Jesus Christ. The church believes that he will "make all things new" (Rev. 21:5); she believes in a "new heaven" and in a "new earth" (2 Peter 3:13; Rev. 21:1). The church of Jesus Christ knows that from now on her destiny is absolutely bound to that of her Lord. Just as Jesus died and arose from the dead, so the church and the world with her shall have to pass through death and resurrection in order that the "reign of God" may come. The old world will not be transformed, neither will it be improved, adjusted, or reorganized. No, it will literally be *recreated*.

In the world, the Christian man witnesses for the kingdom of God as the revolution par excellence. Without being an anarchist, which is a desperate form of protesting, he will never be able to judge that the actual situation of the world is satisfactory; he awaits "the new heaven and the new earth." Besides, his entire demeanor will be marked by a total availability to the commands of his Lord; the testimony of his life already proclaims the great revolution of the kingdom.

"We do not pray, saying: Beloved Father, make us submit to thy kingdom, as if we had to run after him, but rather: May thy kingdom come to us. In fact, the grace of God and his righteous kingdom, just like all values, must come to us if we want to obtain them; we could never go to them; just as Christ came down from heaven to us, and it was not we who climbed up from earth to him in heaven" (Luther: *Op. cit.:* Weimar II, p. 98; *Luther's Works,* Vol. 41).

The second petition of the Lord's Prayer obliges us to consider the kingdom of God as an eschatological reality, that is to say, as bound up with the return of Jesus Christ. Even if, by the grace of God, this kingdom can become actual to the same degree as our obedience, our works will always be but tokens of the kingdom and not the reality itself.

Prayer always refers us from an event already accomplished to an event which is to come. In Jesus Christ the kingdom of God has come; the church lives in the power of this good news, but the consummation of the kingdom is still in the future.

On account of the death, resurrection, and ascension of Jesus Christ, the church is sure of what she preaches; she knows that she does not wait in vain; she is not on the wrong track; she is not going in the wrong direction; she knows that "all is fulfilled" and that the day will come when she shall receive the reward for her obedience and the constancy of her faith. Christmas, Good Friday, Easter, and Pentecost are not ordinary events to which we would give a mere religious significance. . . . "No! They are not nothing. They are all that has happened and stands behind us. Thereby, we proclaim the Word made flesh, and we announce the kingdom of God which has come. When, however, the church is not jubilant, when she is not sure of her significance, she cannot be insistent and she is not insistent. A sad and gloomy church is not the church; for the church is built upon him . . . who has come to say the last word (not the next to the last). This last word has already been uttered. We live upon this event. There is nothing more in it to be changed" (Barth: *Prayer*, pp. 48-49).

The church can only pray while resting upon what she already knows and must never forget. All the work the church does— preaching, administering the sacraments, teaching the catechism —has for its goal keeping alive the knowledge of the kingdom which has already come in Jesus Christ.

The Christian church is never discouraged, no matter what may be the conflict she undergoes on account of her own infidelity or that of the world. God's victory is already won and his final triumph does not depend upon the church. She must only take care that her testimony may be of service in setting up, in the midst of the world, the signs of the kingdom which is coming, so that men can believe in the authority and power of him who is already the Lord of the church.

We will never forget that the church *is not* the kingdom of God. The Catechism of the Council of Trent says: "We beg, therefore, of God, that the kingdom of Christ, that is, his church, may be propagated," and again: "It is not enough that we pray for the kingdom of God, unless men also give their best attention and exertions to its attainment. We must cooperate with the grace of God, in pursuing that course which leads to heaven" (Ch. XI, Questions xii and xviii).

It is worthwhile to quote, in this regard, from the text of Calvin's Catechism, in order that we may rejoice in having been freed, by the preaching of the gospel, from the anxiety of achieving the kingdom of God ourselves here on earth: *"In what sense do you pray that this kingdom may come?* That day by day *the Lord* may increase the number of the faithful, that day by day he may increasingly bestow his graces upon them, until he has fulfilled them completely; moreover, that he cause his truth to shine more and more and manifest his justice, so that Satan and the powers of darkness may be put to confusion, and all iniquity be destroyed and abolished" (*Geneva Catechism*, No. 269).

No, thank God, the kingdom of God is not our affair and the church, whatever it may be, is not the kingdom of God. She can only proclaim it and ask God always to do her the favor of making her proclaim it truthfully. It is with this conviction that Karl Barth could say: "We pray in order that we may receive the gift of seeing the uselessness of this tragic sense which befits the pagans, but not the Christians. May we live at once in tranquillity, in good humor, and in the love that constrains no one, but which may in some way attract a few people" (*Prayer*, p. 51).

¶ QUESTION 124. *What is the third petition?*

"Thy will be done, on earth, as it is in heaven." That is: grant that we and all men may renounce our own will[a] and obey thy will, which alone is good, without grumbling,[b] so that everyone may carry out his office and calling as willingly and faithfully[c] as the angels in heaven.[d]

a. Matt. 16:24. Jesus told his disciples, "If any man would come after me, let him deny himself and take up his cross and follow me."
   Cf. Titus 2:12.
b. Luke 22:42. "Father, if thou art willing, remove this cup from me; nevertheless not my will, but thine, be done."
   Cf. Rom. 12:2; Eph. 5:10.
c. 1 Cor. 7:24. Brethren, in whatever state each was called, there let him remain with God.
d. Ps. 103:20. Bless the Lord, O you his angels, you mighty ones who do his word, hearkening to the voice of his word!

Thy will be done, on earth, as it is in heaven. This third petition reminds us that Christian faith involves us in a strict obedience. When we pray, we ask that something may actually happen, and first of all in our own lives. This prayer can never become an escape into which we flee from the troublesome demands of the Christian witness.

The third petition of the Lord's Prayer requires us to take seriously the faith which we confess so that our acts of obedience will proclaim the kingdom which is coming. Even though the kingdom is really God's business and his dominion, we are not excused from doing what depends upon us; it is our duty to raise up signs of the kingdom of God among men. "Christian obedience is an anticipation of the kingdom; it is a verification of the fact that we take our hope seriously, for can one truly wait for something, can one really desire the presence of someone, without acting in his absence as if he were present? We would not really be anticipating the kingdom if we were not making right now every effort to live as citizens of the new age by doing the will of God on earth, that is to say, if our expectation of the kingdom were not a continual straining toward this kingdom in all that we did" (de Pury: *Notre Père,* p. 57).

It is important to pay attention to this: to say "May thy will be done" does not mean to sink into passivity or resignation. We ask that the will of God actually be done, but that this really be his will. We do not give up doing it; we ask God that what we do actually express his will and no longer ours. The Catechism of Calvin says: "In so doing, do we not renounce our own wills?" and answers, "We do, not only that he may overthrow our desires, which are at variance with his own good will, bringing them all to nought; but also that he may create in us new spirits and new hearts, so that we may will nothing of ourselves, but rather that his Spirit may will in us, and bring us to full agreement with him" (No. 273).

Our will is not annihilated, but our obedience must be such that our actions will always be in agreement with God's own will. Luther said: "Yes, to be sure, (God) has given you a free will. But why, then, do you want to change it over into your own will and not allow it to be free? If you do what you want with it, it is not free, but becomes yours" (*Op. cit.:* Weimar II, p. 104; *Luther's Works,* Vol. 41).

When we pray, "May thy will be done," we confess before God and before men that we do not claim the use of our will for ourselves; we ask God to make it, like everything else, serve to glorify his name alone.

Luther observed that God makes use of this prayer to teach us that "we have no greater enemy than ourselves" (*Op. cit.:* Weimar II, p. 105; *Luther's Works,* Vol. 41).

This third petition is our prayer of self-renunciation. Paraphrasing it Luther says: "O Father, let me not fall so low that my will may be done. Break my will, put obstacles in the way of my will, come what may, so that not my will but thine be done. For, just as it is in heaven, where there is no will of one's own, so may it be also on earth" (*Ibid.*).

Let us never forget that the obedience of Jesus Christ is the norm for all obedience to God. Our obedience must be in the image of that which he himself practiced and still practices "in heaven." No more than Jesus Christ has claimed to assume personally the consequences of his obedience, do we have to do it. We must do what God asks of us according to his Word, rejecting any kind of consideration which might keep us from it. If this will appears difficult for us to discern in a particular instance, let us consult the others in the church. The Christian community ought to be such that a sincere search for the will of God will be possible within its fellowship. The Christian is not an isolated individual. He is not a lonely prey to all the difficulties which accompany the struggle to be loyal to the faith; the believer becomes a member of the body of Christ.

The third petition of the Lord's Prayer reminds us that in this world we have the responsibility to be the church of Jesus Christ and nothing else. "May we cease contradicting and falsifying the gospel again and again, in an attempt to make of it a new kind of law. May we renounce behaving like bad servants. May we employ thy patience for our conversion instead of toying with a humanistic Christianity and a Christian humanism, instead of continually provoking thy wrath. In the execution of thy plan, liberate us from this endless imperfection of our obedience. Come to give us freedom and, some day, extricate us from these contradictions in which we find ourselves—we who know that thy will is done and how it is done in heaven" (Barth: *Prayer*, p. 54).

This is truly all that we ask when we pray, "Thy will be done, on earth, as it is in heaven."

❡ QUESTION 125. *What is the fourth petition?*

"Give us this day our daily bread." That is: be pleased to provide for all our bodily needs[a] so that thereby we may acknowledge that thou art the only source of all that is good,[b] and that without thy blessing neither our care and labor nor thy gifts can do us any good.[c] Therefore, may we withdraw our trust from all creatures and place it in thee alone.[d]

a. Ps 104:27-28. These all look to thee, to give them their food in due season. When thou givest to them, they gather it up; when thou openest thy hand, they are filled with good things.
Cf. Matt. 6:25-34.

b. Acts 14:17. "He did not leave himself without witness, for he did good and gave you from heaven rains and fruitful seasons, satisfying your hearts with food and gladness."
Cf. Acts 17:25.

c. 1 Cor. 15:58. My beloved brethren, be steadfast, immovable, always abounding in the work of the Lord, knowing that in the Lord your labor is not in vain.
Cf. Deut. 8:3; Pss. 37:3-11, 16-17; 127:1-2.

d. Ps. 55:22. Cast your burden on the Lord, and he will sustain you; he will never permit the righteous to be moved.
Cf. Pss. 62:8, 10; 146:3.

Give us this day our daily bread. In requiring us to say, "Give us," Jesus is helping us not to forget that we are creatures. Our old man (Adam) is thus alerted to the command of God who wants everything to depend upon him and him alone. The fourth petition is the practical consequence of the first three: the man called to confess rightly the God of Jesus Christ so that he may hallow his name, the man who puts all his hope in the king who has already come and is coming, and who completely surrenders his will into the hands of his Lord, that man can only say to God also, "Give us," and count upon his faithfulness with full confidence, absolute and unconditional. By this petition we are brought back to the concrete sphere of our daily existences, and it is at that level that the testing of our faith is brought about. Facing the realities of life, and no longer abstraction, will we have the courage to pray, "Give us this day our daily bread"?

What is this bread that we have to ask for? Luther, in his Small Catechism, understood it to mean, "everything required to satisfy our bodily needs, such as food and clothing, house and home, fields and flocks, money and property; a pious spouse and good children, trustworthy servants, godly and faithful rulers, good government, seasonable weather, health, order, and honor; true friends, faithful neighbors and the like" (*The Book of Concord*, p. 347).

To be sure, this first and mainly physical meaning of the word bread is not to be underestimated, unless we are led thereby to miss the fact that all the things that Luther needs seem to belong more to comfortable middle class propriety than to the necessities which God gives to the birds of the air and to the lilies of the fields!

In his *Explanation of the Lord's Prayer*, Luther appears to be much more moderate in his description of the "essential minimum" indispensable to man. He speaks no longer of other things, but only of the bread, insisting especially upon the fact that the physical bread is the sign of spiritual bread, that is to say, of the Word of God in Jesus Christ (John 6). "All preaching and teaching," he says, "which do not bring Jesus Christ to us and which do not place him before our eyes, are not the daily bread and nourishment of our souls. They would be no help at all when some need should arise or some trial should occur" *(Op. cit.:* Weimar II, p. 111; *Luther's Works*, Vol. 41).

Thus we are put in the position of having to ask for our bread, so that in receiving it, we do not forget the fact that it does not come by itself. It is necessary that this temporal and material sign bring us back to the everlasting grace of God. The bread reminds us that everything comes from God and that he gives to everyone who asks of him (Matthew 7:7). "Of this teaching," Luther added, "the whole scripture is full, full, full."

As to the word daily, it seems that it is necessary to translate it "for tomorrow," thereby reminding us that in the account of the creation, the "day" begins in the evening: "And there was evening, and there was morning, one day" (Gen. 1:5). Strictly speaking, in the evening we ask for the bread which we will eat the following day. We are not able to make provision for a longer period of time. So it was with the manna in the desert, of which the Jews could gather only enough for one day without the worms appearing in it. God intends to remain the master of his gifts.

Whether it is a question of physical nourishment or of the living bread which comes down from heaven (John 6:33), God does not allow us to claim ownership of it, nor to capitalize it, so that we would no longer have to put our trust in him. Nothing belongs to us in this world, and we cannot be sure of anything, unless it is what God gives. But we have to ask him for it. Luther recalled that if in his time the church knew so much wretchedness, it was due to the fact that the faithful did not *ask for* the bread of heaven. It is the same even today, where we must demand that preaching serve us the Word of God, Jesus Christ the living bread and nothing else.

As to the "us," it reminds us that the believer prays not only for himself but also for all the others who must have bread. The fourth petition forces us to assume our share of the disgrace of this world where three fourths of mankind lacks the necessary bread. We are summoned to do everything in our power so that human indifference and egoism do not come to throttle providence, the "almighty and ever-present power of God whereby he still upholds, as it were by his own hand, heaven and earth together with all creatures" (Question 27).

We are convinced that the problem regarding bread in our world does not, in the first instance, depend on economic philosophies. It is essentially a question of preaching the gospel. In the very measure in which the church faithfully distributes the living bread of the Word of God to men, this Word works to move us to resolve such problems.

When we say, "Give us this day our daily bread," we are praying both for our life and for that of the world.

❑ QUESTION 126. *What is the fifth petition?*

"And forgive us our debts, as we also have forgiven our debtors." That is: be pleased, for the sake of Christ's blood, not to charge to us, miserable sinners, our many transgressions, nor the evil which still clings to us.[a] We also find this witness of thy grace in us, that it is our sincere intention heartily to forgive our neighbor.[b]

a. 1 John 2:1-2. My little children, I am writing this to you so that you may not sin; but if anyone does sin, we have an advocate with the Father, Jesus Christ the righteous; and he is the expiation for our sins, and not for ours only but also for the sins of the whole world.

Cf. Ps. 51:1-7.

b. Matt. 6:14-15. If you forgive men their trespasses, your heavenly Father also will forgive you; but if you do not forgive men their trespasses, neither will your Father forgive your trespasses.

Forgive us our debts as we also have forgiven our debtors. The embarrassment that this petition causes us rises out of our manner of praying. How many times do we hear said that: "We ought to forgive—as much as it is necessary for us to be forgiven"? However annoying this claim may be, we do not have to pervert it in order to make it acceptable. The affirmation of this reciprocity in forgiveness is not the only one of its kind, and it is this fact that prevents us from trying to remove it from the Lord's Prayer. Paul bids the Ephesians to forgive one another, as God in Christ forgave them (Ephesians 4:32). This is also the meaning of the parable of the unforgiving servant (Matthew 18:23) and of its conclusion: "So also my heavenly Father will do to every one of you, if you do not forgive your brother from your heart."

Thus the forgiveness that we ask for is the very same as that which our neighbor expects from us. If we are not ready to grant it, we will never understand the meaning of the forgiveness that God offers us, free of charge, in Jesus Christ; not believing in it, we will not receive it. Thus we condemn ourselves to remain outside of God's mercy.

Clearly God does not impose any condition upon his forgiveness; it is free and unconditioned. That must continue to be an unshakable assurance for us. We are not going to fall back again into the anxiety of a religion of works and merits. God expects nothing from us for forgiving us. His forgiveness is there, and is available, it has been fully manifested in Jesus Christ and does not have to be repeated.

Moreover, here is where the exacting claim of the fifth petition of the Lord's Prayer affects us in all its rigor; if we do not forgive others, we thereby make ourselves incapable of laying hold upon God's forgiveness. It remains for us a reality that is strange and completely foreign. The forgiveness of the neighbor is the means which God gives us, in his grace, that we may have some comprehension of his work of mercy. It is hardly necessary to insist upon pointing out that this is the heart of the gospel message. "How shall I hope," says Karl Barth, "for something for myself if I do not even grant it to my neighbor?. . . By so doing, I shall simply validate my hope and my prayer" *(Prayer,* p. 68). Although God's forgiveness is here, it is essential that the validation of our salvation be made at the level of our daily existence. By forgiving my neighbor, I make my confession of faith in the good news attested by the holy Scriptures, that God forgives sins.

May we never forget that there exists no common measure between what we are called to forgive in others and what God actually forgives in us. The figures that Jesus quotes in the parable of the unforgiving servant are meant to emphasize this with all possible clarity: on the one hand a debt of ten thousand talents, that is, a half a million dollars is remitted without any payment being demanded; on the other hand, a man has his brother thrown into prison for less than fifty dollars!

Barth invites us in his own way, full of cordiality and serious good humor, to take a look at the meaning of these proportions: "In the light of the divine forgiveness, we see those poor creatures who have offended us, and even in difficult cases we think that, after all, the matter is not so serious. Let us not settle down to enjoy the offenses done to us; let us not nurse our grudges with pleasure. Rather, let us retain some humor with respect to our offenders. Let us have toward others this small impulse of forgiveness, of freedom. . . . He who does not have this very small freedom is not within reach of divine forgiveness. It might be said of him that he does not know how to pray, that he cannot then receive anything" (Prayer, p. 67).

Thus the fifth petition requires us to act in this world in relation to all men, no matter what they can do to us, as free men, that is, men freed by the marvelous, staggering news of the remission of our debts by God in Jesus Christ. If God did that for us, who could prevent us from doing it for our brothers? If we refuse to do it, it is because we have not yet understood the newness of the gospel.

The fifth petition helps us to forgive those who have offended against us at the same time that we are beginning to understand our own offenses toward God. If each day we must ask God to forgive us, it is because we offend him every day: "we doubt his Word: our unbelief is a very serious offense. We misuse his grace and we consider it scandalous that he takes it from us: our lack of gratitude is a very serious offense. We do not cease to be preoccupied with ourselves and to make everything revolve around our dear selves: our egoism is a very serious offense. We believe ourselves masters; we seek in ourselves the source of our life and we invent for ourselves a righteousness of our own: our pride is a very serious offense. We do not stop judging and condemning men who are at the mercy of our passions: our lack of mercy is a very serious offense. . . . Our life is just one long offense made against this Father and this Creator to whom our prayer is addressed" (de Pury, *Notre Père*, p. 89).

We cannot and must not forget that we are offending God. We owe an infinite debt to him and one that increases each day from the weight of all our offenses. We ought, therefore, to seek forgiveness from God, begging him to set us free from it. If we can do it, if we dare to bring ourselves before the one who accuses us with deceitful conduct, it is by virtue of Jesus Christ who has "fully paid for all [our] sins" (Question 1). Thus God invites us in Jesus Christ not to faint under the burden of our offenses toward him; he bids us ask him for forgiveness and not attempt anything whatever to try to free ourselves from our faults through our own means. God simply enables us to say, "Forgive us," so that we can live in his presence.

At the same time God emphasizes the earnestness of our petition by forgiving the offenses of those who have offended us. The gospel does not permit us to withdraw at little or no cost; God demands that we make some concrete decisions which require sacrifice.

It will never cost us as much as it cost him "who was put to death for our trespasses and raised for our justification" (Rom. 4:25).

"May we, therefore, live our life such as it is, that is to say, united with his; may we take our place where he has placed us, where we are in reality, where he has suffered, obeyed, and lived for us. May we put on this new man whom God has begotten in Christ. May we not live in just any way, but in the reality of what God has done for us" (Barth: *Prayer*, p. 70).

What we seek from God, in the fifth petition of the Lord's Prayer, is the very possibility of living "in newness of life" (Rom. 6:4).

℘ QUESTION 127. *What is the sixth petition?*

"And lead us not into temptation, but deliver us from evil." That is: since we are so weak that we cannot stand by ourselves for one moment,[a] and besides, since our sworn enemies, the devil,[b] the world,[c] and our own sin,[d] ceaselessly assail us, be pleased to preserve and strengthen us through the power of thy Holy Spirit so that we may stand firm against them, and not be defeated in this spiritual warfare,[e] until at last we obtain complete victory.[f]

a. John 15:5. "Apart from me you can do nothing."
   Cf. Ps. 103:14; Rom. 8:26.
b. 1 Peter 5:8. Be sober, be watchful. Your adversary the devil prowls around like a roaring lion, seeking someone to devour.
c. John 15:19. "If you were of the world, the world would love its own; but because you are not of the world, but I chose you out of the world, therefore the world hates you."
   Cf. Eph. 6:12.
d. Rom. 7:23. I see in my members another law at war with the law of my mind and making me captive to the law of sin which dwells in my members.
   Cf. Gal. 5:17.
e. Matt. 26:41. "Watch and pray that you may not enter into temptation; the spirit indeed is willing, but the flesh is weak."
   Cf. Mark 13:33.
f. 1 Thess. 3:13; 5:23. [May he] establish your hearts unblamable in holiness before our God and Father, at the coming of our Lord Jesus with all his saints. . . . May the God of peace himself sanctify you wholly; and may your spirit and soul and body be kept sound and blameless at the coming of our Lord Jesus Christ.

And lead us not into temptation, but deliver us from evil. Much could be said here about the way in which this petition has been interpreted. The very fact that the Lord's Prayer is the prayer of the Lord does not stop us from saying at this point: "Do not let us fall—do not expose us—do not let us fall prey to temptation!" The least we could do would be to begin by not yielding to the temptation of accommodating the Bible to our own way of thinking, at the very moment when we ask to be protected from it! The one great temptation, the only one ultimately, is of not taking God's word for it, of not taking him at his Word. If everything in the world happens as if God were no longer the Lord, if all the temptations threaten us, is it not, in the first place, because the church of Jesus Christ has stopped believing in his sovereign Word and because, in what she says and does, she herself acts as if Jesus Christ were not Lord, as if his Word were only a human word to which each one can impute his own meaning?

The temptation of the church is in not believing. It is a trick of Satan which he uses to keep us worried about all the little temptations, while we succumb to the worst one, without our even realizing it.

Satan is never such an evil one as when he persuades us that nothing is really important, that everything is relative, that it is dangerous to take the Word of God too seriously and that we will inevitably end by confusing the letter and the spirit. Satan is never so sure of his triumph as when he succeeds, according to the expression of Luther, in making us "throw out the baby with the bath water." His joy knows no bounds when he sees us doing it with the best intentions in the world, either to keep peace in the church, or to avoid other people's temptations, not to risk offending reason or hurting the feelings of modern man. Satan does not waste his time on trifles, he attacks the main issue, he knows very well that he will get everything else if he succeeds in making us doubt the Word of God.

When we pray, "Lead us not into temptation," we beg God to keep us from believing that we can make of his Word what we want; we ask him, above all else, to give us simplicity of heart and spirit that will permit us to believe him in all that he tells us; we plead that God himself keep our eyes and our ears open, so that Satan does not lull us to sleep in the illusion that we are no longer capable of being tempted, that we are strong enough, we, our customs, and our traditions, so as not to yield to temptation nor to believe him when he speaks to us.

When we pray the sixth petition of the Lord's Prayer, we recall before God the very perilous situation in which we stand, and we ask him to keep watch over our faith so that it remain truly "the faith."

We know that God himself "tempts no one" (James 1:13), but he can, in order to test our faith, *lead* us to the place where we may be tempted by the devil. "Jesus was led up *by the Spirit* into the wilderness to be tempted *by the devil*" (Matt. 4:1). (Notice that Jesus replies to the satanic temptation of wanting to take God's place by quoting the Word of God itself!)

When we pray, "Lead us not into temptation," we ask God not

to put us in the situation of having to face the assaults of the evil one but to spare us this test of our faith which we know is already shaky. What else can we pray for, realizing that we have built our house on the shifting sands of our own human securities? What can we ask of God but to help us recover the solid rock of his Word, the sure "foundation" (Isa. 28:16; 1 Cor. 3:11) named Jesus Christ?

This is our situation: we are always in danger of giving in, of falling prey to the most shameful temptation.

To pray "Lead us not into temptation" means: Confirm us in the one who has delivered us from all temptation. We know that this deliverance has taken place and is already accomplished. Then remove from us all illusion about ourselves; keep us from thinking that evil or the evil one is not so great after all, that everything will come out all right and that we will get out of it by ourselves; remind us that our situation is too involved for us and that we are ripe for utter defeat; do not lead us where he who will make us fall is raging, that is to say, into the desert of unbelief, of doubt, and of fear.

This is what we confess to God. "We can be sure that when we follow thy Word, we shall not be led into great temptation. By following the path which thou hast prepared for us and which thou hast revealed in thy Son, we shall always be shielded from this aberration. Thou wilt deliver us from the evil one" (Barth: *Prayer,* p. 75).

The sixth petition is not entirely negative. We also ask God to bring about the positive result of making us take with utter seriousness the Word of our deliverance in Jesus Christ. Therefore, we pray that he give us good preaching, good instruction, and the sacraments to confirm our faith. By praying thus, we confess our faith in the God who never abandons his own. In a word, we do not ask for anything other than the presence of God in our midst. It is this presence that delivers us from the fear of sin, from Satan, and from death.

❑ QUESTION 128. *How do you close this prayer?*

"For thine is the kingdom and the power and the glory, forever." That is: we ask all this of thee because, as our King, thou art willing and able to give us all that is good since thou hast power over all things,[a] and that by this not we ourselves but thy holy name may be glorified forever.[b]

a. Rom. 10:12-13. There is no distinction between Jew and Greek; the same Lord is Lord of all and bestows his riches upon all who call upon him. For, "everyone who calls upon the name of the Lord will be saved."
Cf. 2 Peter 2:9.
b. John 14:13. "Whatever you ask in my name, I will do it, that the Father may be glorified in the Son."
Cf. Ps. 115:1.

The doxology, that is to say, the glorification of the name of God, which concludes the Lord's Prayer, is the reply of the community itself to this prayer which Christ has taught and made possible for us to use. This confession of faith takes us back to the invocation of the prayer: the faithful community acclaims the one who, in Jesus Christ, came to be revealed as the Father of all mankind. The church tells him that she believes in him and that she puts all her trust in him, that she knows how to hallow his name, that she recognizes his rule, that she can do his will, that she received from him the bread of life, that she is able to share with others the forgiveness which she has received; the church knows that she is delivered from all temptations by the power of Jesus Christ, the Word made flesh. She proclaims that all her hope and all her trust are in God. She knows that nothing can happen to her that is contrary to the will of her Father. The faithful community is not deterred by the poverty, the inadequacy, the lack of fervor in her prayer; she raises herself resolutely above all her wretchedness in order to cling to the one who guarantees this very prayer; "to remind us again," says Calvin, "that our prayers are altogether grounded on the power and goodness of God; and not on ourselves, for we are not worthy to open our mouth in prayer; and also that we may learn to close all our prayers in his praise" (Geneva Catechism, No. 294).

❡ QUESTION 129. *What is the meaning of the little word "Amen"?*

Amen means: this shall truly and certainly be. For my prayer is much more certainly heard by God than I am persuaded in my heart that I desire such things from him.[a]

a. 2 Cor. 1:20. All the promises of God find their Yes in him. That is why we utter the Amen through him, to the glory of God.
2 Tim. 2:13. If we are faithless, he remains faithful—for he cannot deny himself.
Isa. 65:24. "Before they call I will answer, while they are yet speaking I will hear," says the Lord.
Cf. Jer. 28:6.

This last word of the whole prayer means "certainly, truly, surely." It is the word of the end but it is also the word of the beginning. "Truly, truly I say to you, you will see heaven opened and the angels of God ascending and descending upon the Son of man" (John 1:51). This word is the seal of truth affixed by Jesus Christ at the close of every human prayer. Luther said: "O God, my Father, these things which I have asked for in my prayer, I do not doubt them, they are surely true and will be done, not because I asked for them in my prayer but because thou didst command me to ask for them and hast promised them in all certainty. So I am sure of thee, O God, thou art trustworthy; thou couldst not lie, for it is not the dignity of my prayer, but the certainty of thy troth which affects what I firmly believe; and, for me, there is no doubt that there will be born from it an Amen and that that will be an Amen" *(Op. cit.:* Weimar II, p. 127).

The word amen is the word of faith which nothing can shake, because it is founded on the grace of God in Jesus Christ, proclaimed in the Word of God, attested by the Holy Spirit and confirmed by the sacraments.

How in the face of this affirmation, which has been declared to us, would we not say: "Amen, truly, certainly I believe because thou dost say it to me; thou art my Father, now and forevermore"?

To him who loves us and has freed us from our sins by his blood and made us a kingdom, priests to his God and Father, to him be glory and dominion for ever and ever. Amen (Rev. 1:5-6).

BIBLIOGRAPHY

For Heidelberg Catechism

Niesel, Wilhelm. *Bekenntnisschriften und Kirchenordnungen der nach Gottes Wort reformierten Kirche,* "Heidelberger Katechismus." Zurich: Evangelishcher Verlag, A. G. Zollikon, 1938.
Tercentenary Edition: *The Heidelberg Catechism,* in German, Latin, and English. Charles Scribner's Sons, 1863.

For Commentary

Asmussen, Hans. *Le Combat de la Prière* (The Encounter of Prayer). Neuchâtel-Paris: Delachaux & Niestlé, 1952.
Barth, Karl. *Church Dogmatics,* Vol. II (The Doctrine of God), I. Edited by G. W. Bromiley and T. F. Torrance. Charles Scribner's Sons, 1957.
————. *The Faith of the Church.* Translated by Gabriel Vahanian. Meridian Books, 1958.
————. *The Heidelberg Catechism for Today.* Translated by Shirley C. Guthrie, Jr. John Knox Press, 1963.
————. *The Humanity of God.* Translated by John Newton Thomas. John Knox Press, 1960.
————. *Prayer,* according to the Catechisms of the Reformation. Translated by Sara F. Terrien. Westminster Press, 1952.
————. *The Teaching of the Church Regarding Baptism.* Translated by Ernest A. Payne. Student Christian Movement Press, 1948.
Bartmann, Bernhard. *Lehrbuch der Dogmatik* (Textbook of Christian Doctrine). Paderborn: Bonifacius Druckerei, 1932. (*Précise de théologie dogmatique.* Translated by Marcel Gautier. Paris: Castermann, 1944.)
Calvin, John. *The Catechism of the Church of Geneva* (1541). Translated and edited by Thomas F. Torrance, *The School of Faith,* pp. 3-65. Harper and Row, Inc., 1959.
————. *Commentaries: On a Harmony of the Evangelists* (1558), *On the Gospel According to John* (1553). Translated by William Pringle. William B. Eerdmans Publishing Co., 1949.
————. *Institutes of the Christian Religion* (1559). Edited by John T. McNeill, Library of Christian Classics, 2 vols. Westminster Press, 1960.

Council of Trent. *Canons and Decrees.* Translated by H. J. Schroeder.
B. Herder Book Co., 1950.

――――. *The Catechism.* Translated by J. Donovan. Lucas Brothers, 1829.

Cullmann, Oscar. *Baptism in the New Testament.* Translated by J. K. S. Reid. Henry Regnery Co., 1950.

Evdokimov, Paul. *L'Orthodoxie* (Eastern Orthodoxy). Neuchâtel: Delachaux & Niestlé, 1959.

Kierkegaard, Sören. *Attack upon "Christendom."* Translated by Walter Lowrie. Princeton University Press, 1944.

――――. *The Journals.* A selection edited and translated by Alexander Dru. London: Oxford University Press, 1938.

Lightfoot, J. B. *The Apostolic Fathers.* London: Macmillan Co., 1863.

Luther, Martin. *The Book of Concord,* the Confessions of the Evangelical Lutheran Church. Translated and edited by Theodore G. Tappert. Muhlenberg Press, 1959.
"The Large Catechism" (1529)
"The Small Catechism" (1529)

――――. *Luther's Works.* Vols. 1-30, edited by Jaroslav Pelikan. Concordia Publishing House. Vols. 31-55, edited by Helmut T. Lehmann. Muhlenberg Press, 1957 ff.
"Disputation Against Scholastic Theology" (1517), Vol. 31 (Weimar I)
"Explanation of the Lord's Prayer" (1519), Vol. 42 (Weimar II)
"Good Works" (1520), Vol. 44 (Weimar VI)
"Heidelberg Disputation" (1518), Vol. 31 (Weimar I)
"The Seven Penitential Psalms" (1517), Vol. 14 (Weimar I)

Maury, Pierre, *et al. Les Sacrements* (The Sacraments), Collection "Protestantisme," No. 3. Paris: Je Sers, 1942.

Melanchthon, Philip. *The Book of Concord,* the Confessions of the Evangelical Lutheran Church. Translated and edited by Theodore G. Tappert. Muhlenberg Press, 1959.
"Apology of the Augsburg Confession" (1531)

Pury, Roland de. *Notre Père* (The Lord's Prayer). Neuchâtel: Delachaux & Niestlé, 1945.

Pury, Roland de, *et al. L'Ordre de Dieu* (The Ten Commandments). Geneva: Roulet & Cie, 1941.

Saussure, Jean de. *Cours supérieur d'Instruction religieuse basé sur le Catéchisme de Heidelberg* (advanced course of religious instruction based upon the Heidelberg Catechism).

Weber, Otto. *Karl Barth's Church Dogmatics.* Translated by Arthur C. Cochrane. Westminster Press, 1953.

GENERAL THEOLOGICAL SEMINARY
NEW YORK